# TIN SOLDIER

C.T. Benning gives us a war story with a difference. From Ronsdorf to Tyneside — a whole lifetime of a very ordinary German soldier — his day-to-day life on the battlefields during the 1914/18 War, his reactions to the war, his injuries, narrow escapes, those unofficial leave passes . . . followed by what it was like to live in Germany during the post-war years of galloping inflation when the Mark went mad.

And then to England. Setting up in business and being accepted here — until the advent of the Second World War, and then internment. What it meant to be a pro-Allied enemy alien! the years of internment and then eventual reunion with his wife and daughter, to be interned yet again on the Isle of Man.

Throughout it all runs the strong thread of determination; here is a man who could not help but survive on a desert island, whose very life demonstrates just how much necessity is the mother of invention; who used his brains — and wits — as and when the occasion demanded.

Perhaps, after reading this book, those of us who are British by birth may have gained some insight into the lives of those who become British by choice.

# TIN SOLDIER

**CHARLES T. BENNING**

*Charles T. Benning*

ARTHUR H. STOCKWELL Ltd.,
Elms Court　　　Ilfracombe,
Devon

© C.T. Benning, 1975
First published in Great Britain, 1975

To
**MARIANNE**

ISBN 7223 0823-X
Printed in Great Britain by
Arthur H. Stockwell Ltd
Elms Court    Ilfracombe
Devon

# INTRODUCTION

The Author was born at the end of the last century in Western Germany, where he spent the first 35 years of his life. Not many people would therefore be better qualified to give a detailed description about the pros and cons of a race, in which by fate he was born. He grew up through the years before the first war, observing the marching of the Germans in peace-time at every minor opportunity, being gradually absorbed into the biggest fighting the world has ever seen. He saw the World War from a worm's-eye view from the bottom of the muddy trenches as an ordinary private in the Infantry of the Kaiser's army. Before this war came officially to an end he deserted the ranks and went home.

The roaring twenties brought him face to face with high living, revolution and inflation, culminating into the worst Dictatorship mankind has ever witnessed. In 1932 the writer made his domicile in England, slipping away from the jackboots of the Nazis, finding freedom at last in a democratic country, in his occupation as a Company Director in a Hyde, Cheshire textile factory. He was prepared for peace for the rest of his life. However the long arm of the Third Reich from Berlin followed him wherever he went. He was severely warned about having joined the Rotary Movement, which was, to the Nazis, illegal and punishable. He was not allowed to become a British Subject and was also warned that he showed far too much British tendency.

The Author ignored the warnings and carried on with his democratic life until the fateful day, September 3rd 1939. On this day he put his and the fate of his family into the hands of the British and followed his work in England during the phoney war. 1940, in May, his freedom stopped, being locked up behind barbed wire. He describes the days as an Internee and P.O.W. in camps in York, Lingfield, Canada and the I.O.M. — We have read many stories about British soldiers in German P.O.W. Camps, but little has come out about the Allies' treatment of their German prisoners. This is the second chapter of the writer's experiences.

Fighting for freedom all the way the writer came home to England in 1943, became a British subject and lived happily ever after amongst the folks of Northumberland, where he and his family still enjoy life up to this day.

## CONTENTS

**Book One**

| | |
|---|---|
| The Early Years | 11 |
| Education | 14 |
| The Weaver | 21 |
| The Tin Soldier | 31 |
| Real War | 39 |
| Flanders | 50 |
| The Siegfried Line | 59 |
| The Artois | 74 |
| The Battle of France | 79 |
| Homeward Bound | 99 |

**Book Two**

| | |
|---|---|
| Peace in our Time | 125 |
| The Country of Adoption | 141 |
| The War to end All Wars | 153 |
| The Internee | 158 |
| A Free Trip to Canada | 172 |
| The Return Journey | 212 |
| Reflection | 230 |

*Photographs set between pages 192 & 193*

**BOOK ONE**

# THE EARLY YEARS

Most of the inhabitants of the small town of Ronsdorf, in Western Germany, were preparing their souls for the coming year, 1897, by attending New Year's Mass at the local church. However, this was not the case with a certain Magdalena, who was confined to her bed awaiting the birth of her second child. It was the fervent hope of Magdalena, and her husband, Josua, that this child should be a boy.

Josua Bender was a draper in a small way of business, with a habit of transacting every commodity into finance. He even converted unborn babies into hard cash, by hinting to his wife that girls were worth less than boys, financially. This conclusion was reached by reckoning up their contribution to the family's budget in later years.

If the new baby were a boy, it made a great difference to his future whether he was born at 11.59 p.m., 1896, or 12.01 a.m. 1897. As mere humans are unable to foresee the future, no one, at this time, could be aware of the significance to this unborn child. However, if he came on to this earth after midnight, it meant he had to join the 1914-18 war a whole year later than his future comrades born a few minutes earlier. Many of the latter were to have sacrificed their lives on the battlefields of France long before those born in 1897 even joined the army ranks.

Fortunately, for this baby boy, he was born after twelve, and in the following narrative, we shall describe, in particular, the course of his life. Had he but known, at this juncture, that he was to live through two bloody wars, to be faced eventually with possible annihilation through the Hydrogen Bomb, given a choice, he might well have decided to return to the unknown.

He was christened Karl Theodor. A Bender by heritage, they called him Theo. When, eventually, he learnt to walk, and to think for himself, he found it a pathetically slow-moving world, compared with the speed and hurry of today.

His mother he remembered as a gentle, religious woman, with an eagerness to help others at any opportunity. With her lovely eyes and features he believed her to be the most wonderful mother in the world.

To Theo's childish mind, his father presented a very different picture, his most prominent feature being a bushy moustache protruding from a somewhat small face. When sitting on this parent's knee, he would hold on to this protrusion with his tiny hands, like a pair of handlebars.

As time went on, the family grew in size; first another girl, then a boy.

With the years, Theo's brain became more mature, and he began to see things in their right perspective. He learned the reason for the existence of his father's shop, and that people had to live on the money they earned.

Soon he came to know his father's daily routine. It was Josua's custom to open his shop by 9 a.m. Then, after giving instructions to his only assistant, he would walk to the post office. Apart from a bicycle, which his father found too strenuous to pedal, mechanical equipment was non-existent. Motor cars were unknown in the cobbled streets, and children could play to their hearts' content without being knocked down and killed, while sparrows still found their daily food in the digested oats in the cart-horses' droppings.

From the post office, Josua would make his way to the 'local' where, around 10 a.m., the town's business fraternity would meet every day of the week, every week of the year. Here, the grocer, millwright, carpenter, barrister, draper and sweep, gathered together round the *Stammtisch* (Table of the Guild). Their main topic for discussion was politics, but the daily newspapers, magazines and journals were at their disposal and provided food for thought and conversation.

If one could have been an invisible observer at any of their meetings, one could have imagined oneself to be present at General Army Headquarters, where strategical and political policies for the whole of Germany were decided upon. Here, the wise men of the town, in their aprons and overalls, their faces bedecked with beards and Kaiser Wilhelm moustaches, were shaping the course of their Fatherland, to the accompaniment of numerous glasses of schnapps and lager, which were liberally poured down their gullets. In those days, in every village, town and city all over Germany, a *Stammtisch* was found in every ' local '. It was here that politics were discussed, and made.

Having spent half his day in this way, Josua would join his family for lunch. Then, after his customary snooze, he would spend a couple of hours in the shop. Feeling lively again, he would make his second trip to the ' local '. Of the few hobbies he had, the chief one was singing in the male voice choir, where he performed as a brittle and wiry-sounding tenor; another was amusing his company by telling jokes. The best places to perform these talents were, without doubt, the public houses, where he was always welcomed as a jovial and likeable chap, and could be sure of an appreciative audience. These nightly excursions invariably extended into the early hours of the morning, straining both his financial position and family relations to the limit.

# EDUCATION

Josua always stood by the principle that his first-born son should receive a good education. It would cost him a great deal of money, but he was sure Theo would make the grade. We cannot be certain that his views on this subject were not mainly due to his desire to make an impression on the neighbourhood.

The boy, however, had very different ideas on the subject. His school life proved to be a flop from start to finish. Not that Theo lacked intelligence or was incapable of learning, on the contrary, he was a quick-thinking and witty fellow. However, his mind was so full of his latest escapade or adventure that, to the detriment of his father, his studies became of a secondary nature.

Even Josua's cane did not help very much. It seemed as though the father wrought pleasure from beating his son, as punishment was meted out on every possible occasion. Theo would be marched down to the cellar of the house to avoid his mother interfering, and where the screaming boy could not be heard. This punishment, however severe, had no effect, and instead of encouraging him to improve at school, Theo became worse and grew stubborn.

At the age of six, Theo's teacher had to inflict the first hiding during the first hour of the boy's school career. Although he displayed a lively interest in his new surroundings the lessons received very little of his attention. He had the urge to explore — in the same way as he had pulled off the tail of

## Education

the expensive rocking horse he got for Christmas, only to find that it was filled with sawdust. So it was that on his first day at school, discovering the inkpot in his desk, he picked it up for closer inspection, only to spill it over his new white collar and fashionable bow-tie. No wonder there followed the hiding!

Generally, life was pretty much the same from his sixth to fourteenth year. He was always in trouble, even to the extent of teasing his teachers, which usually reflected in his school reports. These were poor, and prolific with grades five, four and three. Only in singing and languages could he manage a grade two for ' good '. Whenever he brought home his report at the end of each term, the cane would be brought out, and down to the cellar he would have to go. The question of punishment has been with us ever since, but to Theo it proved of no avail; had his young life not been dogged by the threat of a beating, he might have done much better.

The father's dream of a well-educated boy, leaving the sixth form with all possible honours, did not materialize. The money he had spent on High School education was wasted. Shortage of money, through his own shortcomings, did not permit further wasteful expenditure. When, for the second time, Theo was sent down to the fourth form, his father took him away from school, and, at the age of fourteen, he started an ordinary apprenticeship in the weaving trade.

All these years the boy had mixed with the well-to-do. Now, shunned by his previous pals, he found himself in completely different surroundings, where he had to grope his way to become a manual labourer. He was soon to learn that there were two different classes of people in the world.

Mainly, he only had himself to blame for his apparent failure, owing to his adventures and versatilities outside school. He liked to jump from one topic to another, making his grandfather, Elias, remark that the boy was no good — too unsettled to get anywhere in life.

A tiny backyard was his playground with tall buildings towering up on every side. The place was full of rats, which at an early age he would chase with his father's scraper, hacking them in two, or catching a large one alive in a cage trap would take it to the near-by cobbler for cremation.

It was in these surroundings that he grew up, with all the

amusements and hobbies a boy could wish for, whether white mice, pigeons or squirrels.

When he was a few years older he opened his own cinema in the backyard with the aid of a magic lantern. Consisting of a crude contraption of canvas and old carpets, he could seat ten, and charged two bones entrance fee for the circle, and one for the gallery. In this way, he learnt how to make money by selling the bones to the rag-man for pop and fireworks for the end of holiday celebrations. Some of his friends in a near-by street did even better than him. However, they resorted to even greater lengths, using a trap-door leading to a cellar. There, they advertised the 'Naked Lady' and, for a bone or two, one could see a young girl in the nude.

In winter his backyard became an ice-rink. Blocking all holes and drains, he filled it with water with the hosepipe. Here, the whole juvenile neighbourhood learned to skate, until one day Theo ran into a girder and broke a tooth.

In those days, when anaesthetics were unknown, patients receiving attention were usually taken to the barber, who used tools similar to the ones we use nowadays for pulling out nails. The sixteen-stone barber's wife, held Theo's head in a vice-like grip, and, by hook or by crook, the tooth had to come out. No amount of yelling on the part of the victim would alter this.

Another aspect of life soon became apparent to Theo. People did not live for ever. While playing red indians, his friend Fritz, overbalanced, to fall on the sharp triple spikes of a fence. Pinned by his ankles, he hung, blue and lifeless, head downwards. When Theo found him, he calmly unhooked the poor Fritz and, unperturbed by the dead-looking body, managed to revive him.

Amongst the girls in the ' gang ' there was a wee little one from a poor family. Instead of growing up she grew thinner and thinner owing to galloping consumption — or, in modern terms, tuberculosis. She died. All the tiny youngsters were called into the little bedroom where Elsie lay. She was dressed in a white robe and lying in a small, cheap coffin. Her little hands were folded in prayer, and her face was as white as chalk. Four small Sunday School pictures, depicting scenes from the Bible, decorated the upper part of her shroud. It was a most solemn affair and beyond the youngsters' understanding. With tears in her eyes, the mother tried to explain that the soul had left the girl's body and gone through the ceiling, upwards to Heaven, where it would be safe for ever. When Theo walked home he had to think hard to puzzle this out.

At the age of twelve, he had to join his church, and was taught the Catechism by a peculiar parson. The Benders belonged to the Reformist Church, which, at the turn of the last century, still harboured a fanatically religious assembly, to which an outsider was hardly able to join.

The foundation of the town of Ronsdorf goes back to the year 1737, when a creative and pious genius, Elias Eller, a sectary and visionary, was searching for a place where he could build a town of a super religious nature. So successful was he, that soon he gained the estimation of the then ruling monarchs and princes.

To his followers he declared himself their God-sent leader. The movement quickly grew to immense proportions, the members of which had a fanatical faith in Elias, and even went so far as to call him the new Messiah. To this day, this religious aspect is still reflected in Ronsdorf's nickname 'Zion'.

The sect adhered strictly to the words of the Gospel, while all Christian names had to follow the pattern of the Bible. Theo, therefore, found himself amongst relations where names like Abraham, Jacob, Nathanael, Eva, Joel and Sarah were in abundance. Josua Bender's family seemed to be an exception; more modern in his ideas he named his children: Luise, Theodor, Lydia and Heinrich.

The minister who taught Theo's class the Catechism was of the old school; a man of the highest standing, he knew his Bible by heart. His actions, however, were different, in that he would never marry one of his followers to a member of the Catholic Church. Neither would he keep to the written word when one of his congregation ceased to live. When ready for the journey to the cemetery, the dead person would be treated by the pastor according to his, or her, belief in life. If, in his estimation, the person had lived a good life, the corpse had nothing to fear. He would preach as though he were opening up the very gates of Heaven itself, as an example to the whole congregation.

However, if it came to pass that the pastor had to bury, what he thought, a bad member, he would not follow the horse-drawn hearse to the cemetery, but walk on the pavement or in the gutter, well away from the procession. At the grave-side, his sermon would be befitting to an individual low in his own estimation. Not one word would he utter in that person's defence, but would endeavour to pave the way to Hell for the unfortunate deceased. Apart from this serious failing, his correctness was otherwise without fault, and three-quarters of his salary went to feed and clothe the poor.

During his ramblings, Theo had, by now, familiarized himself with the layout of his home town. A fairly small, pretty place, it harboured approximately 17,000 inhabitants. It had a rural setting, with undulating country in changing patterns of woods and fields. Surrounded, as it was, by attractive farming villages, in the middle of the otherwise busy and industrial life of Rhine and Ruhr, it came to be known as the 'Garden Town'.

As they grew older, Theo and his friends tired of the backyard as their playground, and earmarked the market square for their activities. Regardless of the fact that it had generally been understood to be a quiet place for older people to relax, football matches were staged with appalling noise, which resulted in attracting the gendarmes from the near-by Town Hall. At the early age of seven, therefore, a fine was issued against Theo, not to mention severe concussion through running into a goal post in the form of a lime tree.

His brother fared no better, and ripped open his stomach on a sharp spike. When Theo eventually managed to carry him home, the blood was running out of his trouser ends. It was a very serious case. The white-faced boy lay in the surgery, while the doctor, a man of over eighty, prepared the needle and the knife. When some of the superfluous fat was cut away from the wound there was no anaesthetic in use. When it came to stitching the wound, the stiff brittle hands of the surgeon were unable to pierce the skin with the needle, so Josua was forced to take over the task of stitching his own son himself.

These mishaps, however, did not deter the boys and their friends from further daring. They switched their activities to the outskirts of the town, where they came across a railway bridge crossing the highway some thirty feet up. Here one of the boys had traced a small opening close to the steel rails. It was considered a daring adventure to creep under the rails which carried the heavy traffic of goods trains. It became a matter of heroism to sit in this aperture, with the top of one's head touching the base of the iron rails, waiting for a train to approach. The first sign was a slight rumbling which gradually grew louder until it eventually reached a crescendo, as it passed over the adventurer with the most earsplitting roar, the speeding wheels only separated from the boy's head by eight inches. This represented a challenge which every member of the gang had to perform. The weaklings were taunted and teased until, feeling ashamed, they too, had gone through the chamber of terror.

This was only one of the gang's escapades. Many often proved dangerous and not a few, frequently caused damage. The harder and more hazardous the feat, the more keen were the boys to perform it.

Entertainment during the long winter evenings was home-made. There was no television, radio or electric light, though Josua with his modern gas-lights, was well advanced over most people, who enjoyed themselves in their lounges by the dim glow of a paraffin lamp. People then were not synchronized or plasticized as they are in this new age. They were more alive, exercising their own brains, not being fed with artificial amusements. Practically everyone in the family played a musical instrument, and relations and friends would gather together for an evening's concert. Home-made chamber music was the vogue, whilst the elderly folk unfolded their stories of bravery during the 1870/71 war.

During these pleasant diversions, Theo would be made to sit still, but he would become gradually more fidgety, until he could bear it no longer. Once, when the room was packed to capacity and the shrill sound of the fiddlers was at its height, he crept out of the room and down to the cellar. Bent on mischief, he espied a piece of rubber hose, and fitting it on the gaspipe, opened the tap and blew down the hose. The gas was forced back, inch by inch. When the din of the music stopped upstairs, he knew he had succeeded. The gas-lamps had gone out, leaving everyone sitting in the dark, wondering what had been the cause.

# THE WEAVER

Having completed two years in the parson's class learning the Bible and the Catechism, the fourteen-year-old pupils were now ready for their Confirmation. According to tradition, two Sundays were set aside; one for the examination in front of the congregation, and the following week, the Confirmation.

On both these solemn occasions, the church would be packed with fathers, mothers, uncles and aunts, all eager to see and hear their offspring. All were dressed in black for this important event, Theo looking very odd in his long pants, crowned with a bowler hat. On the first Sunday everything was going according to plan, with precise answers to the parson's questions, until he came to ginger-haired Paul, the dud of the class, and to whom he had taught the answer beforehand. From the pulpit the question came: "Through which water did Moses lead the people of Israel?" Paul hesitated, whilst Theo sat behind him whispering, and to the astonishment of the congregation, came Paul's reply: "Through the Rhine, sir." When both events were over, Theo took home his parchment document, a guide for his life: The Lord is my shepherd, I shall not want.

Theo was now ready for his working life. How different he looked in his outfit when going to work. Gone was the smart, scarlet school cap and uniform and, in their place, he was dressed as a proletarian in ordinary working-class clothing, with a cloth cap pulled down over his left ear. Morning after morning, six days a week, from 7 a.m. to 7 p.m., he had to learn how hard it was to earn six shillings a week.

His place of work was not in a factory, as these were very few and far between in those days, but in a workroom of a private dwelling house. Every member of the family helped, in one form or another, to process the textile fibres obtained from one of the warehouses. In this way, silk ribbons of the highest quality were produced, and shipped all over the world.

It was a pleasant family atmosphere, which Theo joined. His master, Herr Winter, an elderly man with a large hump on his back, took charge of the boy for the next three years. Never without his two foot long, dangling pipe, Herr Winter fumigated the small workroom with his stinking tobacco, causing the flies to drop from the ceiling. He was a good soul and appreciated the fact that, in his young apprentice, he had found a great help.

Theo grew to like his new job and, still conscious of his failure at the Grammar School, was determined to make this a success. Only once did he let his master down, and that was one morning when the old man found him flat on his back, unconscious, his machine still running. The previous evening he had been playing football with some of the lads down a side-street. In his usual fervour he had missed the ball, kicking, instead, a brick overgrown with grass. His big toe was broken in two, but he dared not tell his father. Theo's brother took him home and quietly helped him into bed. When the injured boy got up the next morning, the pain was agonizing, and his brother helped him to hobble out of the house. A walk to work was out of the question, so with one shoe on one foot, and his father's large slipper on the damaged one, he climbed on to a bicycle. Once at work, it was not long before the excruciating pain caused him to lose consciousness and fall flat on his back. When he found him, his master was very perturbed, and had the boy's prostrate form carried to the doctor. The diagnosis was a fractured big toe — the cure, several weeks rest.

Theo soon found his ground in his new environment, and made new friends amongst the working-class. They proved decent pals, with no snobbery attached. The years passed by quickly and Theo was soon mature enough to study the behaviour of his elder fellow-men. Like any other town in

Germany, Ronsdorf was always full of activities.

There was an abundancy of societies and organizations, and whenever even the smallest bunch of townspeople gathered together, the flags were out, bands were playing, the folks were marching. This appeared to be, as he was later to find out, a typical habit of the German Nation. This was understandable regarding military formations, but he detected that the civilian behaved in the same fashion, whether it concerned the voluntary fire brigade, the football or swimming clubs. He came to the conclusion that the Germans loved marching. Given a military cap, a band, some flags, they would march through a brick wall, if their leader so decided. Even the male choir was no exception. Theo detested these frequent festivities when the members, partly in morning dress, with peaked caps on their heads and emblems on their chests, tried to put on a military formation in their own right as subjects of their Fatherland.

As 1914, the year Theo finished his apprenticeship, drew nearer, the more prominent this kind of marching became. His elders read their newspapers, and were thereby better informed on the political intrigues in the world. He listened to their stories about the opposition of the British, the French, and the Russion Empires, all in opposition to the expansion of the German Reich. This young apprentice had never given a thought to politics. Like many of his pals, he did not even know who was the German Prime Minister at that time. What did he care about who was at the top of the political and military administration?

He realized of course, that should there be a war, he would eventually be in it. Already he had made the resolution that the main thing was to avoid getting himself shot, and killed. Normal military exercise, a chance to get away from home and see places, would be a good opportunity for adventurous youngsters, but shooting with proper rifles and maiming, or perhaps, even killing one another was a different matter altogether.

It was in this spirit that he approached 1914. On August 4th of that year, while crossing the market square, he met Adolf, a much older friend, who told him that England had declared war on Germany. He had read the newspapers, and the only political fragments he could piece together were that an important chap from Austria had been shot at Sarajevo. Austria, Serbia, Russia, France, England and Germany seemed to be at loggerheads over this. Bad as it was to assassinate someone, in Theo's mind, it was no reason for educated men to start a world war.

Those were the days of the strong Germany, when the characteristics of marching came to the fore. The Kaiser and his Ministers were impatient and, when all other countries were striving to avoid it, in spite of all the formidable opposition she had to march forward and declare war on Russia and France. Nobody expected then, that in the outcome, the whole world would be fighting against Germany. The national stubbornness was prevalent again, as the Germans attempted to batter their heads against brick walls.

The remaining four months of 1914 were rather exciting ones for wartime Germany. Hardly a day passed without all the bells of every church in the land ringing out to herald yet another victory of the Kaiser's armies. At top speed, their mighty forces swept through Belgium and France, grinding to a halt short of Paris. The same was happening in the east, where Hindenburg was chasing the Russians straight into the Masurian Lakes. What a strong and mighty Germany to endeavour to defeat the whole world!

Although the ringing of victory bells can be an exhilarating sound to nationally minded people, too often, the pealing can have a reverse effect, causing some sceptics amongst the older generation to predict then: *Wir siegen uns kaputt!* (We conquer ourselves to death.)

In a short space of time most of the men over twenty had left their homes in answer to the Kaiser's call, and some were already in their death struggle, digging their claws into the fertile soil of France or Russia, their blood drained, their bodies dead.

As the cream of manhood gradually disappeared from towns and cities, the male teenagers took over at home. They seemed to grow up much more quickly, and Theo was no exception. Although only seventeen they put on a manly façade, frequenting the public houses and drinking beer like the big chaps. Most of them smoked like chimneys. Many of the women, who past their prime, and deprived of their menfolk, took advantage of their inexperienced youngsters. The fact that they were only seventeen-year-olds did not matter in the slightest. Most of these relatively young boys, becoming wise to this state of affairs, but not looking sufficiently mature, endeavoured to grow some kind of moustache. As long as they could boast hair on their upper lip, their manly status improved.

Hard as he tried, Theo had no success in his effort to grow a moustache, even though, on the recommendation of his friends, he smeared green soap on his upper lip and chin.

At this period in his life, Theo was still in some kind of a psychological flux. Somewhat frustrated through his abrupt change from Grammar School to life in the weaving trade, he felt unsettled. Nor had he forgotten the numerous beatings his father had applied in the past. Those early days seemed very remote, as he had grown too much in strength for his father to apply the cane any more. The way was open to him to go as he pleased.

His apprenticeship completed, he continued for a while in the ribbon weaving industry until, through the outbreak of war, this trade died down to nothing. There was no longer any demand for this commodity and consequently Theo found himself without a job. One day, being tired of his unemployed state, he timidly approached his father, asking him for a loan of ten marks. Never having been out of Ronsdorf, he felt a desire to see the world. With a smile, his father handed over the money, feeling sure that his son would soon be back, as he could not get far on such a paltry sum. However, Josua Bender was mistaken!

Completely ignorant as to its destination, Theo boarded the first train to stop at Ronsdorf. Before his first exciting day was over, he had found a job in a town called Kettwig, many miles from home. The next step was to find lodgings. With only a few marks in his pocket, he checked in at one of the best hotels in the town. He had gambled on a prosperous future but, unfortunately, the job he thought would last for months, finished abruptly through his own misdoings. Suitably dressed, he was able to mingle without suspicion with the residents in this well-to-do hotel. However, when it came to general behaviour and table-manners — not using knife and fork according to etiquette, and introducing himself as ' Mr ' Bender — Theo was completely out of his depth, and was hastily removed from the hotel dining-room. The following day he was segregated from the rest of the guests and ate a lone meal at a table in an adjoining room. He had lasted out two days, but on the third, he slipped up altogether. Before leaving for work that morning, he approached the hotel manager with the request that a small dilapidated tin be filled up with ground coffee, for his tea-breaks. That was the final straw! In a kindly, fatherly way, the manager told him he would be wiser to seek other accommodation, and would he please check out. Here, his brief dream came to an end. After cashing his few days' wages, he paid his hotel bill and made off. However, he was not beaten, yet. He had learned his lesson the hard way. The upper classes do not mix with mere labourers.

Packing his little bag, he set off walking homewards. *En route,* he took odd jobs at roadside farms, until after ten days, tired and hungry, he came at last to his father's house. In one sitting, he polished off a potato salad his mother had made for the entire family. Needless to say his father was more than surprised that the ten marks had lasted Theo so long.

For a very short while Theo was content to stay at home, but before long the wanderlust was upon him again. Once more he set off from his home town to explore the industrial Ruhr, where well-paid jobs were in abundance. For a time he worked for Krupp's in Essen, becoming proficient in turning shells for the army. Then he switched from place to place, changing his job half-a-dozen times, until he finally became a skilled turner, earning more money than he could spend. This suited him very well, because beer and women cost money — for, after all, was not life a thing to be enjoyed?

When finally he came back to his native town, he had a good financial account to his credit. He joined in with his pals again. One could only describe these youngsters as enthusiastic and hilarious, during the early part of the war. They adopted the attitude that they were there to enjoy themselves as much, and as often as possible. Who knew how long it would last? It was a certainty that the longer this wretched war dragged on, their turn would come and they would be in it up to the neck.

Their noisy revelling became more and more frequent, and in the still of the night, the humble townsfolk were invariably roused from their beds by these drunken youngsters. Nobody knew what they would be up to next. One morning, early risers, when crossing the market square, looked in amazement at the famous monument from the 1870/71 war, on top of which stood the bronze figures of the Kaisers Wilhelm I and Friedrich III, with Wilhelm pointing his finger to the ' West ', the danger of France. On this important index finger dangled a large direction sign, inscribed ' To the Ronsdorf Reservoir '. The gang had done it again. Theo, being the lightest one among them, had been lifted on to the platform to shake hands with the Kaisers, and to put the placard in position. For this he got into trouble, his pastor mentioning the incident from the pulpit.

This was only one of the pranks in which Theo played a major part. Many of the jokes his work-mates put over were not always in very good taste, however, and could hardly be termed ' Jokes ' at all.

1915 was drawing to a close. The war had gained impetus, and grown into a world conflagration. Scores of wounded and discharged soldiers returned to their homeland. They told of their fighting experiences, mostly in an exaggerated form, to the teenagers who were, indeed, not far removed from the day when they would play their part in the deadly battle.

All this did not add up to our draper's son, who had learned the Ten Commandments. He had been taught — Thou Shalt Not Kill; Thou Shalt Not Steal. Now, the new policy was completely the reverse. At this impressionable age, it was not easy for Theo to swallow such new and devastating psychology.

At the age of eighteen he had outgrown the surveillance of his strict father, but to his mother he would always turn for advice, knowing full well that without her he would be alone.

Very soon, he would have to go to be medically examined, and he was fully aware that, when that happened, his joyous days would be numbered before the army swallowed him up. He was not alone in this predicament, and he and his friends formed a club for the furtherance of drinking and riotous living.

Having inherited from his father the ability to make people laugh, he became something of a comedian. He would walk on the stage and enthral the public with one of his chief acts, that of a medium in a trance. Dressed in an exotic-looking robe, under which were hidden numerous strong magnets, Theo would fall into a trance, and radiate a magnetic power. Pieces of metal thrown at him by the pseudo hypnotist would adhere to his body with a clang until, finally, a whole cascade of iron chippings released from above, would cling to his body with a clatter. Had it not been for his mother's advice which brought him back to reality, he would have made the stage his new career.

As the eve of his call-up loomed nearer, so the tempo of the nightly escapades with wine, women and song, heightened. Theo became completely exhausted. He became dangerously ill with diphtheria. Night after night, his aunt sat by his bedside applying hot linseed bags to his throat in an endeavour to keep him alive. In those days this was the only known remedy for such deadly diseases. At the same time Theo's bonny sister, Luise, fell ill with congestion of the lungs, and within a week, at the early age of twenty, she died. Penicillin and antibiotics were unheard of then, and with the primitive methods available there was no cure.

Soon after his illness, Theo was summoned for his medical. Thin and frail he attended, expecting to be rejected. However, such were the fatalities in the front line that more and more men were demanded, and our disillusioned conscript was passed A1, ready to march and fight.

Most of his school pals who were born in 1896, had long since left. Through the baptism of fire they had gone. Some were already dead, bringing home to the youngster the realities of this sinister life.

Awaiting his call-up was a stimulant for further enjoyment. He claimed far too much from his weakened physique, until on New Year's night 1915/16, his heartbeats became erratic and grew faster and louder. He managed to shout for his mother who anxiously felt the heartbeats. Certainly something was wrong here. Theo was sure he was going to die, but the old doctor's skill saved him from a heart attack.

This was a lesson which went home to Theo. He recovered from this nasty experience but it left him frightened. Vowing that from now on he would alter his entire way of life, he moderated considerably and adhered to such moderation for the rest of his life.

He took up sport, and soon excelled in football and swimming. With this more healthy existence, he grew stronger and began to look better again, but the wartime shortage of food partly curtailed his progress. Good meat was in very short supply and difficult to obtain, the blockade of Germany having its effect. Human beings now consumed food which in peacetime was fed to cattle. Green vegetables were out, and bunches of stinging nettles were gathered in the fields, though it must be admitted they were both nourishing and tasty. Remnants and waste of barley, which Josua had taken great trouble to requisition for his remaining meagre looking piglet, went through the coffee-grinder, to be baked into a kind of cake for the family to eat. The curtailment of the pig's food supply did not help the latter, who quickly began to shrink, until, when weighing only eighty pounds, it disappeared altogether. Thieving was common, and who could blame folks for this when hungry?

The year 1916 advanced quickly and, for some unknown reason, Theo was still at home. The army continued calling-up, but they just seemed to by-pass Theo's category.

In the meantime, his patriotic relations urged him to join the Youth Brigade, a semi-military organization, which he did, learning to march and play with dummy rifles.

He had settled down in his home town, in a job involving weaving tapes for army matresses and making rifle straps. The humming of his weaving loom would be accompanied by his tenor voice singing all day long. Not only did this attract the passers-by but also Paula, the buxom, nineteen-year-old assistant of the butcher. She went daily to collect the eggs from the hen-pen opposite the lad's workshop.

Whether it was because she liked him, or that she was aware of the extra nourishment Theo required, each day she would slip a few eggs into his pockets. This proved most welcome and, consequently, a friendship developed between them, much to the detriment of the butcher's food supply.

In the past Theo had mainly knocked about with boys of his own age and therefore thought nothing at all about this new acquaintance. She was just a very nice girl.

Instincts of love sometimes develop slowly and Theo had never given this side of things a thought. Then, suddenly, one day, a spark set something on fire. There was more to it than just receiving eggs. He was head over heels in love, and his singing became more impassioned. Telling the girl of his feelings he was thrilled to find that her thoughts were on the same lines. Running straight home to his mother, he breathlessly broke the news to her that he intended to get married.

After this had been digested by Josua and Magdalena, they informed him that this was right out of the question, a draper's son and a housemaid just did not fit. This summer dream, which started like a fireball, eventually burnt itself out, the call-up papers doing the rest in October, 1916.

There was no holding him. All his friends had gone months ago, and now he wanted to follow them. The preparation and final departure from home did not take him long. The world was open to him to unknown adventure.

## THE TIN SOLDIER

Theo was amongst the last batch of the 1897 conscripts. Eight of them in all, they were healthy boys, and had known one another since their school days. Some were well-to-do, while others were just working class men, but in the army there was no distinction, and each became a private soldier.

Little did they know then that, with the exception of Theo Bender, within eighteen months none of them would be alive. Seven young lives frittered away for a nonsensical cause that ended in disaster for the mighty Germany.

Theo was determined to use whatever excuse he could muster to stay out of the front line. It did not always work, however, and on many occasions he found himself in the midst of the bloodiest hand-to-hand fighting.

And so the time came for him to leave his home. Kissing the weeping members of his family good-bye, his last words before leaving were, "Don't worry, Mam, I'll come back."

They were taken to the county assembly point, joined there by other batches of youngsters all bound for the same destination — Heidelberg, where they were to join the Company of the 14th Rifle Regiment. On the 17th October 1916, they graduated to soldiers receiving a weekly wage of Mark 2.30.

The first few days were full of interest for Theo. A sturdy sergeant measured and weighed him. Although 5ft. 8ins., he only touched the scales at 9 stone 6 lbs. The height was all right, but after his illness, he was still far too thin. This could be remedied, and very soon was. His new abode was in an oven factory which had been requisitioned for military training.

Once he had received his kit, it did not take him long to get into his khaki uniform. He presented rather a comical figure, with his tunic drooping from his narrow frame, and the peak cap which was far too large. Despite this Theo was as proud as a peacock when he sat down to write his first letter to his mother, describing all the events.

Sealing the letter, and affixing the stamp, the mail was ready for posting, and it was at this juncture in his military career that he first contacted trouble. Unknown to Theo, there was an important inspection in the offing and the Major in charge, accompanied by the Sergeant-Major, was engaged in getting the battalion into two long rows.

Just at the very moment when both lines of soldiers were still at ease, an order, shouted in the true military style, echoed around the parade ground: "Attention! Eyes left!" Riding on horseback through the main gate came the Brigadier to inspect the columns of men. This was, apparently, an ordinary military procedure, which became extraordinary as our newly-baked soldier, a comical-looking figure, came darting out of the entrance of the barracks to weave his way in the direction of the letter box outside the main gate. The alley he approached was flanked on one side by the Brigadier, the Major and Sergeant-Major, and on the other by the immaculate-looking battalion. This caused a fearful commotion, resulting in poor Theo being chased all over the courtyard by the indignant Sergeant-Major, who put the flat side of his sabre to good use on the unfortunate lad's behind. No further punishment was inflicted, however, when it was realized that it was the young soldier's first day in the uniform of the Kaiser's army.

As the days passed, the change from civilian life into military activity began to work wonders with Theo. He began to fill out and, consequently, looked a lot smarter. His army rations were supplemented when he struck up a friendship with a farmer in the village of Schwetzingen, where he spent most of his week-ends, enjoying nourishing meals in the company of the farmer's lovely daughters. Paula was by now completely forgotten.

Every day, the young privates were put through their paces — walking, running and climbing. This was good for the boys' physique.

Then came the day when Bender became the proud possessor of a rifle, serial No 9915A. He gazed at it admiringly, for was not this the weapon upon which, one day, his life might depend? Theo made many friends amongst his platoon and, in army language, they called one another *Kameraden*. He was generally liked and could always be relied upon to keep the platoon amused.

Amongst the physical-training instructors, there were some nasty old hands. Rough and coarse, in their methods, they could pull the guts out of a new recruit if they thought fit. On the other hand, there were several self-opinionated types amongst the privates who would defy the superiority of their instructors to the detriment of the whole platoon. When this applied, there was only one remedy, that of ' The Holy Ghost '.

This barbaric punishment was well planned beforehand. The sturdiest and strongest fellows were chosen for the sudden attack. At a given moment, somewhere around midnight, the victim would be set upon and his face and upper body covered with a couple of blankets, stifling any noise the poor chap might make. Then, a second lot of strong men would start the real attack, striking blow after blow on the culprit's lower back with the hardest of instruments. When all was over, the poor soldier had no clue as to who had attacked him. If he had complained to the Commanding Officer, he would certainly have received another visit from the ' Holy Ghost ' the second night. This remedy always worked, and succeeded in knocking the offender into shape.

Their army training was rapidly being speeded up and in order to make sure that they stood by their national flag, they had to undergo a solemn ceremony in one of the large churches, where each one had to deliver an oath to defend his Kaiser and the Fatherland.

Any soldier displaying cowardice or trying to desert, received severe punishment, even death. This dedicated and holy pledge in the history to follow became something of a farce. The Kaiser, to whom all soldiers had sworn their allegiance, disappeared from the scene and when the disastrous end of the German war was near, deserting both Reich and army, slipped across the Dutch border.

With two months of solid training behind him, Bender was longing to see his relations just to show his mother what a fine soldier he was. Although leave was out of the question at this early stage, when his grandfather, John Elias, died, he was granted compassionate leave.

As all eyes would be upon him in the funeral procession, he must look smart. It was of great importance to the lads from 'Zion' that their first representative from the regiment had to look outstandingly smart when facing the townspeople. And so it came about that Theo Bender returned to his home town looking exceedingly immaculate in hand-tailored uniform, including a peaked cap which he had borrowed from one of his more affluent comrades.

Looking more like a Commanding Officer than an ordinary private, on his arrival he immediately visited all his relations and friends to show them what a fine soldier he was.

Needless to say, he was a great success with the girls from the neighbouring big city and, on his return to camp, had many stories to tell his comrades of his latest experiences in that field.

Once back in harness again, his leave was soon forgotten through the variety of army life. There was something new every week. Exhaustive bayonet fighting, rifle practice, and new exercises. These were enthusiastic youngsters, with the sparkle of youth in their blood. All looking extremely fit, Bender, a stone heavier than when he first joined, was no exception. His rifle shots hit the target all right, and, to everyone's surprise, he excelled himself in the bayonet duels, knocking the other fellow about with a dummy weapon, a wooden contraption, rifle-like, with an iron rod sticking out of the top, covered with a protective stuffed hard cloth ball at the end.

Many of these instruments were in poor condition, and on some, the protective covering was missing altogether, exposing a rusty rod. The recruits were supplied with special fine mesh face-masks and steel breast-shields, to safeguard themselves during practice, but, more often than not, these precautions were ignored.

The champion of the regiment was a veritable Hercules of a chap, a butcher by trade. He would challenge anyone with his bayonet. The instructor, a corporal, who had witnessed many a blood-bath in frontline fighting in real war, was not impressed by this boast. One day he challenged the sturdy butcher's boy, who readily accepted. Grabbing up the first dummy rifle, with no protection over the rusty rod, the fight began in earnest. Fellow corporals and the sergeant urged the two contestants to wear face and breast-shields, and tried to persuade the butcher to change his rifle for one with a cloth ball covering. However, neither the instructor nor his pupil heeded the warning, and the battle grew rougher and tougher, with hard hitting from both sides. The butcher's boy, not particularly fond of his corporal, employed all his skill in an endeavour to defeat his superior in front of his mates, and soon things began to happen. One more parry, one more attack and the poor corporal fell to the ground unconscious, the rusty rod having entered his mouth and out at the back of his neck. He lay on the grass in a pool of blood, his face deathly white. By a miracle he survived — but now it was a case for the hospital, and the Commanding Officer.

Heidelberg, the wonderful University Town, an attraction to visitors in peacetime, was an ideal place for a garrison for young soldiers. It was a town steeped in history, with many famous relics, apart from an abundancy of modern entertainment. Bender, not particularly interested in the town's historical side was, however, in the latter. Young privates did not possess the resources to entertain the girls of the town, and it was an accepted thing that the girls, who earned high wages in munition factories during the war, should pay for an evening's entertainment. Theo had grown more discerning in his choice of women, and did not choose the first who happened to come along. Their fleeting associations left little impression in his mind. He had a long way to go yet before the girl of his choice, who would be his partner for life, came along.

1917 was well advanced into the spring, and still the Army General Staff seemed to have forgotten the existence of these twenty-year-old riflemen. They were all in fighting trim, but no summons came, whereas much younger men from other formations were tramping through France and Russia. Bender well appreciated the position, for the longer their training lasted, the greater their chances of survival.

Exercises were now at their peak. With full pack, steel helmet and rifle, thirty or more miles was the order of the day. The strain began to tell on Bender and as a result he became run-down, eventually breaking out in boils all over his face and body. For several weeks he lay in the sick-room. Here, also, he gained a new experience of army life. Surrounded by comrades, mainly laid-up with septic heels presumably caused through the strain of marching, he discovered that the malady was self-inflicted. These chaps would go a long way to keep clear of tiring exercises. They would moisten a middle finger and, covering it with dirt from the floor, rub the skin off their heels, until through to the bare flesh. To aggravate it further, they would lay a few hairs into the open wound, causing it to become inflamed and grow septic, the bare bone showing at the base of the matter. When Bender left hospital, it was with a new aspect on a soldier's bravery.

And so life went on, interspersed with the small incidents typical of army life, until the Whitsun of 1917. On that day a holiday had been granted for everyone, with no duties whatsoever. Bender had planned a long distance swim in the river Neckar, so in the early hours of Sunday morning, he and his friend caught the tram which would take them up the course of the river for some five miles. On the bank of this fast-flowing river, Theo stripped, handed over his togs to his pal and with a wave of his hand, dived into the rapid current. Although a good swimmer, he had never known such a strong current, and this nearly brought about the termination of his life.

At the outset he drifted happily along, enjoying the sunny morning. He was the only soul in the vast expanse of water. Approaching Heidelberg, the river flowed faster, passing the old bridge and the castle. Swifter and swifter the current became, making him realize all too well, that this was quite different from the swimming pool. Finally, he gave up struggling against the tearing swirl and was swept along at an alarming rate. Seeing a lone island he tried to swim at right angles in an endeavour to reach the shore, but in vain. He knew that if he missed the island, he would be swept out into the middle of the river again, and that meant drowning. A few yards away from the island he scraped a submerged rock, and grimly held on to it. Pausing to regain his breath, he summoned up all his strength, and in a last attempt, performed a long flat dive, which landed him, with outstretched arms, in the bulrushes.

On the island he sat all day, watching the passers-by only half a mile away, but afraid to make that final bid for safety. By this time, the alarm had been raised in the barracks. A search party eventually found him, sitting cold and shivering in his swimming trunks. The rescue party had to swim across the calmer arm of the river and escort the hapless Theo back to the mainland.

At last real battle was in sight, and the regiment was mobilized for wartime service. Everyone was excited, if a little nervous, and after packing their kits and posting their last letters home, they were bundled into goods and cattle carriages, ready for the journey to the front.

Onwards rolled the long train, further and further south, until it finally came to a halt past Colmar in Alsace Lorraine, behind the utmost southern tip of the German-French battlefront. A long and tiring march landed them in the middle of the Vosges mountains, the quietest part of the western war. Nothing exceptional happened here. It was more like living in a sanatorium with plenty of fresh air, intermingled with the sounds of far distant artillery fire. Each day found everyone waiting expectantly for the command to occupy the front lines. A month passed by in this way, the soldiers having a good time digging trenches. Finally, a signal came for them to board the train for a new destination. To their surprise, it turned out to be Heidelberg. Back they were, none the wiser about a real war.

After three years of war, the Allied and the German armies were locked in stationary battle, the final outcome of which was doubtful. The struggle that had started like an avalanche in the Kaiser's favour had halted in three years of deadlock. On both sides of the lines, the soldiers were dug deep in the trenches and pillboxes, leading a miserable existence. Despite the fact that the Western Front was quiet, men were still dying by the thousand. Over the tops they would jump in local skirmishes, wearing each other down day after day. For the Infantry in the trenches it became a matter of waiting, being exposed to heavy artillery fire against which they had no defence. They sat, like rabbits in their holes — waiting.

Unscrupulous inventors were still at work bringing out newer and deadlier methods of killing. No longer were shell and shrapnel splinters the last answer. They hit upon a new method of fuming the human creatures out, by using the deadly Mustard Gas. This was a terrible death, which dissolved the delicate tissues of the chest.

In the German trenches, soldiers began to wonder what had gone wrong with their leader's strategy. For them, the war, which had started so successfully and should have been over within twelve months, was still dragging on. There were even signs that they might ultimately lose the war. In general, the Germans believe they are the cleverest race on earth. They were the masters in industry, planning and invention. The German Military Intelligence can plan a war; they plan it well, allowing for every eventuality. However, they are too cocksure. Never expecting anything to go wrong, when it does, they have no answer. Such thoughts had by now entered the minds of German soldiers. They became complacent, thinking that after all if they did win the war, it would be a bad thing for those who would become soldiers for life, occupying enemy countries for years on end.

# REAL WAR

Into this atmosphere moved our riflemen, when the General Staff decided, after all, to employ these soldiers in their prime. A regiment of the elite, trained for mountain warfare, originally destined for Roumania, where their main formation had been stationed for many years with little fighting. The war in France demanded Infantry and, reluctantly, they had to change from their green uniform to the field-grey of the common soldier. Zero hour came in August, 1917, when, fitted with brand new equipment, the regiment waited to be shipped to whatever destination Headquarters should decide.

The night before departure every man was out for his last fling until midnight. In the excitement, many of these joyriders overstepped the mark, arriving back, unsteady on their feet and full of beer to find the barracks closed. As they scrambled over the wall they were caught by the guard on duty, and locked up for the night as punishment.

Next morning, the regiment lined up in front of the building looking very spick and span, ready for their march to the station. But they had reckoned without the Commanding Officer. The latter, annoyed about his recruits' behaviour the night before, had his own plans. When the order came that would set the column in motion, it was not, as they had expected, the route along the highway to the railway station, but into a freshly ploughed, rain-soaked field. A breathtaking exercise began. In their new outfits, they had to creep through the puddles of the furrows on their bellies. The ordeal over, they assembled, a ramshackle-looking formation, covered with mud from head to foot, ready for their march through the fine streets of Heidelberg. Soldiers ready to sacrifice their lives had been treated like pigs. The officer in question was earmarked for future revenge and, as had been known to happen before, probably shot from behind by his own men in real battle.

A bedraggled-looking dirty lot, flowers from sweethearts decorating the tips of their rifles, they goose-stepped through the city. Soon the command "Sing!" was given, and expecting the worst if they did not obey, their voices sang louder than ever: *Dem Kaiser Wilhelm Haben Wir's Geschworen* (To Emperor Wilhelm we have sworn). Finally, they were herded into the cattle trucks, and set off for Strasbourg, Infantry Regiment 136.

Theirs was a short stay in this famous city, and soon their journey towards France continued. Like the others, Bender sat in an open cattle truck, his legs dangling out, the landscape passing by. He nearly met his doom when, as they passed beneath a bridge at top speed, the parapet caught his jackboot; frightened, he crept back into the truck. When nightfall came they all settled down on the hard boards of the rattling train, which still bore evidence of its previous four-legged passengers.

Where were Bender's companions from 'Zion'? They were somewhere in the contingent. What were they thinking now that real war was approaching? There was Karl Trambach, who had sat with Theo in Grammar School. The son of well-to-do, highly patriotic parents, he would certainly approach this war in a different frame of mind from Bender. Education to him would make all the difference; no fear of enemy bullets would enter his head as he went over the top. Was it not his duty to help win the war for the Kaiser, whom he and his father held in great admiration? A strong and muscular, manly-looking chap, with a dark moustache, Karl was just made for the German Army.

Then there was Paul Langerback, better known as 'Spider'. Thin and tall, a cause of under-nourishment, but jovial and full of fun, he came from a completely different class of people. Even if the war-machine went down the drain, he had nothing to lose.

Walter Henner was another one somewhere in the train. His working-class parents were a stage higher than ' Spider's '. A well-built boy, quiet and thoughtful with no inclination to shoot others, what would he be thinking on the eve of warfare?

Eugen Stremner fell into a similar category to Walter, but, owing to his upbringing, more on the Socialist side. Such people loathe anything that reeks of Capitalism, and are against being herded together and treated like cattle. What would be his war-dreams, as he rocked along in one of the shaking carriages? Certainly, he would regard the outcome of the war with indifference.

Somewhere in the train was Eduard Plater. In his political views, he fell into the same class as Karl Trambach. A son of very rich parents, should he survive, he would, one day, inherit the formidable engineering works. He would have to fight, if only for the sake of his father's factory. Bender knew him quite well, as he did all the others, but Trambach and Plater at one time sat together with him in the same Grammar School. They had carried on in the traditional conservative way, whereas Bender had dropped, at an early junction, into the class of the working men.

Where was Erich Martin, the sturdy butcher's boy, whose nose was always running? Instead of wiping it with his handkerchief, he would raise his lower lip and catch the drips from his nostrils. This six-footer, was the son of a policeman, belonging to the middle-class. Patriotic — yes. But, in spite of Erich's muscular frame, he would not be the first to overrun the enemy.

The last one of the bunch was Wilhelm Schmied. A tall chap, he was the son of a weaver, who would spend hours dreaming of the future. Would he know that he was to be the first to die for his country's cause?

Here they were, an assortment of young men, all with different outlooks on life, who, without war, would have been confined to their own political and financial category. War had brought them together, the rough and the refined in a mass of field-grey.

At last, the long train drew to a halt at a place called Thiaucourt, south-west of Verdun. For the first time they stepped on to French soil, where they joined the Hanover Infantry Regiment 164, a part of the 111th Division.

It was a quiet sector of the Western Front where immature troops could be acquainted with their new surroundings before being introduced to the real brutalities of war. Here, they occupied wooden barracks some twenty miles behind the front line, but near enough to be hit by the French artillery; also, in reach of the flimsy-looking aeroplanes, a novelty not experienced in past wars.

Immediately upon their arrival, one of these aeroplanes must have smelt the reinforcements at Thiaucourt, for it promptly dropped its load into the vicinity, killing only healthy cattle and horses. This was a novel sight for the newcomers. The animals' carcasses were soon left behind, deprived of the healthy meat which would go to feed many a hungry soldier.

In this atmosphere the troops began to acclimatize themselves. At night, they were plagued by multitudes of rats, roaming through the wooden structure. Soldiers, dreaming about their far away homeland, would brush what they thought to be a sweetheart's curl from their faces, only to find on waking up, that it was the tail of an over-size rat. These pests were dealt with by a shooting gallery, set up in the barracks during the evenings. Bait was laid at one end of the hut, while the soldiers with their rifles, retreated to the other end. It was a matter of waiting until scores of rats congregated around the bait, when a hail of bullets would descend upon them, leaving many a rat lying dead on the floor. Quite a harmless game, and it kept them in training. The victims — just rats.

This was one of the first experiences to be faced. But there was another one caused by the thousands of fleas and lice which tormented the soldiers' bodies. Out in the open, in the dark of the night, they would run in the nude, shaking their vests and shirts to get rid of this pestering annoyance. The lice were more penetrating than the fleas, digging holes in the skin and hiding beneath it, sucking the blood. This special type of louse was thickish and strong in appearance with a kind of cross on its back and, when killing and flattening one between the nails of the thumbs, a sharp crack was audible. They were tough, and very difficult to extract from the skin. They could be boiled and still not die, their only extinction *en masse* being accomplished by the official delousing chambers established behind the front line. Even then they would not all die, some surviving in the nicks of the leather purses.

Bender, as so often before, got into trouble straight away. He had slept in France for the first night, only to discover the following morning that his brand new jackboots had gone. It never occurred to him that a Kamerad could have stolen them from him. Making his way to the store he clicked his heels, and said to the Quartermaster Sergeant, "Good morning, sir. I must have a new pair of jackboots — mine disappeared during the night." This was innocence at its highest and he just managed to get out of the store before the Sergeant's boot came in contact with his behind. This brought it home to him that his jackboots had been stolen after all, and that he had to get new ones before the next rollcall. By the evening, he was the owner of a brand new pair. They were two inches too large, so he ingeniously wore larger socks, tying a big knot into the toe ends, so filling the vacuum inside the boots. In these he marched for the rest of the war.

By 1917 the whole of Germany was strangled by the blockade. Civilians were starving, whilst the fighting forces were fed on the barest essentials. Their main diet consisted of cabbages, potatoes and swedes, with very little bread. In place of butter, which was practically non-existent, they were issued with ' monkey fat ', an indescribable substance. Added to this was a tiny ration of jam. This comprised the diet of a soldier during wartime. Napoleon once said that soldiers fought with their stomachs, and accordingly, there could not be much fighting spirit left in the German armies. It was no wonder, therefore, that when Bender saw how a couple of soldiers increased their rations with boiled chicken and rabbits, he was curious to know from whence they came. He was well aware that they must be stolen, but who could blame the hungry ranks for so doing? In any case, were not the terms good and bad reversed during war? Most soldiers had had to accept this conception when wholesale killing and plundering became the order of the day. The common private was allocated the barest of rations. A sergeant, with authority, might get a little more, whereas an officer, with the help of his batman and the swill of the company kitchen, could rear his own chicken and rabbits. Even in the army, class distinction had to be maintained.

With this kind of psychology in mind, the hungry Bender set about investigating where these tasty fowl came from. One evening he approached the two chaps as like Henry VIII they were hungrily tearing away the flesh from the legs of the chicken. Paul Karmann was one, Karl Rehman the other. Paul, a native from Hamburg, was only eighteen. Tall and thin, he walked with a peculiar swaying gait, his foot-long pipe following the movement like a pendulum of a cuckoo-clock. Most likely he had been brought up near the shipyards of Hamburg and, never having tasted a good life, he revelled in his element as an easy-going soldier. Even in the thickest of fighting, he never grew perturbed. His stomach was number one, and as long as he had food to fill it, he could not care less where it came from.

Karl was a different character altogether. Well into his thirties, he was a strong fellow, who looked smart even in his worn field-grey. He was a real battle-axe, having been in the fighting since the first day of the war. His reactions and behaviour were the result of the many shell-shocks he had endured. For him, life had changed since he left the plains of northern Germany for service in the army. One thing, however, he and Paul had in common was their complete indifference to life.

Bender opened the conversation by asking where the chicken came from. Paul and Karl both smiled, and invited him to accompany them the following night to see for himself. The adventurers hurdled over hedges and fences until they landed in the yard of the Artillery. There, they found what they were seeking. It was the usual custom of the kitchen staff to have a small trailer attached to their kitchen waggons, carrying the few chickens for their officers. Out came the hens in a flurry of feathers, Karl, Paul and Theo each grabbing one. Back over the fences they flew, but not soon enough. A hail of rifle bullets followed them. This was the first time Bender had been at the receiving end, and as he heard the live bullets hissing close to his ears, he realized that this was a dangerous business, requiring courage. He was now assured of his future food supplies, this stealing escapade providing him with a new stimulant.

From the day of its arrival, the 111th Division had been split into three, the 76th and 73rd Regiments holding front line and reserve, while Bender's formation, the 164th, was exercising far behind the first line, affording yet another week's respite. Bender was allocated to the 9th Company where, for the first time, he met his new Company Sergeant, a soldier according to the textbook, worthy of a cartoon. His name was Molendam, his face almost covered by a large, bushy moustache. Tucked through the third and fourth button of his tunic was a fat wallet and pencil. Little did he know then that in the days to come he would have many encounters with Private Bender.

After a week in reserve, one dark night the regiment was herded into small trucks to be taken by a diminutive army train close to the front, from where they would march the last lap to their destination. It was a dark, deathly quiet night, almost as if there was no war at all. They occupied their dug-outs, dark holes hewn into the bare rock, without any wooden support. Wooden planks covered the bottom, which was full of water. This was to be their domicile for a week to come. How far away home seemed at that moment!

It was not long before the silence was shattered and the first shells began to drop. They fell on the roofs of the shelters, shaking the whole of their hide-outs and causing stones to fall from the ceiling. This was war in earnest. The end was near, they thought, and many a quiet prayer was uttered. What with the noise and the rats, there was not much sleep during the first night.

In spite of this extreme adversity, the men had to acclimatize themselves and, with the light of the first dawn, they crept out of their holes to explore the trenches. Bender, with his insatiable curiosity, had to see where the fireworks had exploded and with artillery shells whistling overhead, he climbed on top of the trench to investigate. This was a dangerous and prohibited procedure which earned him a sharp reprimand.

At midday, it was his first turn for sentry duty. What a proud feeling this was. He, a tiny unit in the massive German

Army, guarding his country. Although in this sector they never saw an enemy soldier, they were still close enough to kill one another. The Frenchmen opposite, with their telescopic rifles, were always on the look-out for the slightest movement. Bender, soon alert to this danger, kept his head well down behind the large steel shield, and looked through the small peep-hole. Through this he watched no-man's-land, observing occasionally the spray of dirt in front of his nose caused by an enemy bullet. The sentry next to him took no precaution when investigating the spray of the bullets, and was shot through the head and killed by an accurate French rifleman. One German soldier less; the end of the war one step nearer.

Bender began to learn the mechanics of war quickly. His next sentry duty was at midnight. All alone, his eyes pierced the darkness in front of him for any sign of movement. There were flashes in the far distance, followed by a hail of rocks and steel in his immediate vicinity. The artillery from St Mihiel was aiming at his sector. Remembering that light travels faster than sound, he jumped for cover the moment a flash was visible, so safeguarding his body from eventual injury.

Each night, during the one week that the company occupied the front trench, the enemy were being harassed by voluntary patrols sent out in the dark and by the end of the week, every man of the unit had volunteered with the exception of Bender. Despite the fact that Sergeant Molendam labelled him a coward, Bender had no inclination to volunteer for such a stunt. If compelled, he would have to go, but to step into no-man's-land voluntarily, sacrificing his life, went against the grain.

Bender preferred to upset the enemy when there was no risk to himself. He had an opportunity for this in his first week. Being trained on the mine-thrower he joined a batch of soldiers as 'The Shot' in one of the secure and solid concrete pill-boxes, specially constructed for this kind of warfare. The mine-thrower stood on a concrete platform inside one of these pill-boxes. In the stone ceiling was a small escape hatch. The mine was put in the socket, the string pulled and, with a roar, off it went, through the hatch, high up into the sky, to descend in a steep dive bang into the enemy trenches. This was fine practice-shooting, but it did not last long. The German boys had reckoned without the retaliation of the enemy, until they found themselves in a very vulnerable position, and being smothered with artillery fire. This put an end to the mine-thrower.

The second week, the reserve were marched into a dense wood, hidden from observation in elaborate dug-outs. This was more like a holiday where the troops could roam at large through the autumn forest. The only drawback in their lush shelters was the absence of artificial light. Candles were useless, but officers were supplied with electricity. Bender soon found the remedy. Somehow, a connection had to be made between the double line of high-tension wires which led to the front of the massive concrete headquarters of the division and his own shelter. There was no electric cable available for this purpose, but barbed wire would conduct electricity just the same. Through the trees, like monkeys the lads climbed, fastening the connection from branch to branch, while with thick gloves they hooked the ends of both wires over the live lines. Requisitioning a bulb from somewhere, the installation was ready. It worked, with far too brilliant a light in Bender's shelter. Here, they could laze about and read, just like a holiday resort. It did not last, however. The rain set in, soaking the trees and the wire. Through the electric current being diverted, officers at headquarters began complaining at the dimness of the lights. Soon the repair gang turned up and when they spotted the elementary connection, the vacation came to a hasty conclusion.

The fortnightly baptism of fire, if one could call it that, was over, and they were back in the vicinity of Thiaucourt. As it was impossible to find a means of supplementing his rations while in the front trenches, Bender was growing increasingly hungry. Having learned something from Paul and Karl, much to the others' surprise, he decided to try his own hand at the game. Strolling along the village street one day he encountered a flock of hens and cockerels. Here were some good meals. But how did one get hold of a live hen? Bender pondered. Seeing a plump-looking one, he tried to catch it, but it was too quick for him. Catching sight of a brick lying in the street, he picked it up and threw it into the midst of the feathered mass. It accounted for one casualty; a weighty bird lying on its side, gasping for breath. Bender grabbed it up, but by now the whole village had come to investigate what all the noise was about. With the cackling bird under his arm, Theo made off, with the villagers close on his trail. Nipping out of sight down a side entrance which led into a large garden, he hid the bird under the hedge. Coming out at the other end, Bender was back in the street, joining the crowd in an endeavour to find the culprit.

During this episode, Paul and Karl had been sitting comfortably in the platoon's quarter, on the first floor of an old barn. Slowly, the door creaked open to reveal Theo. They could hardly believe that their friend had actually caught a live hen in broad daylight.

However, repercussions were bound to follow as the incident had been reported to the officer in command of the village. In the meantime Paul lost no time. He collected the bird from under the hedge and brought the boiling pan into the barn. Soldiers lying about in the straw soon lifted their nostrils, everybody anticipating a bite. This, however, did not arise. With a bang the door burst open, giving Paul just time to throw the boiling pan, together with its contents, into the far corner of the barn, where someone hastily covered it up with plenty of straw.

In the doorway stood the Company Commander and Sergeant Molendam, the tasty aroma of the half-cooked hen weaving round their noses. Very red in the face, the officer roared — "Where is that bird?" Everyone stood to attention. No matter how much the officer persevered, no one replied to the question. Molendam, knowing his thieves, shouted: "Karmann! Step forward. You will do duty as night sentry, to be followed by a day of hard work!"

Paul countered: "If you permit, sir, can Bender come with me?"

Perplexed, the sergeant made his way towards Bender, looking him up and down, then he came out with one of his typical expressions: "Look! Look! Look!" he said. "We have a third thief in the company. On sentry you go!" he shouted to Bender. "You and Karmann, will guard the kitchen's food supplies."

In two hourly sessions, Bender and Paul switched their duties during the night and, by the morning, a good deal of the iron rations had disappeared from the kitchen into the barn; a welcome additional food supply for all the occupants.

## FLANDERS

The introduction to war was now over! It was late September when, one morning, the bugles sounded the alarm for new marching orders. This time the train took the division further and further north. Older soldiers amongst them, fearfully whispered, "Flanders — the blood-bath of the war." They were right in their predictions, the final stop being Lichtervelde. The older ranks began to swear. "——— awful!" they said, on seeing the name-plate of the station. They had landed at the hot-point of the Western Front, where soldiers suffocated in the mud and died by the thousands. Only one week of rest was granted, after the light skirmishes in the south, before they were marched to Roulers, the town once famous for textile goods, but where mills now lay in smithereens. Here they idled, preparing for the real thing.

On a late evening in October the division was set in motion — destination, front line. From far away the rumbling of many guns was audible, lighting up the dark sky and painting brilliant patterns into the clouds like a far distant thunderstorm. By now it was pitch dark, and they moved into single file. The fireworks gradually came nearer, but still the men were out of reach of the exploding shells.

They passed Westrosebeke and those in the know were aware that Passchendaele, the hottest spot of all, was near. Close in line they went, balancing on the rims of crater after muddy crater, which had been created by the millions of shells that had fallen there since 1914. The landscape was disfigured by the skeletons sticking up out of the mud. A low-voiced command came: "Stick closer together!" The soldiers held the handles of each others' spades. This was the only way to avoid the men falling into the water and blood-filled holes. The whispered commands, coming from the leading man, sounded sinister in the darkness, as they were passed down the line. "Wire on the left; deep hole on the right." All this fitted into the pattern of this nightly inferno.

That night, it almost seemed as though the Lord held the fate of these soldiers in his hand. For, through some inexplicable reason, by the time they stepped into the belt of bursting grenades, the whole line of fire just stopped. Unmolested, they kept trudging along, until Bender and his company reached the line of reserve, the remainder marching on to the very front. Once more, he was lucky to fight the war in the less vulnerable second line, where he and his mates were housed in a fairly safe-looking pill-box, a twenty feet square cubicle of solid concrete, with a top some twelve feet thick. Into this box, through a three feet square entrance, crept Bender and his seven companions. The only entrance, this was a veritable death-trap. Relatively, it was a comfortable place, with just sufficient air to breathe. The heat of their bodies and some ersatz wool blankets kept them warm. In here they waited, day after day, for something to happen.

Having occupied their den without a shot being fired, they settled down playing cards, expecting a quiet week. The inside of the shelter was filled to capacity. The ceiling was no more than four feet away from the floor, and a couple of candles supplied a primitive light in an otherwise dark hole. At one time this concrete cubicle must have been well sunk into the ground, the very top below the mud. Like ants trying to unearth something, human beings, with their long-range missiles must have cleared the soil away, leaving the shelter standing on top of the ground like a cigar-box. A perfect target, visible for miles.

In here, the eight occupants became prisoners for practically a week. No sooner had they settled down on the evening of their arrival, than Hell was let loose. Shells and shrapnels, big and small, were bursting around the box with such intensity that nobody dared to put his head out of the only small exit. Even ordinary human needs could not be accomplished. It was too great a risk to endeavour to visit the non-existent toilet facilities outside. The result was, that after a few days, it was practically impossible to use the exit of this death-trap, the entrance being filled with a repulsive stinking mess up to elbow-depth.

The climax came when, on the 25th October, one of the heaviest long-range shells hit the concrete box fair and square. Fortunately it was a dud and did not explode. Had it done so, no one inside would have remained alive. The impact was such, however, that the whole shelter tilted over, making the exit even smaller. Everybody was asleep at the time when the percussion came, throwing the eight bodies inside up against the hard stone ceiling with tremendous force. The only sound after this was Bender's screaming, the others lying lifeless on the floor. Bender had been saved by a miracle. The vertical concrete wall, against which the boys' heads had been resting, was covered with old wooden boards, with rusty and pointed six-inch nails sticking out everywhere. It was one of these nails, bent downwards, which saved his life. Through the impact, his body was jerked upwards, his head, fortunately, in the path of one of these nails. It pierced into the skin of his head, scraping part of his bony skull, and coming out again two inches away. There he was hanging, conscious and screaming just as if he had been fastened to the wall with a large rusty safety-pin. He shouted to the others, but no one replied. Somehow, he managed to release himself, blood spurting all over the place. Pushing his way through the excreta in the exit, out into the open, he completely disregarded the exploding shells around him. Raising his voice, he shouted in the direction of the pill-box, some fifty yards away, which housed the company officer and some men. Fortunately, they heard him above the noise and waved to him to crawl the distance through the murderous artillery fire. One of the men met him half-way and dragged him along, unable to recognize him as Bender, as his eyes peeped out of a face encrusted with drying blood.

Pulling him into their shelter, they cleaned his face and bandaged him, whilst a team was organized to help rescue the other seven left in the death-box. They found them, some already recovered from unconsciousness. These were the light cases, suffering from concussion. The others remained lying on the concrete with cracks in their skulls.

By the evening Bender had recovered from the shock and with a clean dressing on his head, leaving two tiny spaces for him to see, he was ready, in spite of the Hell of fire, to find his way back to the reserve in Roulers in the dark. The officer agreed, and put him in charge of two other dazed and concussed fellows. With shells exploding all around them, they walked, crept and scrambled along the brims of the dirty shell craters. Eventually they reached the first Red Cross post, a dug-out with four entrances leading fifty steps down into the bowels of the earth, where doctors were working like Trojans in an endeavour to patch up and repair the mutilated bodies.

Just before Bender's party arrived, a huge shell with delayed action had hit the ground half-way above one of the entrances. Penetrating the soil it had exploded in the middle of the stairs, occupied from top to bottom with wounded soldiers awaiting their turn for medical attention. The result was absolute chaos. The steps were strewn with countless dead bodies, and over these Bender had to struggle to reach the bottom quarter of the provisional surgery.

After a short examination by the doctor and the application of a fresh bandage, a ticket was attached to his tunic and he was ready, just like a post-parcel, to be despatched. Bender made his own way up the stairs into the open. As luck would have it, a four-wheeled, horse-drawn army cart was about to leave in the direction of Roulers. As Bender clambered into the cart, the driver warned him of the hazardous journey ahead.

With Theo lying in the back of the cart, the driver whipped the horses into a gallop, the exploding war contraptions spurring the horses to greater speed. Every second was vital here in an endeavour to get out of the fire and reach a quicker and proper road. It was a nightmare ride. They flew over the shell craters, sometimes with all four wheels on the ground, other times none at all.

Finally, they did reach the highway, and out of the line of fire. The horses slowed down to a gentle trot to cool their steaming flanks. Entering Roulers, the cart slowed down and halted. Stepping out of the cart, Bender thanked the driver and began to walk the dark streets. Slipping into a shop doorway, he struck a match and read the writing on the label pinned to his tunic. 'Back to company rest-room for recuperation.' This was too bad. He had expected to have been ordered on the first train home to Mam and Dad. Bender stood for a few moments in reflection. One thing he was not going to do was go back into the land of Hell. Dropping his ticket down a convenient drain, he made for the largest hospital, from where transports of wounded soldiers were shipped to Germany. It was 3 a.m. in the morning when he knocked at the door. He was admitted and examined by the doctor. The result was the same, and out Bender came with another ticket. Once again, he lost it, and tried another hospital. But, even here, the result remained the same. Feeling very dejected, he finally knocked at the door of his Company Sergeant. Out came the latter, half asleep and clad only in his underpants. Thrusting his face close up to Bender's he uttered his usual phrase, "Look! Look! Look! The first private back from the front!" Molendam examined the ticket on the tunic, and directed him to the company sick-room.

Here he joined some more privates, all with minor complaints, sufficient to keep them in the rear where they did nothing but peel spuds. Bender took advantage of the fact that, with his head still bandaged, he looked like a severely wounded soldier. Newcomers arriving continually from the front, described the appalling conditions. For those in the first line, there were no trenches at all. For a week at a time, they stood in shell holes, some of them up to the hips in water. Here they fought, dozed and slept in a vertical position, without any kind of shelter. Had he not been injured, Bender would have been there now and hearing their stories, he was more than ever determined to stay out of it. He had had enough! He could see nothing wrong with this line of thought. For were there not thousands of soldiers strung out behind the front as far as Germany who by influential recommendation held their positions without any fighting at all? *Etappen-Hengste* (Stallions of the Etappe) they called themselves.

On the day that his exhausted regiment came back, Bender removed his bandage, and tucking it away in his kit, joined his friends again. Neither Paul nor Karl knew where Bender got lost. Hair-raising stories were told, many of them boasting of the number of Tommies they had shot with their own rifles. Private Reimer, a smallish chap from Krefeld, and an officer's batman, circulated his own tale of having shot fifty-two Englishmen in one evening in the presence of his superior.

What a terrible deed, for which in peacetime a man would have been hanged. However, this hero was immediately decorated with the Iron Cross.

The regiment was enjoying a well-earned rest after the fight. Everyone was expecting to be moved to a quiet sector of the Western Front for further recreation. Now, there was plenty of time available to walk the streets of Roulers or just laze about and do nothing.

In the meantime, Theo and Paul had found a new occupation. With hammer and jemmy, they roamed through the many bombed mills, knocking off the brass and copper bearings from war-damaged machines. They made good money out of this but, unfortunately for them, Molendam was responsible for all scrap, before the money was paid out. As far as he was concerned the two lads were making money too fast, far more than he could earn as a sergeant. And so the business was stopped. Nevertheless, by then the two had made enough to put away for a rainy day.

One day the bugles sounded for the men to assemble in the large square. Rumour had it that all was not well at the front owing to the heavy casualties. When Bender heard this, he rummaged through his kit and got out the dirty bandage. Wrapping it all around his head again, he put the steel helmet on top.

Standing at ease in one long line, they awaited the Company Commander. "Attention!" came the command, and in walked Lieutenant Oetker. A schoolmaster by profession, in civilian life he must have been a first-class type. He was a born leader, never shirking his duties, and treated his troops fairly and justly.

Until then, Bender had not come into contact with this superior. Half apologetically, Oetker addressed his troops, telling them that, once again, they would have to repair to the front-line. Wishing to ensure that everyone was fit for the coming ordeal, he walked from man to man, asking each one: "Are you fit for front-line service?" And, in every case but one, the answer came, "Yes, sir!" It was not until Oetker reached Bender, a strange-looking object, with his steel-helmet sloping over his dirty bandage, that the reply came in the negative. "Why?" asked the Lieutenant.

"Occasional sickness and severe headache, caused by concussion in the concrete shelter!" came the prompt reply.

He won the day, for as he sadly watched his company disappearing in the direction of Passchendaele, for their second battle, he was the only soldier left behind.

Dejectedly, he turned and walked back to the sick-bay, where he had no right to be. Was it cowardice that had made Theo Bender fabricate an illness that did not exist? It had taken a certain amount of courage to take this step however, as he knew full well that he would land in jail, if the doctor passed him as fit. Sergeant Molendam told him plainly what he was in for, and eagerly awaited the doctor's diagnosis the following morning.

However, there was no examination next day. Accompanied by a corporal, Bender trudged towards the large hospital in the town. They had almost reached it when a long-range shell from a Naval gun scored a dead hit on the hospital. Debris flew everywhere and the hospital was razed to the ground. Doctors, nurses and patients were buried under the rubble. This tragedy provided Bender with a respite of several days while the damage was repaired.

When next Bender was called for examination, he had time to prepare himself the night before. Knowing that failure would mean a court martial, he did not go to sleep that night, but sat smoking and drinking strong black coffee. The following morning they were late and had to run to reach the hospital in time, the corporal being the driving force. As an exhausted and fatigued Bender stood facing the doctor, there was no doubt in the latter's mind that the private was ill, accounted for by a weak heart and high temperature. He treated Bender very kindly, telling him to go back to the sick-bay and rest there until further notice. Inwardly smiling, the phoney soldier went straight to Molendam with the doctor's report.

## Flanders

"Who the ———— do you think you are, idling your time away at the expense of the German Army? I'll soon put you to work!" the sergeant burst out.

Bender was growing a little too big for his boots, as he knew that regulations were against a soldier being employed while on the sick-list.

In the end the sergeant's patience completely gave out. He had received an order to send a team of eight workers to the front to repair a concrete bunker. He could manage seven men, including a corporal. Who should be number eight? Defying all regulations, he appointed Private Bender.

At 4 a.m. the next morning, with the corporal in charge, the group set off. Mile after mile they trudged along in neat formation. Gradually men began falling out, until the line became longer and thinner until the last few chaps were out of sight. Bender was still with the corporal, asking where the bunker was? Were they still out of reach of bursting shells? As they topped a rise in the ground, they saw soldiers milling around in a field below. They were, apparently, building what looked like a concrete shelter. This could be the job to which they had been allocated. Bender induced the corporal to find out for himself. Obviously, those fellows were building a pill-box all right, but the position did not tally with that on the instruction sheet. The corporal hesitated for a moment, probably thinking of the shells bursting around the real shelter on his order. It was quiet here, and . . . . On the spur of the moment, he clicked his heels, and reported to the officer in command: "Eight men for work from the 9th Company, Infantry Regiment 164!"

Although the officer had received no advice of such a group to help him, the bluff worked. Bender rolled up his sleeves for a good day's work. The others followed suit, and they all enjoyed a wonderful day's work in brilliant sunshine, unhampered by war.

That evening they reported back to Molendam, the chit duly signed by the officer on the site confirming their daily work. The sergeant was very pleased.

The backwash came the following morning. Molendam was furious when he received a nasty message from Headquarters, informing him that the eight men never turned up — for the boys it was another war-day less. What a stupid mistake it was to have turned up at the wrong site.

November had now arrived and still Bender had not fired a shot. The bulk of the division had been engaged in senseless slaughter, and they came back without their dead. Wilhelm Schmied from ' Zion ' was no longer amongst them. He had been hit in the chest by an English grenade.

The well-deserved rest came, and the division was moved to the neighbourhood of Tourcoing. At long last, the men were in decent quarters again. Theo, Paul and Karl soon got into their stride, and supplemented the diet of many a soldier with some fat geese. They sat together, singing and playing on the mouth-organ. Once again, they were enjoying life — but for how long? They had experienced the cruelty of war. Many a man who had joined with the highest of morals would return from it completely demoralized, no longer knowing the meaning of 'Mine' and 'Thine'. How many would succeed in rehabilitating themselves, and finding their own level again in the aftermath of war?

## THE SIEGFRIED LINE

Soon there was yet another move. Headquarters could not afford to allow the troops to rest for too long as, after three years of war, soldiers were growing scarce. Into the train they were loaded, the 164th being landed some eight miles north of the main Arras-Cambrai-Lecluse road on the 13th November, 1917, ready for the battle of the Siegfried Line.

The men had just occupied their digs, and Lieutenant Oetker was settling into his quarters, when he discovered that two of his rabbits had disappeared. Little did he know that they were already in Paul's boiling pan. After roll-call, the men were instructed to stand to attention whilst a house-to-house search was made for the missing rabbits. They were never found — neither, for that matter, were the thieves.

After this abortive search, Molendam came out with a special announcement. Headquarters had instructed that each company in the division should supply one man for the deadliest of all formations — the storm troop. "I want one volunteer," he shouted. To his amazement, with a click of heels, Bender stepped forward. Slowly the sergeant moved towards him, thrusting his nose into the private's face. With a peculiar look he said, "Look! Look! Look!" He was too astonished to say more. The cowardly Private Bender had actually volunteered for the storm troop.

Theo had made up his mind to show the sergeant that he was, after all, a real fighter. Next day, leaving his comrades, he went to join the dreaded storm troop in their quarters, the last mansion at Lecluse on the main road to Bapaume.

From now on life became exciting. There was training and exercises each and every day. Bender was the smallest man amongst the men, who were mostly hand-picked for this exacting job. Running and throwing dummy hand-grenades, and rolling up faked enemy trenches, was a physical demand for even the fittest and strongest. How long would Private Bender last amongst this crowd?

The 164th Regiment had enjoyed only a very short rest, and whilst Bender was passing the time throwing grenades, the division had moved into the thickest of fighting, to the north of Cambrai. Fate, apparently, again had its hand in Bender's plans. This time, he had wanted to be courageous but, by leaving his formation, it looked as though he had played the coward. By coincidence, the whole division ran into the battle which went down in history when, on the 20th November, the English, for the first time, attacked with a large formation of tanks — previously unheard of in battle.

Day after day, the division was in the thick of the fighting and instead of the anticipated rest, once more they had to shoot it out against implements of war they had never seen before.

Busily engaged enjoying his duties far behind the front, Bender knew nothing about this state of affairs until, due to an emergency, the sleeping storm troopers were commandeered in the middle of the night. Evidently, they had run out of certain ammunition at the front, which Bender's troop had to supply. This really was exciting. Groping about in the dark, the group loaded up their truck with cases of hand-grenades. Driving as far as they could, the last lap was sheer hard labour. Over uneven and muddy ground they trudged, each man loaded with boxes full of ammunition, whilst every couple carried between them an additional box of hand-grenades. On and on they stumbled, occasionally tripping over pieces of barbed wire. Finally, completely exhausted, they sat down for a short rest in the darkness. The rumbling of the guns presently drew nearer, but the explosions were still out of reach. They squatted down on the cases containing the live ammunition to have a snack and a smoke, feeling as safe as in mother's garden.

## The Siegfried Line

In the darkness, the glimmering tip of a cigarette can be seen from far away and does not escape the keen eyes of an artillery observer. Our gunpowder-plot did not have long to wait. A great bang sounded in the far distance, and then came the familiar *z-z-z-zumm* through the air as a heavy artillery shell passed over their heads. The first shot was far too wide; then came the second, exploding much nearer. With one accord everyone scrammed into the invisible surrounds. Another burst, and into deeper holes they crept, everyone for himself. When all was quiet, the storm troopers cautiously returned to where they had left the boxes, which were undisturbed.

They were ready for their last lap to the front. Grabbing up their loads, they were about to set off when they realized that one man was missing. In the distance, they could hear a faint voice calling. After searching the dark surrounds, they eventually came across Private Bender, his chin pinned to an iron spike in the midst of a tangle of barbed wire, and bleeding profusely. In his hurry he had thrown himself flat on his face to avoid the flying red-hot shell splinters, and landed in the rusty entanglement.

It was obvious he was unable to continue and after the sergeant had bandaged his wound, they left him behind. For several hours he sat waiting in agony and pain, for his comrades to return, expecting fresh bursts of firing any minute. On their return, the storm troopers collected him and took him back to Lecluse.

The injury soon healed and by the time Bender was fit again, the 111th Division had returned from the exhausting battle near Cambrai. How glad he was to talk to his comrades once more, telling them about his experience in the storm troop, while they, in turn, told him of the tank attack.

When pay day came, they received three weeks wages. It was a small amount, but a lot for a common soldier. That same evening they all had an enjoyable time together in the canteen. They spent all they had, Bender eating everything he could get hold of — sausages, grapes and chocolates, intermingled with sweets and beer. In other words, he made a pig of himself, and as a result, was sick all night. The following morning, feeling very weak, he took his upset stomach to the army doctor.

In a primitive room, many other sick patients sat awaiting their turn. The doctor examined man after man. Bender found this an intriguing spectacle. A chap at the head of the queue was suffering from a boil in a most delicate part of his behind. "Bend down!" commanded the doctor, and turning to his assistant, instructed him to apply iodine. On the table stood a bottle of this antiseptic, out of which a long stick protruded, with cotton-wool at its end. This seemed to be a magic stick applied to the boils.

"Next please," the doctor shouted. And when a fellow stepped forward suffering from a septic tooth, the same stick, with the same cotton-wool was first of all thrust into the iodine and then into the patient's mouth. It was hygiene of the highest order.

"Next please!" Before Bender could open his mouth to explain his complaint, the doctor was examining the patient's still swollen face. After a quick diagnosis of blood poisoning, caused by the rusty spike, he set to, without an anaesthetic, and lanced the swollen area. After his head had been covered with yards of bandage, he was given a bottle of bitter-tasting medicine for his stomach and told to call again the following morning.

Into the open street our soldier stepped, with only his eyes peeping out of small holes, looking every bit of a badly wounded soldier just back from the front. When his pals saw him they poked fun at him, asking how it was he always managed to get wounded without seeing a battle.

As soon as Bender's face was healed and his stomach had recovered, he made straight for the office of the storm troop. After being cross-examined by the Officer in Command, he was pronounced unfit and inadequately trained for the large military operation due in a couple of days.

The storm troop had been training incessantly for an attack to roll up part of the British line. It was a big affair, to be supported by a barrage of artillery fire, involving numerous guns in the rear. The object, was to surprise the enemy, snatch a few live Tommies and bring them back to Headquarters. Such skirmishes frequently took place on both sides.

Through his absence while sick, Bender was out of this

manoeuvre. According to the Commanding Officer, he did not have the physique for such an exacting formation as the storm troop, and to his dismay, he was ordered back to his own regiment. Disillusioned, he returned to his company, to be greeted in surprise by Lieutenant Oetker and Sergeant Molendam. Weighing up Bender's two extremes, his cowardice in Flanders and his guts to join the storm troop, the sergeant now, more than ever, was doubtful as to Bender's war tactics — after all this time the private had not fired a shot in the battle at Cambrai.

The 9th Company, through weeks of bloody skirmishes, had knitted together as a solid unit. They knew one another inside out. The Commanding Officer and Non-Commissioned Officer understood their men and shared their hardships. Theo was welcomed back to the unit, his nearest acquaintances anticipating a supplement to their army rations. They did not have long to wait. Already, Paul, Karl and Theo were plotting a plan of action. Whilst these three were around, canteen managers made sure of locking their doors.

The formation was still stationed at Lecluse — not a pretty place in wartime — with all the population gone and most of the buildings flattened. The near-by river Sensee was the only attraction, where, with the aid of a live hand-grenade, an occasional meal of fish could be caught. Here, the troops were left for some considerable time, far away from relations, home and friends. Some grew moody and depressed, whilst the more cheerful amongst them, could not care a damn. However, Bender the comic, even managed to make the dismal ones laugh with his funny extravagances.

One day, while prowling around, he ran into the cook who was an acquaintance of his. This gentleman told him, on the quiet, that he had some extra meat to spare, and if Bender could organize it, the men could have a dinner party in one of the army huts.

In they all came, ready to partake of the deliciously aromatic freshly-slaughtered calf. They all dug in, filling their stomachs to capacity, and washing it down with thin, watery lager. What a meal it was! Afterwards, they shook hands with the cook, congratulating him on the fine meal. To their horrified amazement, he produced the fresh skin of a German pedigree dog — the 'Dobermann'. Despite the fact that it had been an excellent meal, their reactions were psychological at the thought that they had eaten a domestic pet.

By now, new reinforcements were beginning to arrive from the rear, and soon masses of troops were congregating at Lecluse. This was a sure sign that the 111th would soon be heading for the front again. Meanwhile, Bender had discovered that some of the new chaps were from 'Zion'. Immediately, he arranged for a grand reunion to be held in the canteen. The men from Ronsdorf numbered thirteen, and an enjoyable evening was had by all.

It was a bleak December day when Bender once more found himself marching with his old formation towards the battle-front, reaching the dug-outs just before dawn. Not far from the town of Remy, they were in the third line of defence in a wide open landscape. As a direct hit was a thousand to one chance, there were no trenches or pill-boxes to protect them from artillery fire. Here and there huge squares had been dug into the ground some nine feet deep to allow shrapnel splinters to sail over the top. Under the open sky they lay, covering themselves up with whatever was available. For some time to come they spent a most monotonous existence in this relatively calm atmosphere.

Something, Bender decided, had to be done to relieve the monotony. One morning, he and Walter, an old school pal, scrambled into the open to explore their surroundings. They were a good distance from the first line and, as they thought, out of sight of enemy artillery. They soon realized their mistake when light shrapnels flew overhead. The guns obviously had their sights trained on the lone figures.

They treated this as a game — if a highly dangerous one. Bearing in mind the value of the precious metal in the copper grenade rings and brass fuses, they hurried back to their trench and collected a couple of sand-bags and spades. They then walked out into the open, attracting the enemy's fire. Shell after shell burst around them, each one exploding with a hissing noise and sending the top fuse through the air, to hit the ground with a dull thud in the neighbouring vicinity. That was what they were after. Digging them out of the ground, still hot, they filled their sand-bags.

This went on for several days. The kitchen wagon would collect the scrap in the evenings, to be paid for later. The highlight of the escapade was when they traced a huge sixteen inch, unexploded shell, with the three large copper rings still attached. Fetching their rifles, they hid behind a bank and aimed at the rings, knocking them off one by one. Two copper rings, which they had torn from the live missile, were already in the bag. Once more they tried, this time shooting off the third ring when, like an earthquake the whole lot went up into the air, covering Walter and Theo with a heap of soil.

No doubt, during the week, Walter and Bender had encouraged the enemy artillery to shoot more than usual and when the horse-drawn field kitchen drew up one evening to feed the hungry soldiers, the British artillery scored a bull's-eye, smack into the kitchen, killing one of the horses. Not for long was it left lying there, however. One by one the privates arrived on the scene and, with long knives, cut chunks of meat from the animal's buttocks, this being the most tasty part of horse meat.

After a week the regiment moved on towards the front. Bender, together with three other chaps, was allocated no more than a small hole in the ground, a ragged piece of tarpaulin, acting as a curtain, in the entrance. The whole contraption was nothing more than a means of keeping out rain and wind. It was certainly no protection against shells or splinters. This was a different kind of warfare here, only a few yards short of the village of Cherisy, now no more than a mass of rubble. This was paradise for the British mine-throwers. As they fired their shot, it could easily be seen in the daylight, sailing through the air like a large potato-masher, to land with a terrific explosion.

Here, in their miserable and nerve-racking conditions, they lived and slept. For warmth, they fixed a tin, resembling a brazier, with fuel collected in the neighbourhood. One morning Bender was up first, and pulling aside the dirty curtain, saw to his horror, that a huge unexploded mine had landed plumb in front of the entrance. How they had slept through the impact, he did not know. One thing he was certain of, however, if it had burst, no one would have come out alive!

Life in general was uninteresting, with two hours on sentry duty and four hours off. As long as the British followed suit, this was all they had to do. One morning while Bender, suffering from an attack of melancholia, was standing on the sentry platform, Walter looked him up, being surprised to find his pal on watch. Evidently, this private had succeeded in avoiding this duty by volunteering, each and every evening, for night patrol into no-man's-land. Bender's reply to this was that he had no intention of offering himself on a plate to the enemy, and asking to be shot. He could not quite understand the attitude of Walter, who was a quiet, gentle person, and would not hurt a fly. Then the secret came out. Urging Theo to join them, he explained that whether corporals or sergeants they had no other object in mind than to walk through their own barbed wire and relax in the first deep shell hole for a quiet smoke and a chat. All that was left, was for a fictitious report to be sent to Battalion Headquarters on the lines of: 'All quiet in the Sector.'

Immediately, Bender saw a chance of making life easier, and promptly volunteered for the following night's patrol, once again leaving his sergeant to scratch his head and puzzle over this private's unpredictable bouts of courage.

The night was frosty and cold, with a full moon lighting up the snow-covered landscape. At midnight, a lance-corporal together with eight men, including Bender, crawled over the top of the first trench, making their way through broken barbed wire into no-man's-land. Everything was against them. The air was clear, and by the cold light of the moon, the visibility was good for many yards. The men, in their dark uniforms, were thrown into sharp relief against the whiteness of the snow. As usual, they made for the deepest shell hole, and, squatting down, invited the leader to a smoke and a chat.

This was one time when it did not work. The lance-corporal, who had recently joined the division, was patriotic to the core. Since 1914 he had fought in Russia on many fronts, and, although he had not yet received the Iron Cross, this was the medal he most coveted. Here, was his golden opportunity. Being in command, he proceeded to point out the duties of a German soldier and completely ignoring the privates' entreaties, gave the order to advance. Realizing the futility and danger of approaching over the snow-covered land, they very reluctantly began crawling towards the British line. Walter kept close beside the corporal, Bender following at a distance, whilst the rest straggled along faint-heartedly in the rear. They approached the British strung out in a long line, the corporal, Walter and Bender forming the spearhead. These three lay on their stomachs right up against the British barbed wire, some thirty yards away from the nearest Tommy. So close were they, that odd English words drifted across to them from the front trench.

For some time all was quiet until, suddenly, out of the trenches, marched a British patrol, consisting of sixteen fully-armed men. Over the top they came, straight towards the three German soldiers. The corporal sized up the position in a flash — three against sixteen were no match. Simultaneously, three hand-grenades whirled through the air, only to fall far short. Then, it was every man for himself, back to the German lines. The privates bringing up the rear, heard the explosions, and seeing their three comrades running in their direction, they too, turned and headed back to the German lines. By now, it was really getting hot. No one knew who sent up the first Very light, but more followed close behind. The green, the red; signals for the belligerent artilleries. The Germans were apparently expecting a bold British attack, and their machine-gun fire by some serious miscalculation was trained on their own patrol, still in no-man's-land. Frantically, the nine men threw themselves on the ground and, with their bare hands, began digging themselves into the earth like moles. Bender, by himself in his hole, was sure his end was near. He lay still, watching the fireworks from the bottom of his burrow — dirt, stones and steel spraying over the top. There was now a real war on, but nobody seemed to know what it was all about. Certainly something had gone wrong at the German end. For nearly two hours the nine men had to bear the brunt of every gun, and mine-thrower covering the small vicinity. Despite the cold winter night, Bender was in a hot sweat.

It was the courage of the corporal who saved them. Worming his way along on his stomach through the murderous fire, he reached a quiet sector, from where he was able to shout to a German sentry to stop the annihilation of a German patrol. It took a long time for everything to quieten down before the nine exhausted men could crawl back, through the barbed wire, into their trench. Their uniforms in tatters, they were ready for a few hours sleep. Everyone was asking where the operation had gone wrong. The answer was simple, but far-reaching. One German sentry forgot to tell his relief that there was a patrol in no-man's-land. As a result, not only did it almost cost nine men their lives for no apparent reason, but thousands of shells had been wasted in defending themselves against what proved to be a non-existent attack.

Calm reigned once more. Bender got up expecting to enjoy a leisurely day in the trenches. Unfortunately, however, Walter's prophecy did not come true and a few hours after his ordeal, he was posted to sentry duty.

It was a crisp, sunny morning, and Bender was endeavouring to observe the landscape through hand-made collapsible telescopes, fitted with mirrors, which extended over the top. It was preferable for an enemy bullet to hit this wooden contraption rather than his own head.

Soon he heard a commotion in the trench behind, and recognized the voice of his Sergeant, saying: "There he is!" Then another voice requested Bender to step down from the raised platform. In spite of the note of authority in the newcomer's voice, Bender knew that it was against regulations either to turn his back on the enemy or step down from his post before being replaced by a relief.

Not until another chap came along to take his place, did Bender jump down into the trench. To his surprise, he realized he was confronting a colonel from Regimental Headquarters, who had been sent specially to substantiate the evidence of the lance-corporal's report. Each of the nine men had to be scrutinized, in order to obtain a true picture of the night's events. The colonel's voice held a note of reproof that they had not managed to seize a British soldier alive, so enabling the Germans to establish the identity of the regiment in front. Bender thought this attitude very high-handed, as they had been extremely lucky to get away with their lives.

At that time, however, Bender did not know what was in the

colonel's mind, nor was he aware that a report was on its way to the division as a result of this. To Theo Bender's amazement, in front of all the men, the Iron Cross and the Cross of Merit were pinned to his tunic, on the highest recommendation of the Duke of Brunswick, Ernest August. Bender had no clue as to why he had been awarded the crosses, but was of the opinion that it was meant to act as an encouragement for better performances. What would Sergeant Molendam think now?

On Christmas Day, 1917, Bender felt the need for a proper wash. Feeling uncomfortably dirty, he gathered some snow and melted it on a brazier. Stripping down in the cold frosty air, he performed his ablutions and, feeling much better as a result, settled down to enjoy the day. It just dragged on and on, and even on a festive day, duty had to be done. However, it was very quiet on both fronts all day long. Both the British and German soldiers felt the need for a little peace and meditation on that anniversary of Christ's birth. Their thoughts straying to their loved ones, they longed for home at that time, more than ever before.

Boxing Day greeted Bender with a great surprise. He and his pal, Paul, received marching orders, and were told to report to base for a new allocation.

Off they marched to Bruille, a mining district a couple of miles from Aniche. Here, the French population, out of reach of war, still occupied the town, and they found digs with a coal-miner and his family. They slept in the attic in double bunks — very soft and warm. Perhaps not up to the standard of an hotel, but compared with the dirty holes they had lived in, this was paradise. They were joined by a sergeant from the Machine Gun Company, two more privates and their own sergeant, making six in all. It did not take long for the miner's family and the six German soldiers to become the best of friends. The hard training on the machine gun, a heavy machine, started immediately. Being attached to the 1st Company, the six soon experienced the miserably small amount of rations allocated to them. To do hard work, one requires good food and plenty of it. Here, this was out of the question. Not one of the kitchen staff knew the six soldiers in the attic, and they served their men first, giving the machine gun men what was left.

Paul and Bender did not like this state of affairs and began to plan how they could obtain a supplement. What better place could they choose but the company's kitchen itself? Sergeant Ottermann, knowing that he had two of the best pilferers in his group, agreed to the plan and he soon convinced the machine-gun sergeant and the rest of the men. They all prepared for the big raid.

One night, Paul prowled around the kitchen's shuttered windows, which were each held secure by a large bolt. During their investigations the day before, they had seen into the room, where sausages and bacon hung from the ceiling, and kegs of monkey fat and jam were stored on the floor. Paul twiddled the large bolt until the wedge inside fell out, causing the shutter to spring loose. Scraping away the putty, he took out one window frame — the way was open. Clambering inside, they discovered they were in the wrong room, a stout padlock barring the way. A large pair of pliers soon snapped the lock, and into the food store they went.

In the middle of his garden, the French miner, with the aid of his family, had dug a large, deep hole, big enough for a coffin. Out came the food, passing from man to man, and into a wooden case already inside the grave. The lid on, soil was shovelled in, and flowers were placed on the top. Apart from the missing supplies and the padlock, the kitchen looked untouched.

The following morning, the culprits were awakened by a great deal of noise. The 1st Company assembled in an adjoining field, whilst furious officers scrutinized the ranks. The offenders were never found, and the kitchen staff was sacked. For weeks to come, the little French-German colony had no food worries.

It was a pleasant interval for Bender and Paul, doing their exercises, whilst their own company was hammering it out at the front. The training course with the machine gun lasted four weeks. How they all enjoyed practising with the new piece of equipment. It was good fun running from the top of the hill to *ack ack* into the valley, knocking down cardboard soldiers one by one. All over the world, youngsters like nothing better than to be presented at Christmas or birthdays with a toy rifle

## The Siegfried Line

or gun. The louder the bang, the better they like them. Is it any wonder, therefore, that when the real thing comes along, these young men are in their element?

The same applied to Bender's group. They revelled in their training, which had now practically come to an end. The two sergeants and four privates had lived amicably together until now, but in the end the friendly quiet blew sky-high. On the 27th January 1918, Paul and Theo had gone to Aniche, where their old pals from the 9th Company had occupied reserve quarters. It was the Kaiser's birthday, and this called for a celebration. They turned up equipped with food parcels for their friends, and beer was in plentiful supply. With the prolonged war, the beer got thinner and thinner, and one had to drink twice the quantity before it had an effect on the human balance.

Bender had also taken with him, scores of packets of roasted coffee, the proceeds from the pilfered kitchen. This commodity was very scarce — practically unheard of — the soldiers' brew being made from roasted acorns, which grew on German soil. Theo had also sent packets of coffee to his friends and relations at home, in Ronsdorf. Circumventing the postage rules, they arrived just in time for Mam's and Dad's Silver Wedding, eighteen cups being consumed, that very day, by Aunty Anna.

It turned out to be a wonderful evening for Bender and Paul. They kept in full swing until midnight, when they had to hit the long trail in the dark back to Bruille. By this time, Paul had had more than enough beer, and could hardly walk. Bender was hard put to it to keep him on a straight course in the middle of the road. Reaching open country, they came to a point adjacent to the Divisional Army abattoir, where cattle were slaughtered day after day. Equipped with most primitive drainage, the liquids just ran through open land, filling the ditches near the road up to drowning heights. It was here that Paul lost his balance once more and, before Bender could catch him, his friend had disappeared in to the smelly mess of the cesspool. Had not Theo pulled him out immediately, he would have surely drowned. There on the road lay a stinking bundle in the form of Paul Karmann. Too bad to be transported, Bender left him alone and made for home.

It was in the early hours of the morning when the door of the digs opened. Everyone, including Bender, was fast asleep when Paul fell in the door, upsetting the group in their peaceful slumber with his noise and smell. More particularly annoyed was the instructing sergeant, who was faced with a long day only a couple of hours away. Silently he swore his revenge, and when the duty started, it was obvious that he had his eye on Paul and Theo. The latter, who had not been paying attention to the sergeant's deliberations, heard his name being shouted.

"Bender!" roared the sergeant, for the second time. "Repeat what I have just said!"

Unfortunately Bender could not do so, and the tension mounted. From then on he became the victim of the sergeant's wrath and the events which followed had nothing to do with army drill. Across the field he was made to run with the heavy machine until he had had enough. Completely exhausted, he dropped the machine gun, only to hear a new command: "Pick it up and run!"

Bender did not move. Very red in the face the instructor walked up to him. After lecturing him on army discipline, and explaining that to ignore a command from a superior in front of the ranks meant a court martial, he again ordered the private to lift up the machine gun and run. There was no reaction.

Bender was taken out of the line and marched to his Commanding Officer, followed by witnesses proving his disobedience. The verdict was that Bender should appear before a panel of judges the following day.

This brought the morning drill to an end and silently the group made its way back to the miner's attic. Here, there was an uproar, with Sergeant Otterman and the privates all swearing at the instructing sergeant's unmilitant behaviour. Trying to get a soldier with an Iron Cross an army sentence was nothing short of mutiny. Still the offending instructor stood his ground. Then, everything else having failed, Bender and Paul played their last trump card — the pilfering of the company's canteen. They threatened to split the whole affair wide open. They were all in it together, as even the sergeants had aided and abetted. This did the trick and the instructor was forced to apologize. It was clear that something drastic had to be done to avoid a sentence being passed on Private Bender.

All through the night they were on their feet, pouring strong coffee and alcohol into the unfortunate man until, by the following morning, he was a physical wreck.

The officers judging the case sat early. Bender was brought before them, looking pale and haggard. His disobedience was clearly proved, but it also seemed obvious to them that they were dealing with a sick soldier with a weak heart. Subject to the doctor's decision, he was released. The diagnosis was that Bender was unfit for such strenuous employment, and the instructing sergeant received a curt note not to strain the private's capacity in the future.

## THE ARTOIS

The interim machine gun training over, Paul and Theo were glad to see the last of their instructor. On the 1st March, they rejoined their company in the small, badly shelled village of Recourt. The machine gun group left most of the pilfered food behind in the grave, and when the time came for them to say good-bye, the miner looked very sad at seeing his German friends leave, and his wife openly wept.

Recourt was a dismal place. Nothing could be found here to supplement their meagre rations. Paul, however, soon found a solution. Only a few houses remained standing, but decorating the outside of Paul's derelict mansion were stone vases laid in the walls, with the open neck protruding — ideal breeding places for the many sparrows. Once a ladder had been found the hunt was on. Paul would watch the parent birds enter one of the vases. Closing the top, he would wait for the couple to come out again, and after screwing their necks, throw them down to Bender, who popped them into a sack. By lunch-time there were twenty-four of them, strung up on a thin wire over a red-hot brazier, all nicely plucked and cleaned. The soldiers sat around the fire eating delicious sparrow-pie, bones and all.

The next day the division was on the march again towards a new sector of the front. A surprise was in store for Bender, who had been recommended by one of the lieutenants to become the batman of a newly-joined officer. This was not so much on account of the private's soldiering abilities, but more because of his skill at pilfering. The officer in question, coming from a poorer class family, knew that having picked an ace of a soldier, he would supplement his food rations and keep him in trim with shirts, vests and socks.

Bender and Officer Bellmann fitted well together. One thing they had in common was that they had both sat in High School.

In the Artois they soon settled down in the trenches again. Through his promotion, Bender found himself in much more lush quarters than before — it was amazing what a pip on the shoulder could do. The whole of the front was calm. Night after night Officer Bellmann, accompanied by his batman, patrolled no-man's-land. Every evening they jumped over the top to explore, in the dark, every crevice, trench, cave and hole. This went on for some time until, one night, they discovered a sole British soldier, lying in ambush in one of the trenches in no-man's-land. This was a most valuable chance for Bellman to earn his first medal. He instructed Bender to make a large sweep through the landscape and approach the lone Tommy from the other side. At a given signal, both were to jump on him and capture him alive without a shot being fired. Each one armed with an army revolver and a hand-grenade, they silently crept in opposite directions towards the unsuspecting victim. At Bellmann's muffled shout, they simultaneously jumped upon the British soldier. There was no fight or resistance, for the Tommy had been dead in his uniform for a long, long time. Had he been shifted, he would have disintegrated. Even taking the number of his regiment would not have helped German intelligence for he had been dead far too long.

Although the battle in the Artois, at this period, was mostly quiet, it did not mean that nobody was killed. The intermittent artillery salvoes went on, and although many a grenade misfired, there was the odd one that did find its target, and many a soldier died this way without ever seeing the enemy.

Bellman and Bender continued with their nightly mission, and in the end, the officer earned his laurels and was stamped a brave man. As a result, he was transferred to another company as Officer in Command.

At the end of February, in the company of a small group, Bender made his way back to Aniche to reserve quarters for the 9th, who would soon be returning from the front. With still a few days remaining in his role as batman, naturally he reserved for Bellmann and himself the best quarters obtainable. A fine mansion, occupied by an elderly French lady who could brew real black coffee second to none, was his choice, with a well-furnished bedroom containing two single beds. For the first time in fourteen months he was able to sleep between white sheets again like a normal human being.

When the regiment came back, Bellmann complimented Bender on his choice, his only regret being that they would have to part company in a couple of days, when his new job as Company Commander was ready for him. Even though their association had been brief, they parted with some sad feeling, the officer taking with him a few of the brand new shirts his batman had acquired by some devious means. Entirely against army rules, Bender remained in the old lady's mansion after his superior had left. The French woman liked the German soldier's company, as he could carry on a conversation with her in her native tongue through what he had learnt of the language at school.

The warm, cosy bed, however, proved his undoing. One morning, when the entire regiment had assembled in the square for roll-call, Bender was still fast asleep. After checking Oetker reported to Sergeant Molendam that one man was missing.

"It's Bender!" Molendam replied, and in a flash, he was off to the digs. Barging into the bedroom, he tore the bedclothes from the recumbent form, shouting: "What the hell do you think you're doing?" Then, taking in the quality of the private's surroundings, he roared: "Look! Look! Look! A better bed than mine. Get out and get ——— well dressed. I'll show you what the army is made for."

Jumping out of bed, Bender threw on his uniform and was marched down to the square, unwashed and unshaved, by the sergeant. After a dressing-down in front of all his comrades, he was allotted a top bunk with a straw mattress near Paul and Karl. Needless to say, he never saw his soft bed again.

The training at Aniche was somewhat different from

previous occasions. Everybody was whispering about a large offensive which was to be launched. An ominous sign was the testing of gas-masks in specially built chambers. The conventional mask, in use from the early days of the war, seemed to have become obsolete since the invention of the deadly mustard gas. Whether one wore a gas-mask or not, these poisonous fumes would penetrate. In the hope of preventing this, a device had been made in the form of a special lid which fitted to the ordinary mask, so preventing the fatal vapours reaching the soldiers' lungs.

For three weeks, the division trained hard around Aniche, Bender on the smaller machine gun, the 08/15. Each day they roamed the surburban fields playing at war, first with dummy cartridges, then the real stuff. It was at this time in his army career, that Bender first came into contact with Non-commissioned Officer Mayerberg. A small man, with a clean-shaven face, he would wear a very high peak on his officer's cap to give the impression that he was taller than he actually was. He could run like a hare, and would chase the privates all over the place. Never having actually met him before this, Bender only now found out what kind of a terror he was. The Non-commissioned Officer was the type of person who, as a means of punishment, would order a private to sweep the officers' bedroom floor with a toothbrush, a job which Bender had had to perform once before on the instructions of another man of this type. During his training on the light machine gun he was certain to get involved with Mayerberg for the rest of the war.

By the end of the day, the privates were exhausted, and usually spent the evenings resting in front of their quarters, playing, singing or listening to the accordion. It was the middle of March, and spring was in the air. On one of these nights, Oetker appeared in front of Bender's hut and stood chatting informally to the soldiers. At that very moment, Paul, Theo and Karl were busy roasting the hens they had stolen. Seeing the officer, they hurried outside, in case he should decide to enter their hut to speak with them. However, this alert officer had already smelt something cooking.

"How many birds in the pan this time?" Oetker asked Paul.

"Three, sir!" the private replied.

"All stolen?" came the question, for the officer knew his men too well.

"Oh, *no,* sir!"

With a smile on his face, Oetker left them to get on with the cooking. He was well aware that the fowl had been stolen, but as long as no legal complaint was received at Headquarters, he was quite prepared to turn a blind eye on the proceedings. Young men needed good food if they were to survive the hardships to which they were subjected.

By the middle of March, the division had been moved into a new position. They had received no special instructions, but by then, everyone knew that some unknown massive onslaught was in the air. Bender was down with flu in the sick-bay at the time and, try as he would, he could not dodge the issue. The order was that even sick soldiers had to fight. On the eve of the alarm, the doctor discharged him.

When Bender returned from sick-bay to join his platoon who had been resting in the neighbourhood of Ecourt, they were already packing their kits. It was 19th March, the day before the mightiest battle on the Western Front — the endeavour, on the part of the Germans, to annihilate the *Entente's* superiority in men and material. The 'Battle of France' was rapidly drawing near.

## THE BATTLE OF FRANCE

During the evening, the trucks began to roll in, to be filled immediately with soldiers ready for the slaughter. Driven part of the way, the rest was done on foot. They closed ranks, and as far as the even ground allowed, marched in formation in the dark. There was no pushing or forcing the issue; it was more a matter of keeping the troops relaxed, preserving every ounce of strength for the coming event. Even in the middle of this exercise, half-an-hour's break was enforced. They halted for a rest in army fashion, their rifles put together, three at a time, to form a long line of little pyramids, just visible in the dark. They lay on their backs in the lush grass.

Bender lay gazing up into the starry sky. How quiet it was, he reflected, and what a grand world this was. How vast the universe, with its endless distances, where belligerent armies disappeared in the vastness like the smallest of dots. His mind went back over his past life, trying to analyse the difference between good and bad. All through his life he had been brought up to believe in Christ's teachings, but since the war, these ideals seemed to have fallen by the wayside. Presumably, killing and plundering walked hand-in-hand with Christianity, but where was the dividing line? In the first instance, his reflections caused him some uneasiness, but as he gazed into the heavens above, the silence and vastness of it all calmed his troubled thoughts, and he relaxed in the cool grass. Then, quite suddenly, on an impulse, he started to sing. There, amongst the mass of resting troops, his crystal clear tenor voice was the only sound to break the silence of the night. Not another sound could be heard on this battlefield, as the soldiers lay listening to the liquid notes. From *pianissimo*, his voice rose to *fortissimo,* as the song carried through the still air. The whole of his feelings went into this fashionable, though simple, German Army song — "In the field-quarters, on hard stones, I stretch my tired feet." As the last notes died away, Lieutenant Oetker came towards him. Deeply touched, he clasped the young private's hands, congratulating him on his very fine performance. In the darkness and silence of the night, many a quiet tear was shed by these hardy soldiers — but they were not tears of which to be ashamed.

Almost immediately afterwards, they were on the move again. With knapsacks on their backs and rifles over their shoulders, the long march to the front continued. As they progressed, the going became more uneven. Once again they were balancing on the rims of shell holes, just as they had in Flanders. Not yet recovered from his attack of influenza, Bender was beginning to feel the strain. Mayerberg had allocated him the Machine Gun 08/15, which meant additional baggage. Not only had a machine gun man to carry the usual knapsack and rifle (weighing some 80 lbs.) but, in addition, two steel cases, containing heavy cartridges. With all this weight, he struggled weakly on, the ground worsening and becoming muddy. On and on he struggled, his boots sometimes sticking in the clay.

Finally, he could stagger no further. Catching his foot in the root of a tree, he tripped and fell, face downwards in the wet clay. He did not have strength left to get up, so there he remained. The soldiers behind passed him by, some kicking against him in the dark, until one shouted for the man with the first aid. Two of them came, and turning Bender on to his back, their tiny torch shone into a muddy face, completely unrecognizable. Bender feigned unconsciousness, and one of the men poured some brandy down his throat. Opening his eyes, the indomitable private crawled to his knees, and dragged himself upright. The two Red Cross men loaded his baggage on to their shoulders, and handing him a walking-stick, the three of them followed on at the tail end of the regiment.

Bender and his two companions did not arrive at the reserve line until some time after the platoon had occupied one of the deep dug-outs, with fifty steps and four entrances for safety. The bunk was full, with soldiers sitting on every step, in which positions they had to sleep for the whole night. Bender sat down on the last step, half in and half out of the dug-out, and prepared for the night. Gradually, he became used to his uncomfortable position, and dozed off. During the night it began to rain, the drips of water from the overhanging soil running behind his collar. On awakening the following morning, he found his pants soaking wet. Mayerberg, on his early inspection tour, traced the unhappy soldier, and let loose a stream of invective at Bender's cowardly behaviour.

It was March 20th. All day the soldiers sat in their holes, waiting for something to happen. When darkness fell, zero hour drew nearer, and they moved to another dug-out closer to the first line. Here they sat again — waiting uneasily. Nothing had leaked out from the top about events to come. At 3 a.m. every soldier was allowed out in the open for a few minutes for the last time.

As they returned to the dug-outs, the atmosphere was electric. Listening to final instructions from their superiors, they synchronized their watches to the very fraction of a second. In dead silence, the minutes ticked by until, at 4 a.m. precisely, the whole earth began to erupt. Thousands of German guns simultaneously belted the enemy lines over a radius of some eighty kilometers. Bender's dug-out began to vibrate, tins and bottles falling off the shelves. By the thousands, shells, large and small, detonated not far away, a dull thud amongst them, indicating the explosion of the deadly mustard gas. A westerly wind was blowing that night and the gas was being driven back into the German trenches and pot-holes. It could not do any harm, however, provided the gas-masks were all right and the special lids were on. The air becoming very thick, made it difficult to breathe, and some fellows tried to put their fingers behind the elastic of the mask. The aperture was immediately closed again, as they coughed and spluttered with some of the gas in their lungs.

Dawn found the soldiers still underground. Final instructions were issued — 9.20 a.m. ready for the onslaught;

9.40 a.m. over the top. Hourly, the inferno grew fiercer, as the troops prepared for the start. By nine o'clock, all was ready. What a hell it was to stand in the trenches staring at one another like monkeys, their faces covered by the masks, two large glass eyes protruding.

At zero, commands rent the air. Up the ladder they climbed and out into the open country. It was a typical March morning, with a slight haze hanging over the vast undulating landscape. But what a spectacle of fire and death. By now, the Germans had removed their gas masks and as Bender emerged from the trench, he paused on the top, his heart beating furiously. Trambach, watching him, saw the arteries on Theo's temples bulging out, fingerthick, with every stroke of the heart. There was no time for reflection, however. They all had to run towards the British lines. There was not a Tommy to be seen. The gas had killed them all.

As far as the eye could see, an unending line of German soldiers slowly proceeded towards the enemy line, while shells and grenades burst some hundred yards in front of them. The whole mass of exploding fire looked like some huge fiery snake, stretching from north to south as far as the eye could see, rolling slowly towards the west, the infantry following. Karl Trambach and Theo Bender were in the same small group, together with a number of seventeen-year-old reinforcements. The patriotic Karl, wanted to get as near as possible to the exploding snake, but Bender opposed his suggestion on the grounds that he wanted to keep the youngsters away from death as long as possible. There were soldiers running all over the place. Bender, suddenly spotting Mayerberg running around in circles like a frightened whippet, shouted out to him, "Are you scared?" It was obvious the Non-comissioned Officer did not like it. Bender's tactics began to pay dividends, for he was able to hold the young boys back, including Karl. However, many a German shell short of its target, exploded amongst the Germans, causing many deaths. In spite of the distance between Bender's party and the explosions, one of these missiles landed straight amongst his group. Fortunately, it did not explode, but sent one of the youngsters flying through the air for some ten yards.

They walked on, catching up with the first line, passing the first British trench, which was empty. Following the connecting trench from the first to the second line, there an indescribable sight nearly made them sick. Hundreds of dead British soldiers were piled on top of one another. In an effort to reach the second line, it was obvious that they had died in the connecting trench, the mustard gas penetrating their masks.

They passed the second line — again empty. An hour or so had gone since the onslaught had started, and in this time Bender had seen only three live Englishmen. By now, the 111th Division was in open country. Gone were the days of trench warfare. At about 11.30 the British reserve sector was reached, the troops finding time to investigate the enemy dug-outs. What a haul they discovered. White bread, bully beef, real cigarettes and tobacco, genuine tea and coffee, all commodities which were unknown at that time in Germany. The flow of the offensive was suspended as everyone fell over the eatables. They stuffed their kits to the hilt, ready for a long day ahead. Bender had just climbed out of a trench with a full knapsack, when he saw a German private standing on the top of a trench, biting into a fresh white loaf. At that moment the British machine guns counter-attacked with a rain of bullets, and the private fell head-over-heels into the trench below. A bullet had hit the fellow's hand, passing through the loaf and into his mouth, eventually to emerge from the back of his neck. Jumping down, Bender bandaged his comrade, and after a few words of comfort, handed him over to a near-by Red Cross man.

Owing to the unexpected food, the offensive in this sector had practically come to a halt. The officers were now trying to bully the men into action again. With some effort, the 164th had reassembled in a hollow, in the otherwise open country. They were faced with a steep incline on the top of which was a British machine gun nest, keeping the Germans in check. Then orders came from the battalion to storm the hill. Lieutenant Oetker, the officer-in-charge, shortly addressed his men saying that they were counting on everyone's valour. Their officer stood on top of the bank and gave the signal but, before he could finish his command, he dropped back dead into the mass of soldiers, a hole in his head.

A second officer took over, and suffered the same fate as his predecessor. A third did no better, making a total of three dead in as many minutes. A courageous sergeant took command. He seemed to fare better, at least holding his own on top of the bank. Others followed suit until the whole of the 9th was on open ground, preparing to storm the hill in front of them. The British had, apparently, held their fire until everyone was out of the dip in the land. Now it was an open target for the British gunners, who mowed the privates down by the dozen. This time the shooting was in earnest. No cardboard dummies falling backwards, but live creations. Flat on his belly, Bender crawled forward inch by inch. Private Schmieder, on his left, suddenly let out a piercing yell as a bullet went through his shoulder. Foot by foot they advanced, regardless of the dead. Steeper and steeper the incline became, making it increasingly difficult for the enemy to hit the few left on the target. Finally, there was silence. Then, one by one, the Tommies emerged from their strongholds, their arms above their heads. They marched to the rear of the German lines, leaving behind their machine guns, the barrels red hot and the cartridge cases empty. They had fired the last shot, and a brave lot they were.

From now on the way was open again for the 111th Division. No further obstruction held up the advance for some time until, by mid-afternoon, having covered several miles, they faced another incline. This time, however, there was no machine gun to hold them back. Gradually, the mass of leading soldiers crossed the highest point to see a gentle decline stretching far away into open land, dotted in the distance with thousands of British soldiers.

The German spearhead had advanced well over the top and was making for a near-by dale when, suddenly, many British machine guns covered the slope of the hill. Bender without any further cover, lay with his comrades in open land, the bullets flying all around him. With his spade, he endeavoured to dig himself in, forming a mole-hill in front of his head. There he lay, while many of the other chaps who ran in a desperate bid to reach safety, were mowed down under the furious fire, one man falling straight in front of Bender. He crept up close to the dead body, using it as a shield. A multitude of bullets whizzed over him. Closer and closer they came, one bullet passing through his whole knapsack close to his skin, jerking him backwards. As people often do when faced with death, he began to perspire, frantically digging himself deeper into the earth. From behind him there came a loud clang and turning his head, he saw his aluminium cooking-pot flying through the air, shot from his knapsack. It was now or never, he thought, and ran like a whippet some hundred yards through the bullets, back over the top. He made it. Once more he was amongst the main formation, and sheltered by the top of the incline.

For the first time that day the offensive was halted properly, as in a football match, the other side taking the initiative. In this sector, the German troops were hemmed in, the slight incline just sheltering them from gun fire — but not for long. Masses of troops were milling around flanked on both sides by the corn left standing from the autumn before. Gradually, the British artillery began to fire into the mass, hitting many a human target. Then there came the first roar overhead, heralding the approach of enemy bombers. They were small in those days, but efficient enough to do a lot of damage. They flew over, finding a perfect target. Right and left, the incendiaries came down into the dry corn, setting both flanks into a burning fury and blocking the soldiers' escape. Another squadron arrived to drop a string of heavy bombs into the middle of the scattering troops. The bag had been cleverly closed by British strategy. Their advance cut off, no opportunity for escape was left on either side, the only way open being to the rear. Slowly the German units began to retreat, the swell quickening, when suddenly, at the rear, officers on horseback appeared, their revolvers drawn. That stopped the rot. The division confined to a closed space, turned to fight or die. They held out until dusk fell, when shooting on both sides ebbed out into a night of silent peace.

Bender had become separated from Karl in the heat of the fighting, and so he joined up with two strange fellows with a 164 on their shoulders. One called Buss, the other Tesche, they both hailed from Hanover. The three privates settled down in a hole covered with pieces of tarpaulin, ready for a good night's rest. Buss then proceeded to repack his knapsack, filled with English cigarettes. Bender and Tesche, who were still puffing the beech-leaves allocated to the German Army, begged him for some of these delicate smokes. Buss, however, was a mean blighter and informed them that, when the attack was over, he intended sending them all to his relations.

More soldiers began to trickle in, but when the final count was taken, there were only eight left from the 9th Company, which had started the attack with a complement of one hundred and twenty healthy men. Rumours came through from other soldiers who had seen many falling by the roadside. The gentle Walter Henner, was dead, the explosion of a large shell having thrown him head-long into one of the deep dug-outs, causing him to break his neck. Eduard Plater, who one day would have inherited his father's factory, lay dying somewhere near by. All that would remain tomorrow to mark the spot where, like so many others, Paul Langerback, Eugen Stremner and Erich Martin had been struck down in their prime, would be a crude wooden cross to mark their war graves. Of the eight young men who had departed from 'Zion' such a short time before, only Theo Bender and Karl Trambach, who was, apparently, still with the formation, remained alive.

Before nightfall, the three under the tarpaulin were feeling very thirsty. Without water they could not brew up, so Bender volunteered to go out and explore to see what he could find. Coming across a dent in the ground filled with a yellow watery liquid, decaying bones lying around the fringe, he filled his flask and killed any germs there might have been, when boiling it for their acorn coffee.

What a day lay behind them. An event of the greatest mass-murder the world had ever witnessed. Within just twelve hours, thousands of healthy lads were wiped out, just for the sake of conquering a few miles of French soil.

Under their canvas roof, the three were joined by another chap, Hermann from a neighbouring village of 'Zion'. He had his own stories to tell of the fighting. Like the others, this private had been in the thick of it, and a machine gun bullet had whizzed through his tunic, close to his shoulder. Feeling dead tired, the conversation petered out, and they fell fast asleep. Except for one short burst of machine gun fire near by, the night passed uneventfully. The machine gun men had expected an attack, and seeing the silhouette of a shadow in the dark, imagined it to be a lone English soldier. When daylight came, a German infantryman was found hanging in the wire, riddled with bullets like a sieve. He must have run too far the day before, and made his way back in the dark.

That morning, the sun shone brightly on an unnaturally calm sector. An officer began to count his men who were reduced from batallion strength to less than an ordinary company. Under the tarpaulin, the boys began their wash with the dirty water Bender had found. As Hermann stripped down, he noticed a hole in his shoulder. The tale he had told the night before of a bullet going through his tunic was inaccurate as the shot had actually pierced his shoulder, beneath the collar-bone. That was all of twenty hours ago, but in the excitement of the battle he had not felt it. Packing his bag he bade farewell to his comrades, and off he went, a wounded soldier, in the direction of Germany.

Meanwhile a voluntary patrol had entered no-man's-land in an endeavour to locate the whereabouts of the British Army. They returned after a couple of hours, having walked miles without finding a trace of a single enemy soldier. What they did find several miles ahead, was an empty English slit-trench, a perfect cover compared with the holes in which they were lying. The order came and, once more, they all packed up. In the brilliant sunshine the front line moved forward again. Not a shot was fired. It was almost like a stroll through the countryside in peacetime. Little did the officer-in-charge know then that the slit-trench was a trap laid by the British.

Completely unsuspecting, they all occupied the perfect trench. No sooner had the last man disappeared below ground level, when the sluices of fire opened up, a hell of steel covering the whole of the trench. Like rats the Germans were sitting in the trap. It was murder again, but this time, with no avenue of escape. Some lay flat on their bellies, covering themselves with anything they could find. Bender was in a sitting position, with his back towards the enemy. Karl

Trambach was with him again, and Buss a few yards beyond. Once the British artillery had found their target, the shelling became more severe. Conversation in the trench stopped, as everyone waited for the end. Then came the biggest bang, the first medium-sized shell bursting inside the trench, in the midst of the soldiers. Looking round, Bender could see Karl was still there, as was Buss, but the latter without a head, blood spurting out of his open neck, his knapsack still full of British cigarettes.

Nobody knew what was going on in front. For a fraction of a second, some brave fellow popped his head over the top, recognizing the British in line-formation, just beyond the belt of exploding shells, their bayonets fixed, ready for battle. Through the trench the order came, the youngsters drew their long, sharp knives ready for a bloody massacre. From now on it became a battle of nerves, both sides at the ready.

The German trench was in a peculiar position stretching from north to south over the top of a slope. From low down in the furrow one could see the landscape far beyond, and observe other German formations, to the left and right of the 111th, chasing the British before them at top speed. The German war-machine was rolling again. Horse-drawn carts, lorries, and the whole baggage could be seen pursuing a retreating enemy. The front became a large loop, the British, with their bayonets, in the midst of it. Observing the danger of being cut off, they turned tail, catching up with their main formation, leaving Bender and his comrades another breathing space.

Once again, the way in front was clear. They emerged from the trench, grateful that they had, at least, escaped a knifing. Leaving the many dead and wounded behind, they walked in open land again, Bender and some other fellows forming their own group. The patriotic Karl had to be restrained, for he was always eager to follow hot upon the enemy's heels. Bender would have none of that, for there was plenty of time for them to win or lose this war and, even if Germany won, it would make no difference to him.

In a slow walk they followed far behind the German spearhead. Four men in all, Karl, Theo, a fellow from Barmen, christened Eduard, and a chap from Solingen.

Finding a large shell-hole, at Bender's instigation, they squatted down for a rest. That was a tactical mistake, for the enemy artillery soon put a belt of shrapnel fire behind the first advancing German line, blocking any reinforcement. Here, the four privates lay with missiles dropping in their vicinity. It was too late, though, for escape. They had just dug down, when a shrapnel exploded in the air above them, shedding the whole load of lead bullets into their hole. Screams rent the air, and Bender ran out as quickly as he could, his legs carrying him swiftly over the fields in a south-westerly direction into a sector which no German troops had yet touched. A lone soldier in open space, following the bulk of the British troops. Crossing the main road between Ecoust St. Mein and Noreuil, he ran for shelter towards the village of Vaulx Vraucourt. Not a soul was in sight, as he cautiously approached the place. Some of the houses were still standing, and behind a wall he discovered a battery of British guns, the barrels still hot. Keeping close to the walls for protection, he made his way from house to house. Not a British or German soldier was in sight. Seeing a light in the entrance of a cellar, he peeped in to the basement. Putting himself in rather a vulnerable position, he climbed down the steps, shouting, but there was no reply. What a sight met his eyes when he reached the bottom. In the middle of the cellar stood a large table laden with plenty of nutritious food. Bread, ham, bully-beef, jam — everything. Even the tea in the pot was still warm.

Shedding his army equipment, he sat down and enjoyed his best meal for many years. It was after he had eaten his fill that he suddenly realized the danger he was in, from friend or foe. Anyone approaching this cellar would, undoubtedly, throw a hand-grenade into the basement to make sure that nobody was there. By the time the thought had occurred to Bender, it was too late. Hearing voices from above, he jumped up and pressed his body in a far corner, flat against the wall, listening intently. He cursed himself for not having thought about his own security before tucking into the food. The voices were louder now and, to his relief, they spoke in German. Using his native dialect, which no Englishman would have understood, he bellowed at the top of his voice. "Come in fellows. There's a German down here."

It worked. The Germans outside, the spearhead of the next southern sector, were flabbergasted to find a lone soldier of their breed already in possession of the village. Introductions were soon over. And no wonder, for everyone was interested in the food. Posting a sentry outside the entrance, they all sat down and ate a hearty meal. When it was over, they made a tour of inspection of the whole house. Luckily they had landed in the midst of a British food depot, most rooms being filled with delicate eatables no longer known in the German Army. When they left, all their packs were filled to the top, and with a sergeant in command, they went in search of their own regiment. By the time darkness had fallen, they had found their company.

Bender was introduced to the company's Commanding Officer, who advised him to stay with them until the battle was over, promising him a letter showing evidence of his whereabouts. They all settled down for the night in open country without tents, holes or bunks. So tired were they after the strain of the day, that even the damp grass did not act as a deterrent to sleep.

Amongst these strange northern countrymen, Bender felt acute loneliness and, try as he would, sleep would not come. He was worried about his comrades' fate, and wondered how his Mam and Dad would feel if he were killed. Had the other three in the shrapnel hole scrammed for safety as he had done? As he later learnt, they had not. The boy from Solingen had been killed instantaneously, while Eduard had been hit by a piece of lead which entered his shoulder, penetrating his whole body and lodging somewhere near his seat. Severely injured, he did, however, survive the war. Karl Trambach got out of the hole but was wounded soon after by a machine gun bullet, and so returned to Germany. Theo and Karl never saw each other again. On entering the battle a second time, Karl died like many other soldiers. Probably a cross somewhere in France still marks his final resting place.

As Bender glanced around at the, now snoring, strangers, he grew more and more restless. In his imagination, he could already see his mother reading the innocent-looking postcard, inscribed with the words — ' Missing on the Western Front! ' At the thought of his family's grief, he became determined to leave his newly-found comrades.

Silently he packed his belongings and moved off into the inky blackness of the dangerous no-man's-land. After two days of fighting, the pattern of this part of the Western Front had entirely changed. There was no real front line left on either side. Both German and British soldiers had settled down where they were when darkness fell. Into this jigsaw puzzle walked Bender, in grave danger of running into an enemy group at any time. Cautiously he advanced, his ears straining to catch the slightest sound. It was midnight when, after covering a fair distance, he heard voices. He lay absolutely still for a moment before creeping cautiously in the direction of the sound. Catching the odd word or two spoken in English, like a frightened dog, he moved back again. At any time he could have landed amongst another British group. By now, he had lost his sense of direction and did not know whether he was moving east or west. Halting in his tracks, he waited for the clouds to clear and, seeing the Bear in the dark sky, he traced the North Star for guidance.

The air was brisk and clear, and the countryside — including most of the soldiers — was asleep. After a further move, Bender rested again. Then, he saw a flicker of light, probably someone lighting a cigarette. Aiming cautiously in that direction, he caught the sound of voices whispering in his own tongue. He bellowed, and they shouted back. Next moment, he was in their midst — home at last.

The group of German soldiers introduced him to their sergeant. Bender received the surprise of his life when he saw the superior was none other than the man who had tried to get him court-martialled for disobedience while training on the large machine gun. He felt far from pleased at this turn of events, while the sergeant, on the other hand, was highly delighted to find heaven had sent him a 'first shot' for the machine gun. Practically all his men had been lost in the fighting. He had received replacements but they, too, had been killed. Now he was left with only a few men, and they were only young lads, who did not know much about the intricate machine. Here was a private who could make that gun spit again. The sergeant was muttering about how he would show the British at dawn. There were still plenty of cartridges left. Bender did not like this attitude at all. He had walked into a veritable hornets' nest, for he was well aware that a heavy machine gun was always positioned at the most critical point of the front, and with a sergeant such as this, it was asking for trouble. It was unlikely that this Non-commissioned Officer had forgotten Bender's offence, which might be even more dangerous for him.

The sergeant reformed his group and gave orders to advance to a place where fighting would recommence at dawn. With his 80 lbs on his back, and with the help of another private carrying the heavy machine, Bender started to walk. On reaching a likely place, each one dug a hole in the ground, just large enough to sit in with one's head below ground level, and placed a piece of canvas over the top. Everyone except Bender soon slept; he, in spite of his tiredness, was unable to do so. Since he had left Ecourt-St. Quentin on the 19th, he had had hardly any sleep during the last seventy hours. He felt sure that some of his own platoon must be near and with that he made a further decision. Leaving his rabbit hole, he started out all over again. As he groped his way in the dark, none of the exhausted soldiers heard him go — not even the sergeant, who would find himself without his crack shot in the morning.

It did not take long for Bender to find yet another group and this time he was lucky to run into Lance-Corporal Winterborn, a man from his own platoon. But where were all the others? Not a chap could be traced whom Bender knew. Joining the men underneath an old piece of ramshackle corrugated iron, some of whom were sleeping, others on sentry duty, he chatted with the lance-corporal, who told him that practically everyone of the 9th was either dead or wounded. The new lads with him were reinforcements. Barely seventeen years old, they were little more than schoolboys.

Slowly the dark night began to give way to a newly born day when, for the first time in four days, the horse-drawn field-kitchen brought hot food to the soldiers of the 9th. A cooked dinner for the original one hundred and twenty men it at least served to fill the empty stomachs of these youngsters. The horses soon departed, disappearing over the brow of the hill in a gallop. The sun rose over the horizon to herald the third day of the 'Battle of France'.

The soldiers were still under the corrugated roof, with a seventeen-year-old on sentry outside, when shells began to burst. Winterborn, being in charge, went outside to ask the chap what were his observations. The young boy had seen it all, but not comprehending what was going on, he had not given the alarm. The German first line had already advanced to the west an hour or so earlier. From his experience of the day before, Bender immediately knew what they were in for. The British curtain of exploding grenades soon came. Thicker and thicker they fell, dangerous, flat bursting, Brisant grenades amongst them, leaving large black puffs of smoke behind. It needed the speed of a racehorse to catch up with the German spearhead, now out of sight. It would be suicide to run through the barrier of flying steel.

The lance-corporal gave the order to the trembling youngsters to run for their lives and catch up. Bender, bearing in mind the proverb — ' He who fights and runs away, lives to fight another day ' — was inclined to run back, regardless of the lance-corporal. The rot set in, and they all ran to the rear, Winterborn, much against his conscience slowly following. The bursting shells urged them on, until even Winterborn was running. When the corrugated hole was some fifty yards behind, a huge missile struck it, the roof landing in their midst. The decision, after all, had been the right one. Had they stayed two minutes more, they would all have been dead.

Breaking through the belt of fire, they thought they had made it, when a low-flying British fighter plane gave them absolute hell, in a landscape devoid of cover. They ran for their lives again, until they were finally exhausted. The plane had gone, and they were able to rest. The group wandered aimlessly about until someone spotted a live head popping out of the ground not far away. Drawing nearer, they saw it was a German soldier in a very deep trench. They had come across a fortification in the ground, with steps leading into the earth. Every inch inside was occupied by soldiers who had lost the initiative to fight. Gone was the iron discipline of the German Army. At a guess, there was at least a company of men present and, suddenly, Bender realized that he was not alone in his cowardice.

He went deeper into the matter when evening came, going

back, in his mind, to his school days when he had been taught the myth of the invincible German armies. From Frederic the Great to Wilhelm II; the first one invading Silesia in 1740, following up with the seven year wars. Bluecher, in 1815, helping Wellington defeat Napoleon I. Wilhelm I in 1864, having the German-Danish war on hand starting the second bout in 1866: the Prussian-Austrian war, and not satisfied, he ran over the French in 1870/71 — Bismark and Moltke in army-command. Now, it was Wilhelm II who had started the largest massacre of all. Yes, the Germans could fight, so long as the Prussian military boot kept the common soldier down. Once the top authority had gone, discipline became a farce, the privates longing for home and to live their own lives.

Late in the evening, Bender took the risk of leaving the comparative safety of the trench to explore the lie of the land. There were three entrances to the dug-out, the steps of which were crammed with soldiers. These fortifications were the safest in trench warfare. Dug deep into the earth, it was unlikely that all entrances would be blocked at the same time. Therefore, if, through one large explosion, the top was closed, having two other exits, there was not so much chance of being buried alive.

His explorations at an end, Bender settled down amongst the rest of his group for his first night of peaceful sleep for some time. It is amazing what the human body can withstand under such adverse circumstances. Here was our private, just recovering from an attack of influenza and, instead of the doctor ordering him to bed, he had been on his feet for several days under the grimmest of circumstances. He had prepared supper for the young boys, his pack containing the stores of food shared out amongst them all. The provisions would last him and the youngsters for several days. All of them had tucked in, the newcomers grateful for having found a Father Christmas. They were eating commodities they had not seen for a very long time. Bender had not cared a hoot where the next meal was coming from, and had let them tuck in to their hearts' content.

In his dreams, Bender's body would jerk spasmodically. Once more, he was fighting the battle in his subconscious mind. Then, his sleep was interrupted by visions — dozens of gallows, with bodies hanging from them, swaying in the wind. He awoke, and jumped up, muttering to himself. Surely, it could not be true that all the men in this bunk — there were over a hundred — would be hanged for desertion? There would not be sufficient gallows he reasoned, and gradually dozed off again, awakening next morning after a ragged sleep. The 24th of March dawned, but all the men were still confined below ground.

Some of them began to get restless, and incautiously made off over the top to investigate the near-by surroundings. That proved their undoing. At midday a new division passed the trench. An officer came across one of these lone explorers and questioned him. Not satisfied with the answers he received, he stopped the marching troops, and made his way towards the deserters' fortification. Pandemonium broke out, the superior ordering his Commanding Officers to investigate this deterioration of the, otherwise, proud German Army. There were far too many to book them all. The officer addressed them in no uncertain terms and, with that, he chased them to the west to locate their respective formations. Spreading themselves out, they endeavoured to contact the fighting line miles ahead.

Bender's small group was still together and, in broad daylight they marched, finally reaching the top of a gentle incline. Up to this point they had been walking over grass and soil. Now, it gave way to yard after yard of ground, strewn with nothing but dead Germans, killed a few hours before in a hellish attack. Sticking close together they picked their way through the gory-looking corpses, whose dead faces grinned emptily up at them. Near by, a horse-drawn wagon had been blown to smithereens, the hind-leg of a horse hanging at the top of a battered tree, its head glaring down from another. It flashed through Bender's mind, when seeing all this, how many wooden crosses would have to be made. This gruesome scene eventually proved too much for the little party, still miles behind the first line which they thought they would never reach alive. Completely overwhelmed, they turned about and, by the evening, were back in the dug-out they had occupied the night before.

Not a soul was inside. Down some sixty steps they tramped,

where, to their surprise, they discovered proper sleeping quarters, with double bunks. Here, they bedded themselves down for the second night.

The next morning, they awoke feeling somewhat worried. What would they do for an alibi? For two days, now, they had been out of the fighting and certainly someone, somewhere, would be asking after their whereabouts. Unanimously they decided, regardless of the danger, to search for the front. And so, after a nourishing breakfast from Bender's provisions, off they marched once more.

Miles and miles they covered; the German break-through had certainly gone a long way. By lunch-time the small group of four, (Winterborn had disappeared the day before) were amongst sporadic bursts of shelling. This time, after a good night's rest, their eyes were wide open. They were cold sober, not filled with the potent army rum, as on the 21st, when it had been issued to every private to make him half-drunk, ready for the attack.

Far in front of them were masses of soldiers and, putting on speed, they soon caught up with them. It was a new formation from the rear. The numbers on their shoulders were well over five hundred, a sign that many brand new divisions had been created. In the main, they were a young lot, interspersed with half-mended, previously wounded, soldiers. The little group mingled amongst them, beginning to dodge the rain of shells. Once more, they were in the swim. Bender began to put into practice the exercises learnt in Heidelberg. Running a short distance, he would throw himself down, digging his elbows into the soil and creeping along on his belly like a salamander. Ever forward they all ran until they reached the top of the slope. There, they prepared for another run, this time through a hail of machine gun bullets. In the distance, could be seen, behind the German line, the town of Bapaume, going up in smoke.

Soon came the target for the next attack. Crouching behind another slope, they waited for the next jump which would lead them into wide open fields, devoid of cover, and where enemy planes circled the sky, sending information back to their artillery.

The British had retreated far — obviously too far — giving

them more time to lead the Germans into one trap after another. When the command came to advance, the Germans ran over the summit, to reach the open plain, practically without a shot. Then, when the whole lot were out in the open, the British opened up with everything they had, including machine guns by the hundreds. Never before, had Bender seen so many comrades fall at once. This time, the shoe was on the other foot. It was the Germans' turn to bleed to death.

Gritting his teeth, Bender continued to run when, without warning, the wooden butt of his rifle splintered and fell to the ground. Finding no cover, and with a knuckle bone protruding from the red and bleeding flesh of his hand, he ran back over the top. A Red Cross man guided him into a deep shell-hole. Bandaged and with his arm in an improvised sling, he transferred his eatables into his haversack and left the knapsack, with all belongings, behind. With the aid of a stick, he made his way to the rear as quickly as his injury would allow.

Out of the line of fire, he noticed a tent marked with a red cross, and made in this direction. The blood-stained bandage, put on while under fire, was removed and a corporal cleaned the wound with biting antiseptics. After a short chat about conditions at the front, Bender was ready again, and the corporal directed him to the nearest and foremost emergency hospital at Aubigny aux Bac. It was a long, long way, and the going was slow. However, his luck was in, for he spotted an old army cart drawn by a couple of horses. With a cheery smile, the driver offered him a lift. There was another occupant in the cart, heading in the same direction. He was a badly wounded soldier, whose foot had been hit by hot steel, and the front half was missing. Bender, who at least was able to move, bedded down the groaning comrade in one corner of the cart.

As they wobbled precariously over the rims of the craters, Bender observed the deep tracks made by the big guns in the ground. What a gigantic operation this whole offensive must have been. The transporting of tons and tons of the heaviest equipment over this uneven ground. Without the heavy artillery the boys at the front were helpless. The guns had to follow — and quickly! Bender tried to reason out the position.

It was apparent that the brunt of the German offensive had puffed itself out. It would not be long before the balance would sway in the opposite direction, and the British chase the Germans.

At this juncture, having reached his destination, the driver of the cart drew to a halt. From here, the two wounded soldiers had to find their own way on foot to the hospital, still a long way off. Bender, the stronger of the two, put his shoulder under one arm of his companion, thereby taking some of the weight off the other's foot. Yard by yard they hobbled along, the blood seeping from the man's stub. In a state of collapse, they arrived at the hospital, where scores of other wounded soldiers were milling around, awaiting attention. At long last, a doctor examined Bender, whilst his pal disappeared into another ward. After the hand had been re-bandaged, Bender came out with a ticket pinned to his tunic. This time it bore the inscription: ' Hospital case for Germany '.

He was taken to a near-by barrack, already filled with hundreds of soldiers waiting for the next hospital train. It was late evening and the air in the room was filled with the sickly smell of drying blood and chloroform. After some time, Bender could stand the atmosphere no longer and stepped through the door, out into the fresh air of the night. Aimlessly, he wandered amongst the houses of Aubigny aux Bac. Everything was pitch black — not a single light to be seen — owing to the enforced blackout. Eventually he saw a sign of life in the form of a small chink of light through the nick of a curtain. Glancing up at the notice above the front entrance, he read: ' Military Police '. Knocking at the door, he went in, disturbing a few soldiers sitting round a table playing cards. Humbly he explained his predicament, and contrary to military police rules, they bedded him down on a comfortable mattress, near the stove. That night our soldier slept like a king.

## HOMEWARD BOUND

Early next morning, the engine, with the usual cattle-trucks, rolled into the station. In the soldiers piled, some under their own steam, many more carried on stretchers into the soft straw of the trucks. In due course, the train pulled out. On and on it puffed through the eastern part of France; through Belgium and on to the German border, where all passengers were transferred to a normal civilian train.

Bender, entered one of the typical German third class compartments, with its wooden seats and baggage racks above. The passengers sat cramped together, five a side. He soon found that, by making room for the severer cases, he could swing himself up into the luggage-net, where he could stretch out for another good night's rest. The train moved off on its long journey. Occasionally, someone would peep out of the window for orientation. As the soldiers travelled through the Eifel, night fell, and Bender dreamed about his Mam and Dad, and his brother and sister. The train might be heading for Ronsdorf — it was going in that direction, passing the Ahr valley. It would not be long, he hoped, before it would stop at Remagen. The morning of the 26th of March was well advanced when, stiff and worn, Bender climbed down from the luggage-net. His immediate neighbour, a chap called Blatzmer, was from Cologne, and the two started chatting together. This soldier's mind was also completely taken up with thoughts of his home, now not far away. The two began to plot how they could get out at Remagen, if the train stopped there. As the train approached that station, it did, indeed, slow down, and crawl to a halt.

According to plan, immediately the wheels screeched to a standstill, they were out on the wrong side, and jumping across the rails towards the next platform. There, they crossed the lines again, until they reached the last platform, from where they started to make their way back through the subway towards the exit. In their minds they were already free, and began telling each other what they would do on reaching home. Turning the last corner, to their dismay they were confronted by two military police who grabbed hold of them and hustled them back into the train. And so, further and further south, away from home, they went.

Bender was vexed at this turn of events. Only half-an-hour ago he had been practically sure that, by lunch-time, he would have given his family, only sixty miles from where the train had stopped, the greatest of surprises. However, it was not to be. Feeling sick, he resigned himself to his fate.

During the long journey, the train halted occasionally when a number of attractive nurses would bustle around, handing out hot cups of ersatz coffee, and food to the wounded. The sight of these stout-hearted, trim looking nurses cheered the soldiers more than they knew. Needless to say, the tin soldier, who had not seen the like for some time, thought these women the loveliest creatures he had ever set eyes on. Thinking ahead, he decided that, if he were to be looked after by such as these, life in hospital might not be so bad after all.

The train had already left Nuremberg far behind, and was travelling towards the Bohemian forest. It finally came to a halt in the country town of Sulzbach in the Oberpfalz. Most of the wounded were carried into the hospital and immediately put to bed. Bender entered the large, clean-smelling building and found his ward. As he was not confined to bed, he was allowed his freedom until the evening. After exploring the building which, apparently, had been a convent in peacetime, he strolled outside to have a look at the tiny town. Through the narrow streets he went and into the fields, where on climbing a hill, he could see in the distance behind the Czechoslovak border. Feeling suddenly weary, he strolled back to the hospital where a clean bed, with white sheets awaited him in perfect surroundings. Lying awake for a while his thoughts went over the last eight days. It was just over a week since that murderous artillery fire started between Monchy and Cambrai. He could hardly believe that he had lived through it.

Next morning, he was amongst the first batch to be called to the surgery. None too gently, the surgeon ripped off the bandage. His hand throbbed painfully. It was a good thing that the corporal in the Red Cross tent had applied antiseptic for the injury was already showing signs of healing. A new dressing was applied, and he was passed on to another doctor who examined him for fitness. When the final details were entered in the register, to his horror, he read the two letters, 'K.V.' (*Kriegs - Verwendungs - Faehig*) meaning, suitable for warfare. Bender did not like this at all. He would be the last one to be dragged to the front again. Without a word he left the surgery and for another day, he wandered disinterestedly around the town, all the while being asked by the locals what it looked like at the front. His replies painted a gloomy picture, and people became aware that things were not too good in the 'West'.

Until mid-morning, the tin soldier's day was pretty much the same as the one before. Then, he read the announcement on the notice board. 'Anyone who is prepared to subscribe a substantial sum for War Bonds, for a period of twenty years, will be granted a fortnight's leave immediately.' A kind of hire-payment, it was twenty marks down, and twenty marks per month thereafter for twenty years.

In a flash, Bender was up the stairs and searching for Blatzmer from Cologne. Together, they conspired whether they could manage this. Then, they found a loophole in the War Bond system. According to regulations, they would draw two marks a day for army leave, making twenty-eight for fourteen days. The first down-payment was only twenty marks, so eight of these remained in their pockets for the journey. They had made up their minds. Walking downstairs, they knocked at the paymaster's door. Entering the office they clicked their heels, and informed the Commanding Officer of their willingness to help the country. The formalities soon over, the documents were signed and witnessed. They ran upstairs to another office, with their certificates granting them a fortnight's leave, and promptly received twenty-eight marks each. From then on, it was easy. Back to the first office, where they settled their first instalments, and by midday, they sat in the train, the railway journey for a soldier on leave being free.

What a glorious feeling it was to be entirely free, and sitting in a train heading for home. The train was far too slow and stopped at too many stations. It was next morning before they reached Cologne, where Blatzmer, after shaking hands, rushed out. Fidgetting with excitement, Bender carried on for the last few miles. In a short time — which seemed an age to Bender — he was back in 'Zion' and heading for Mittel Strasse No 33, the draper's shop. Carefully he let himself in and crept silently upstairs, making for the living-room. Throwing open the door he stepped into the room. There, he saw his family sitting moodily around the table, tears in their eyes. Slowly, they raised their heads and stared, unbelievingly, at this 'figure from the dead'. Not understanding their attitude of shocked silence, Bender stepped forward and picked up the postcard, lying in the middle of the table. It was from the War Office and read — ' Private Bender reported missing on the Western Front. '

When reality began to dawn, and his family realized it was truly their Theo, and not some apparition from another world, their tears of sorrow changed into tears of joy, and what a happy reunion it became. They chatted and laughed, exchanging stories into the early hours of the morning. Materially, it was not much of a celebration, for the cupboards were empty and there were no intoxicating drinks. The whole family looked pale and wan through malnutrition. Father did not look at all well and suffered from outbreaks of boils. No longer was he a prosperous draper working in his own shop. Now, he tramped the streets, to and from work, in wooden-soled clogs. The shop and store, which in 1914 were full of goods, were practically empty. When the goods had been sold, there had been no means of replenishing the stocks — new items just did not exist.

Mother looked better in health. With bright eyes, again and again she would look at her son. He had kept his word, and come back. Magdalena had her worries too. It was not easy to feed a family on the smallest of rations. It was bad enough when Theo had left, but now it was even worse. How much longer would it go on?

Heinrich had grown into a frail, lanky lad, his apprenticeship in the tin-smith shop not helping him much. All day long he breathed in the chemical soldering fumes. Not yet sixteen, he was still too young for the war-machine.

Nineteen-year-old Lydia was a pleasant-looking girl, always full of humour and wit even in these dark days. However, the war had left its mark on her too — the rosy cheeks were missing.

In health, only Theo had changed for the better. In a short time he had grown from a thin boy into maturity. In that respect the army had worked wonders. In spite of the strain of the fighting and the poor conditions, the fresh air and exercise had done him good. His family could hardly credit the change as they looked at him in his worn field-grey.

On hearing how he had managed to obtain leave so quickly, being the business man he was, his father's face grew longer and longer. He pointed out to his impulsive son, that the very small army pay could not possibly meet these obligations. As long as he could manage this leave, Theo had not given the future situation a thought. Now, as he heeded his father's warning, he reviewed it differently. Aware that he had no money of his own, he bluntly proposed that his father should pay the next instalment. Equally as bluntly, his father replied that it was out of the question. However, Theo was not unduly worried. The war could not last much longer, and when the end did come the country, the finance, the lot, would go to the dogs.

The news of Theo's return soon spread through little 'Zion', and neighbours and acquaintances called at No 33 to shake hands with the private from the front. This was all very pleasant, until people called whose sons were in the front-line, and with whom Bender had fought shoulder to shoulder in the same battle. He was heartbroken when the parents of Walter, Eduard and the others, all began to ask questions. Bender could not bring himself to break the terrible news which in any case, would soon arrive through official channels. During his fortnight's leave, he became more and more miserable, especially when the official announcements came through to the bereaved parents.

His mission fulfilled, he was almost glad when the time came for him to return to the hospital. With his pockets empty, he made the return journey.

His first object on arriving, was to make himself useful. His luck was in once more when one of the officers, taking a liking to him, gave him a job in the food store. Here, Bender was in his element. He could eat and drink far more than the allotted army ration. Day after day he had to count eggs, taking care that, in so doing, one or two became cracked. These could not be put back into the cases, and the Commanding Officer advised Bender to swallow them raw, which he promptly did. In the long run, there were more eggs cracking than Bender could consume. These he would put into a small container and take to his ward to feed his friends. Soon, they all began to look well on it, even though the eggs in the store were somewhat on the stale side. The Commanding Officer did not eat them of course. He had a better source of supply from his own hens. In the yard, fifty hens laid fresh eggs each day for the Commanding Officer and his friends, the food for the poultry coming from the hospital kitchen. Just as the army was graded, so were the eggs. Stale ones for mere privates; the fresh for the officers.

Bender was making the grade, and the Commanding Officer soon discovered his capacity for organizing. The private was switched to a better department — the equipment store. In the main this amounted to taking care of army utensils. Fine uniforms hung on the racks. Helping himself to one of the best, he adorned the new tunic with fresh medal ribbons, and became a text-book soldier, so smart did he look. The few in the hospital who knew him, began asking questions. If he could get them, they would all like new uniforms. Seeing this as a chance to make money, Bender began to spread the news that new uniforms were available for soldiers going on leave. The trade began to thrive, as more and more soldiers borrowed the uniforms. However, they were not let off scot-free. For this facility they paid two marks hire charge for a brand new uniform for a week-end leave, and five for a fortnight. The money was certainly flowing in fast.

The new Commanding Officer liked Bender's methods, the store being in tip-top order. (The subordinate did not tell him that he pawned the uniforms.) Bender's organization began to grow, another department being added, which put him in charge of the railway tickets as well. At first, Bender gave little thought to this. Then, one day, it occurred to him what a money-spinner it could be. More and more soldiers came to his bureau, where they produced leave passes. Bender, the office clerk, filled in the railway tickets and the officer signed them.

As long as the Commanding Officer was on the scene, there was no money in that. But even he was human, and wanted leave at times. Every Thursday, the officer would disappear for the week-end to see his family. One Thursday morning, Bender knocked at the door of his superior, and stepped inside. Clicking his heels, he said: "Good morning, sir."

"What is it you want, Bender?" asked the officer.

Producing a new pad of unsigned railway tickets, Bender replied: "Please, sir, could you sign the tickets on this pad? There will be many privates going on leave while you, sir, are away, and then I can fill in the rest."

"That's a good idea, Bender. I'll do that with pleasure!" And with that the Commanding Officer signed the lot.

This became the second source of income. Bender soon spread the news on the hospital grapevine, offering railway tickets for week-end leave. He ignored the army rule that, before a ticket could be issued, a leave pass must, first of all be shown. Any soldier willing to pay him two marks could travel to see his relations without a pass. The scheme worked very well and soldiers swarmed in every week-end.

During his spare time, the private roamed through the hospital. Already, a month had passed since he had returned from the front and, by now, he knew every room in the building, and many of the people. There were the light cases and the bad ones, all distributed over the various wards. In some of them they were singing and making merry, while in others, the atmosphere was morbid and depressing, as many a chap neared his last hour. How often he saw the stretcher covered over with a white sheet, standing outside such a ward. Death still surrounded him at every turn.

When confronted with incidents like these, Bender would make for the main exit, and wander through the streets and out into the open country, where he would find an antithesis. Here was life! The green fields, and the green, succulent grass. Healthy cows still peacefully chewed the cud as they did before the war, and butterflies still danced and fluttered in the spring air. Such sights gave him courage, and he would dare to think of the years ahead when this nonsensical fighting had ceased.

Sooner or later it had to come to an end, although according to the newspapers it did not look like it at all.

For the time being Bender was obliged to carry on in the hospital. At intervals, more and more wounded arrived, the soldiers speaking the truth about the war. Business had been brisk, when Bender received a letter from Berlin, marked — 'For the Attention of Private Bender.' He was well aware as to its contents — the first instalment for his War Bonds was due. It was time to pay up and, although he had earned some money with tunics and railway tickets, it had been used for other purposes.

He sat down, and compiled a letter to the insurance company, explaining that, as a private he only earned twenty-one marks a month, and could not pay. It would be much better, he told the company, if they were to approach his father. Consequently, Josua Bender received a demand note. It did not take him long to reply. His son was over twenty-one and, therefore, responsible for his own financial commitments. For some considerable time, endless correspondence went on in this way, but not a penny could be drawn either from father or son. Finally, the matter died a natural death.

Bender had been able to hold on to his job at the hospital despite the many requests from Headquarters to release every able man. His arm was no longer in a sling and, by the middle of May, only a small bandage was necessary. By that time, the chief surgeon required a new office-help, and on recommendation from Bender's previous Commanding Officer, he got the job. Day after day he now had to stand by in the surgery, marking down a record of the doctor's examinations in the register. It was a comfortable, though morbid, job, and

Bender had not been trained as a nurse. Although his occupation had been that of a weaver, he satisfied his superior, the grammar school having taught him something after all.

With a feeling of foreboding, he carried on with his duties. Any minute he expected to be moved, and he did not have long to wait. One morning, the medical officer shouted: "Private Bender! Will you give me your own records!" Slowly the private thumbed through the file until he reached the folder, 'The Medical case of Private Bender.' As the officer turned over the pages, he gave a gasp, "Bender," he said, "you're in for it. The verdict in here is K.V." Feeling sorry for him, the doctor re-examined the now practically healed injury, and with a tape, he measured the length of the hand, each finger and the circumference of the wrist. All this Bender entered on his own records. When the final verdict came, Bender was told to cross out the 'K.V.' and, in its place insert 'G.V.' — meaning suitable for garrison. The medical explanation for the alteration was written in the register, and the doctor signed the report. Once again, his return to the front line was delayed.

That was the end of hospital life for Theo Bender. In a fortnight he had to quit, and rejoin his regiment at Hamelin. Brooding over his position for a day he had a brain-wave. By now he knew every office in the building. Going back to his previous one he found his railway ticket pad, with some of the blank sheets, duly signed. Making out one for himself, dated 1st June, 1918, from Sulzbach to Hamelin via Ronsdorf, he went back to his doctor, asking for his release papers. The latter patted Bender on the back, and wished him luck. The date of release was entered as 10th June. The same day the private sat in the train with a pass for ten days' leave in his pocket. What a surprise it would be for his family to see him again so soon. This time it was not easy to stay, owing to the dire shortage of food. Being on unofficial leave, he was not equipped with a ration card.

They were a dreary ten days, with no company and no finance. The whole town looked gloomy, more and more notifications were being received from the War Office. By this time, all the parents of Bender's comrades had received the message about their sons' deaths. It was with relief that Bender eventually boarded the train which was to take him to the town of the Pied Piper — Hamelin.

Reporting at the regiment's office, he soon came under military drill again. They could not do much with him yet, as his scars were not properly healed, so he leisurely explored the building, its surrounds and the town. To begin with, the only drill was a roll-call morning and evening, to check that all the soldiers were still there. The building was large, with troops milling around everywhere. Those on crutches were still attached to the local hospital. The food was mainly soup served very thin. The place gave the impression of cleanliness, but it was not.

Twenty-four soldiers slept in a large room on double bunks. Bender made the acquaintance of his neighbour. A young lad, like himself, Peter was a farmer's boy, and had also just returned from the hospital. Soon he would be ready again for the 'West'. The first night they slept, Bender in the bottom bunk and Peter in the top. First thing the following morning, the latter jumped up. He could not sleep and did not know what was wrong. He woke his comrade, and still half asleep, Bender stared at Peter aghast. The poor boy's face was covered with large, red blobs, each the size of a shilling. Smallpox, he thought to himself. If it was, it could kill the lot. Wakening the others, they all examined the unfortunate fellow, and upon investigating his bedding, found the cause. The mattress was positively alive with bugs the size of a sixpence. The tormented chap had been bitten all over and had to go to hospital. Bender looked through his bed, and he, too, found bugs but apparently his blood was not sweet enough as the crawly red-looking creepers had not touched him.

The second day after his arrival, Bender explored the regiment's hospital in an endeavour to find chaps who had been in the 'Battle of France'. He did not find many, but was told that the patriotic Karl from Ronsdorf, had just left for the Western Front again, from whence he was never to return. Then Sergeant Grieger crossed Bender's path, both having fought in the same battle with the 9th. The sergeant's hand was smashed and some of the fingers were missing. Despite this the doctor had signed him 'K.V.' and, in a few days, he would be in France again.

When Bender heard this he grew apprehensive, but being in the military whirlpool again, there was not a thing he could do. To begin with he was due for his convalescent leave, to which every wounded soldier was entitled. And so after three days in Hamelin, he was on the train once more, ready for a fortnight in Ronsdorf. This leave went the same way as the previous one, the only difference being that he had obtained an official ration card. The fortnight passed pretty quickly, with Bender dreading the day of his return to the 164th, when the train would carry him to battle once more.

Thinking matters over, he eventually went to see his Uncle John and discussed with him the possibility of getting his fortnight's leave extended. His uncle had one cow and, by rights, was a farmer, this category having priority for growing food. Uncle John sat down and wrote an application to Theo's regiment. It proved successful and leave was extended for a further fourteen days.

People began to gossip in Ronsdorf. How was it that Private Bender did not have to return to his regiment? Theo ignored the talk. To him every week was one nearer to saving his life. However all good things come to an end, and on the 5th July 1918, he returned to his regiment. Needless to say, he was not received with open arms at Hamelin. A furious physician gave instructions to a corporal that Bender should be brought to the clinic every morning for bone and muscle manipulation. The massage and treatment for movement started immediately. His hand and arm were strapped into a machine and long leaded weights on thimbles were attached to his fingers. They were then swung like pendulums on a clock, making the bones creak. If this continued, Bender thought, he would be ready for further fighting in less than a week.

The second morning for treatment came but, first, there was the usual roll-call. The company sergeant read the daily instructions, following this with a request for one volunteer to be transferred to Munsterlager immediately. Noticing the corporal's absence and seeing his great opportunity, Bender stepped forward, clicked his heels and by lunch-time, he was away. As the train hurtled towards its destination, Theo sat thinking about what the corporal would have to say about his disappearance.

Munsterlager, high up in the north German plain, south of Hamburg and Bremen, was a miniature desert. Devoid of any entertainment or social life, it was a place devised for the training and drilling of troops in an, otherwise, uninviting landscape, plastered with army barracks. Bender arrived late in the afternoon, not knowing what his new allocation would be. He eventually found himself in a large square, surrounded by an eighteen feet high wire mesh. Inside was hut after hut full of soldiers, the Commanding Officer's quarters in the middle. In army fashion he entered the main office and stood to attention. The Non-commissioned Officer invited him to be seated, and proceeded to impress upon Bender that he had come to a prison camp. The two dozen huts harboured approximately fifty inmates each, making a total of some twelve hundred prisoners. He, together with a number of other privates, had the job of guarding them. At that time, our soldier was not told what kind of prisoners they were. It later transpired that they represented the scum of the German Army — burglars, thieves, murderers and deserters.

At the end of this interview, he was taken to his hut, standing in the middle of the prisoners' quarters, and made the acquaintance of his fellow guards. Tough stories they had to tell. This job was no pancake, as the men with whom they had to deal were strong and brutal. The guards always carried guns loaded with live cartridges. One could never trust these fellows, and they had to be treated rough. What a job he had got himself into! Still, better here than at Bapaume.

The next morning started with the inevitable roll-call. The rest of the day was taken up with drill and exercises for those who were not on guard. First Bender received his new kit, along with a new rifle, which he could only lift with one hand, the other not yet being strong enough. With the corporals bellowing at the privates they started the routine practice in an open square inside the camp. They marched and ran; left, right and about turn, finishing up with rifle exercises. This was not in the class of Bender's efficiency, but he tried his best to get the rifle on to his shoulder, when the sharp, cutting command came. Half-way only, could he manage, the rifle

slipping out of his grip and dropping on the ground with a clang.
"What the hell d'you think you're here for?" came a voice, as the corporal furiously approached him. Just as it was in Bruille, Bender thought, as the next order reverberated around the square:
"Pick up that ——— rifle!"
He did, but when forced to make the second exercise, the same thing happened. The corporal, reported his private to the Commanding Officer, standing near by. The latter, a lenient fellow, immediately saw the predicament, and directed the corporal and private to the section doctor. Bender came out with a smug grin on his face, the corporal making excuses, and back to the drill ground they went. The sixteen men stood in line, but Bender was now on the tail-end. Whilst all the others were slinging their rifles to and from their shoulders, he did a left, right and about turn. The picture was a very comical one.
The first day finished pleasantly with the last roll-call somewhere around 7 p.m. Before the end came however, the Commanding Officer shouted out one more request: "Is there anyone amongst this lot who has not had any home leave for the last eighteen months?" To Bender's own surprise, he stepped forward, knowing full well that he had been home only eight days ago. "Report at the office afterwards," was the officer's reply, and with that he dismissed the men.
The tin soldier made for his barrack to search for his military pass-book. He was right. All the army leaves he had had in the past were written and stamped on a square piece of paper, not on the actual pages of the book. The small piece of paper was lightly appended with a tiny strip of gum to the inside of the outer back cover. If that slip could be removed, there was no proof that he had had any leave for the past eighteen months. Out it came, and no one would have known the slip had ever been there. With a stern face, Bender made for the office, rendering his military pass to the Commanding Officer. In less than fifteen minutes, out he came with his pass, ration-card, railway ticket and money in his hand, to start another journey homewards, the following morning.
This time the whole of 'Zion' was surprised, and Josua

amazed as to how his son had managed it. But there was no argument, for the documents were in order. Once more, Bender paid a visit to Uncle John. The pen came out for another application, and the private's vacation was successfully extended to three weeks.

It was the end of July when Bender returned to the prison camp. How long would it be before the war came to an end? Whilst on leave, Bender had read various newspapers and in spite of the victorious messages they contained, one could read between the lines. If one wanted to know the true story, one had only to ask the soldiers, freshly returned from the front line. Their tales differed from the newspapers — it could not possibly last much longer.

Somehow, our soldier had to hold out, even if it was at Munsterlager. Methodically doing his drills, he had by now found out the lie of the land. Many a day when the weather was fine, he and Bierbaum, a new comrade, would explore the countryside. There was not much to see as the landscape was flat, intermingled here and there with sparse pines, starved by lack of moisture in the sandy soil.

The *lager* itself was full of troops all the time. In and out they went, as quickly as possible. Partly mended soldiers were newly equipped here, and then rushed to the front with utmost speed. Bender met many fellows with whom he had fought, far more seriously wounded. Once more, they all had to fight and die, for a cause that was almost lost.

September had passed and October half-way through, and still Bender remained guarding the prisoners. The atmosphere in the camp was one of restlessness. Apparently the news had leaked out that things were going badly for Germany. Special instructions were issued to the sentries to keep their fingers on the trigger at all times. Peculiar incidents began to happen. At about 4 a.m. one morning Bender got out of bed in order to use the toilet. As he groped his way in the dark along the narrow gangway he noticed that the place where his bayonet had been hanging was empty. As he switched on the light, he heard a commotion. Underneath the table sat two long-term prisoners, dressed in uniform, and grasping Bender's bayonet. Everybody jumped up, and drew knives and revolvers. Bender could not help feeling sorry for the poor fellows, as sticks and rifle-butts belaboured the convicts' bodies. Dressed up as camp guards, they had been confident that they could walk out of the camp in the light of dawn.

The following week another incident occurred. As a matter of routine one of the guards took twelve prisoners to one of the latrines. They were long, low-lying wooden structures, with the back wall touching the high wire net and the lids of the cesspool outside the compound. Without counting them the guard led his men back to the barrack. When evening roll-call came it was discovered that one prisoner was missing. This was bad for the guards, for nobody knew where, or when, the man had disappeared. The alarm was raised outside the prison camp, alerting the whole of Munsterlager. Twenty-four hours had passed, and the man was still at large. When Bender took his lot to the latrine, he made sure that he counted his men both on the way in and out. Going into the toilet, he was just about to follow the men outside again when he heard a faint groan. On investigation he saw a head poking out of the dark and stinking cesspool. Raising the alarm, the semi-conscious man was eventually hauled out of the messy hole with the aid of grappling irons. Through a miscalculation, the prisoner had been unlucky in his bid for freedom. At regular intervals, a farmer would come when it was dark and open the lids of the pool for emptying. Had this happened the previous night the prisoner would have been at large. Instead the poor devil had got the days mixed and he had to stand up to his shoulders in the liquid for twenty-four hours. The gasses had nearly killed him. They dragged him into the middle of the compound, a helpless smelly packet, who nobody dared touch. With two fire hoses he was thoroughly cleaned, and then carried on a stretcher to the hospital.

After this regulations were tightened, and the guards were warned to watch for mass break-outs. Somehow, more news leaked into the convicts' huts. The first days of November had arrived, and with them there came chaps from the north, from Bremen and Kiel infiltrating the *lager*. Weary of their officers and the war in general, they had deserted. Mysterious stories were going around, and the rot was setting in. Not only was this the case amongst soldiers but the convicts as well. Bender and his comrades grew apprehensive as, when passing the windows of the prisoners' barracks, the grim figures behind the glass made gestures indicating the cutting of the guards' throats. It was high time to get out of here, Bender thought, otherwise he would be killed at the end of the war.

It was not long before all the existing guards were replaced by new ones. The order came for Bender and his pals to pack their bags and, in charge of a sergeant, they marched off the following day in the direction of the station, where they were to catch the train to Hamelin. Before they set off however, they all had to listen to a strict lecture from the sergeant. "Keep together," he told them. "It is my responsibility to see that every man arrives at Regimental Headquarters." With that, they left the prison camp.

As the train sped along, whether in war or peace, the landscape was the same. Inside the wooden compartments they sat, smoking their pipes — still filled more with beech leaves than tobacco — and enjoying the rest. Station after station flew past until, finally, the train arrived at the large city of Hanover.

The two groups lined up on the platform and prepared to change trains. At an order from the sergeant, they quick-marched down the steps of the subway, Bender the last one of the column. As the dim light underground swallowed them up, Bender tapped Bierbaum, who was immediately in front of him on the shoulder, saying: "I'm off!" With that he shook his friend by the hand for the last time. Turning about Bender disappeared up the steps to another platform, mingling with the crowds. Suddenly, he realized what he had done — he had actually deserted the army. Little did he know then that the Kaiser, himself, would desert a few days later.

Bender had not reached this decision on the spur of the moment. While in the prison camp he had found ample time both for reading and studying politics, and life in general. The army had vastly enlarged his outlook. From the information he had gained he was aware that, in 1917, both Emperor Karl of Austria, and even the German Reichstag, had made bids for peace, instigating his Holiness the Pope to intervene. The Russian politician, Lenin, appealed to the belligerents in the March of 1918. The longer the war lasted the more the Socialists in Germany had risen to power, culminating in the demand for peace as early as spring, 1918.

All this had helped Bender to reach the drastic decision he had then taken. However, the iron discipline was still there, and he had to take care not to be caught at the last minute. Quickly he stepped into an express train bound for Ruhr, without a ticket and loaded with the whole of his army equipment. The train moved off, and Bender took up a position at the end of a long third-class carriage adjacent to the toilet, his back to the outer window, opposite him stood a civilian. As the train gathered speed, the carriage began to rock, the two men doing likewise. Occasionally, Bender glanced in the direction of the toilet door, as this was his only escape-hatch if someone challenged him. The two men began to stare at each other, the civilian breaking the monotony by saying, "How do you do?" Then adding, "I know you, don't I?"

Bender did not recognize the fellow, and shook his head noncommittally.

"You live in Ronsdorf!" the civilian persisted.

"Yes, that's right," replied the amazed private. "How did you know?"

The civilian went on to explain that his name was Janowsky and that he lived in the old-fashioned, detached house which stood on the corner near the Reform church. Bender remembered the house quite clearly, with its iron railings guarding the stone steps.

"Where are you heading?" Janowsky asked.

"Home!" was the reply. "I've just run away from my regiment."

"Hush — not so loud," cautioned the other, placing a finger over his lips. "You are not out of the maze yet — there are military police on this train."

Bender gasped and looked wildly around him. His new friend however, managed to calm him, and they talked of other matters. Suddenly, the door at the far end of the carriage flew open to admit two military policemen. Like a shot from a gun, Bender darted into the toilet, locking the door from the inside.

On reaching the toilet, the policemen rattled the handle.

"Yes, what is it?" Bender shouted.

Before either of the military police could reply, Janowsky stepped forward to explain that it was his civilian friend inside the toilet. So innocent did he appear, that the police made no further trouble and continued on their way to the next carriage.

When the train reached Rittershausen, where Bender had to change for the last four miles to Ronsdorf, he shook Janowsky warmly by the hand, thanking him for his help.

As the suburban train finally came to a halt at Ronsdorf, Bender broke out into a hot sweat, not quite sure of the reception he would receive. Few people left the train, and the platform was nearly empty. Gathering up his steel helmet and rifle, he plodded through the subway. He had expected to knock into more military police, but his face lightened when he turned the corner. War in Ronsdorf, with its majority of Socialist supporters, had seemingly finished. This party had taken over, and welcomed Bender with open arms. Outside the barrier, four Socialists sat around a little table. The formalities were kept to a minimum. Bender explained that he had lost his formation. Getting to his feet, one of the men tore the cockade, the emblem of the once proud German Army, from the private's cap. He was then depleted of his medal-ribbons and told to report for duty next morning at the *Anchor*, a public house requisitioned by the Socialists. It was the last time Bender would surprise his family by a visit home as, theoretically, the war for Bender was over.

As a sign of the times, through the four years of bitter struggle, the political pattern of the German citizens had entirely changed. Throughout those war years they had had to follow the German National Party, the party of the right, the hall-mark of the Prussian Junkers, with the Kaiser as its leader. Disillusioned through the miseries of war, the human losses and food shortage, little by little this state of affairs had altered. The dissatisfied people went completely in the opposite direction, leaving their right wing leaders, and by the end of the war, the masses had joined the Socialists. During the war Bender had learnt much about politics and his leanings were towards Socialism. The following morning, without wavering, he signed a declaration which made him a post-war soldier of the 'People's Court'.

## Homeward Bound

Josua, a staunch right winger, was highly displeased at Theo's behaviour. His son had run away from his regiment — what would Germany do he thought, if everyone did the same? Josua still believed in the old traditional Germany, that of the German Empire, and the strong infallible currency. His shop which in 1914 had not been too bad, had now steadily deteriorated. During the war, prices had steadily risen, with Josua still believing in the value of the German Mark. Being a small-time business man, he had continued to buy and sell as in pre-war days, allowing a marginal profit. In the end not only had his stocks gone, but the money as well. This had happened to many people. Every effort went towards the war, and even gold watch-chains and wedding rings had been sacrificed in exchange for iron ones.

Into such an environment our post-war soldier had landed, with no prospect of work for some time to come. However, as always he succeeded in falling on his feet. Soon he became a paid guard of the People's Court, walking the streets day and night like a policeman, to keep order amongst the citizens. Still the war was not yet over. But, on the 9th November, at the instigation of the Socialists, the German Republic was declared, as a result of which the Kaiser disappeared to Holland. What a farce the whole war had been! The avalanche of the retreating German Army was still to come. It was not long before it started. Small formations trickled back from the west. Still intact, they marched through Ronsdorf and other towns. More and more followed behind, eventually clogging the Ruhr district to bursting point. Each division, regiment and battalion, on the move to their respective garrisons, was not aware that, in Germany, the war was over. The truth soon spread however, causing soldiers to leave their regiments and make for home. Some left their equipment behind, whilst others sold it for cash.

These were heydays for Bender who also bought and sold. At home, the spare room was full of blankets, leather-goods and other army equipment. Horses were running around freely, only to be picked up by the citizens and kept in back yards. Many of these poor creatures were slaughtered and converted into sausages, hunger being still uppermost. Bender had a grand time, but his father, who had only known the good old days, was aghast at behaviour in general. His son's business was against all regulations and sometimes Josua, old though he was, felt an urge to give this young man a good hiding. Through an upstairs window, Josua could observe Theo, looking like a policeman in his new uniform, equipped with a loaded rifle or revolver, demanding respect from the inhabitants. Bender was called upon to perform a variety of duties, such as moving stray army equipment from one end of the town to the other. He could command the aid of the number of men necessary for the purpose, some of whom had doubtful pasts. He would sit proudly on the barrel of a long-range gun, which was drawn by lorry through the middle of the town.

One day Josua could stand it no longer. Calling his son to his office, he tried to hammer it into Theo's head that, through the effects of war, he had become nothing more than a demoralized character.

Theo could not sleep that night. His father's words kept running through his mind. Thinking over his past life, in his heart he knew that his father was right. He had to admit that Josua had done his best in the early days to bring him up to be an honest citizen with a sense of values. The war had put an end to those fine ideals. Theo's conscience began to trouble him — how many others, like himself, would find themselves in a similar predicament? He eventually fell asleep, after deciding that something must be done to put a stop to his present mode of living.

The next morning, Josua and Theo met man-to-man to talk the matter over. The father had also been doing some thinking, and was prepared to sacrifice the last of his savings to enable Theo to attend a textile engineering school, in the hope of preparing for a successful life in the future.

Theo thought the proposal over. He could speak English and French. He was a classified weaver, having served a full apprenticeship, and now in addition he was being offered the chance of increasing his knowledge by studying textile technology, thus putting him on the road towards a prosperous business career. Gratefully, he accepted his father's offer, and after quitting his job as a policeman, he commenced his studies.

His first few weeks in school were far from easy, as he had to fight his ever present urge to roam. His class was comprised of a mixed bunch of young men from all over the district. One half of the district — the Cologne bridgehead — fell under British occupation, while the other was under Germany. The border line was not far removed from Ronsdorf. This created a new aspect, and professional smuggling started. Where Bender lived there was acute food shortage, and the people were near starvation point.

After the Armistice, the position had changed in the near-by occupied territories.

Supplies accumulated by the British Army were being sold by many of the Tommies to civilians.

Cigarettes, bacon, coffee and tea were obtainable at high prices. Under cover of dark, men with loaded sacks over their shoulders, would make their way through the forest to unload their valuables in Ronsdorf and other towns, selling their wares at fantastic prices. This new trade had even spread as far as Theo's school, some scholars crossing the bridgehead border, with their legal passes, every morning. Their purpose in joining the class was not to learn, but to give them the opportunity of obtaining a travel permit, thereby enabling them to smuggle. Every morning, long before school opened, these young men arrived, their pockets filled with thousands of British cigarettes. The demand for this commodity was great, and proved a source of temptation to Theo Bender. With some borrowed money, he bought a quantity and sold them at a profit, making pocket-money which he would not have had otherwise. Then, remembering his promise to his father, he gave it up, and settled down to learning in earnest.

Slowly, life in Germany began to settle down, but there was still unrest amongst people who had not yet grasped the fact that Germany had lost the war. Their arrogance still remained. They could not understand why British, French and American troops were occupying German soil. In their opinion, these foreign soldiers had no right to be there. Whenever they could put obstacles in the way of the occupying forces they would do so. This went on for some time until, one day, the French troops marched straight into the centre of 'Zion', leaving no doubt as to who was master. This calmed the hot-heads and there was no further trouble.

It was the Easter of 1919 when Theo had his vacation. So far he had done very well at school, with excellent marks. He found the first days of his break very enjoyable, wandering around the district and through the forests and meadows. Drinking in the fresh spring air, he thought how peaceful it was, and what a wonderful place the world would be to live in if there were no future wars.

Walking slowly back to the town, he went into a restaurant for a cool drink. While he was sitting at one of the tables, a German soldier in a brand-new uniform came in. Looking more closely he recognized Walter Sauer, one of his old friends. Though still a private, he looked very smart indeed.

Seeing Bender, Sauer joined him at his table and they chatted of their experiences over the past four years. Walter was still with his regiment in eastern Prussia, and seemed to have a good job. The soldier looked surprised when he heard that Bender had left the forces without any gratuity or civilian clothing.

"In fact," Walter pointed out, "theoretically you are still in the army. You've never been officially discharged. Why don't you travel up to your regiment in Hamelin and get the items to which you are entitled?"

"I can't," came the reply. "I have no money for the fare and, besides, I'm studying."

"But you're on holiday at the moment," Walter persisted. With that, out came his ticket pad with official documents from his regiment. He completed it to the last detail. "Here!" he said, handing it to Bender. "Go tomorrow and get the things you want, Theo — the railway fare is free!"

The next day Theo, to his father's surprise, once more changed into his field-grey and left for Hamelin. The following morning he made his way to the first military office. Giving his name, they searched their records, with the result — 'Bender unknown here.' He made for the second office with the same result. In the third one, however, they traced his details and promptly made out the discharge papers. Paying the gratuity, they advised him to call at quartermaster's stores for his belongings.

Leaving the office, Bender made for the park and squatting

down on a form, began to study the documents. Page after page he turned over. His whole military career had been meticulously marked down, with not one item left out. Even the Iron Cross and the Brunswick Military Medal were mentioned. All the battles and injuries were there and, not least of all, was the confirmation, from every formation, that he had been a good and reliable soldier. Satisfied, Bender made for the quartermaster's store. Donning the clothes he was given — an over-large jacket and overcoat, tight trousers and a cap that hung too much over one ear — he left his army uniform behind, and came out looking more like a scarecrow than a human being. With the last free gifts from the army he headed for home, where he could relax for a couple of days before the new term started. Bender was now officially discharged from the army.

The following two days Bender spent in reflection. In the solitude of the near-by woods he would walk for hours, thinking over the last four years. Where was the wonderful and mighty Germany of 1914 now? How long would it take to rebuild the shambles that remained? What had this war achieved? — For the Fatherland, nothing but a lost cause. Even the victors had their own troubles to contend with. They had accomplished one thing however, they had broken the back of the Prussian Junkers which was, in itself, an achievement. The following lines of Kipling's poem ran through Theo's mind at that moment:

> For all we have and are,
> For all our children's fate,
> Stand up and meet the war,
> The Hun is at the gate.

The Allies had followed this call; their case was just! But at what cost? 7,000,000 healthy boys from all sides had fallen to the ground — dead! And what of the wounded? The men who would go through life maimed, crippled in mind and body, unable to run and walk through the woods on a spring afternoon, hearing the twigs crackle underfoot, and the birds singing overhead — as he was then doing?

Ah, yes, Theo thought. He was one of the luckier ones. He

would resume his studies, and look forward to a new life at the end of them. A life, he hoped, that would offer him happiness and contentment, but, above all — peace!

# BOOK TWO

## PEACE IN OUR TIME

Post-war Germany entered the new decade of the twenties transformed from the wealthy nation of 1914 into a country of political and economic chaos.

Gone were the days when the Germans ecstatically prepared for war to glory in the many victories their proud army ultimately achieved over so many nations.

Times had changed. The Germans were well aware that the war was lost but, being the proud people they were, would not admit it. The jackboots, peaked caps and military banners had disappeared from the streets. Now it was an offence to display war medals in public. At that time, one thing seemed certain — Germany would never fight another war!

A characteristic of the German people, is a tendency to swing from one extreme to another, whenever the occasion arises. And so it was in the case of politics. The days of the Kaiser and his nationalist followers were over for the time being and instead, practically the whole nation had swung to the left, putting the Socialists in command.

At this stage, it is necessary to look ahead in order to understand the complex political pattern of post-war Germany. Certainly, for many years to come, the Socialists represented the majority of the people in the German Reichstag, the Democrats and centre party (the Catholics), being in opposition to their regime. However, one must not ignore the, then insignificant, Spartacists on the one hand, and the National Socialists on the other.

Again the German extremity came to the fore. The Spartacists represented the very left wing of the left, which was formed in 1918 under Karl Liebknecht and Rosa Luxemburg, and ultimately developed into the German Communist party.

On the other hand, the National Socialists represented the extremist party of the right — better known in history as the Nazis. Their original manifesto, based on the unification of social and national principles, was, later, blatantly renounced in favour of anti-democracy, fascist principles, militarism, imperialism, race-hatred and dictatorship.

When one speaks about the formation of the Nazi party, people outside Germany are mainly under the misapprehension that this took place in the late twenties or early thirties. Far from it! The Nazi party started straight after the end of the 1914/18 war. Hitler, who joined in 1919, announced in Munich his twenty-five points for the party as early as February 1920.

During the years to follow, it became increasingly obvious that these smaller parties, the Communists and the National Socialists, had one target in common — to upset the political machinery.

Although small at the outset, both these extremist units gained considerably in strength during the many parliamentary elections which took place in May 1924, December 1924, and in 1928 and 1930. By that time the Communists were able to cast 3,000,000 votes, while the National Socialists touched the 800,000 mark.

In order to understand the rise to power of a defeated nation, many other factors have to be considered:

1. During the war years Germany had had a lean time and, in 1919, was bordering upon starvation.
2. The first attempt to overthrow the Government (the Kapp-putsch), was made in 1920.
3. The inflation from 1922 to 1924, when every inhabitant, financially, lost everything.
4. The Allied Occupation of the Ruhr in 1923.
5. Hitler's attempt to overthrow the Government by force, in 1923.
6. The masses of unemployed, reaching a figure well over

6,000,000 in 1932. A far worse slump than experienced by other countries.

Is it any wonder that, under such conditions, the number of parties in the Reichstag at one time reached the fantastic figure of forty-three? These were years of political turmoil, unsteadiness and corruption. A most fertile ground for any politician, who, by hook or by crook, could promise the nation a hopeful future.

History has been written on this subject and, therefore, it would only distract from the aim of this book to repeat all the world shattering events which led up to World War II.

Whilst living through the hectic years of this decade, Theodor Bender observed the political developments and formed his own conclusions. After finishing his course at the textile school, despite vast unemployment, he established himself in his first executive job. As a humble citizen, he started his new career with the hope that Germany would settle down again to pre-war standards. Active politics were of no interest to him. All he asked of life was a safe future, with a comfortable income, and eventually a wife and family.

The textile industry in which he was employed as a designer and draughtsman, began to re-establish itself. A year of peace had made all the difference. The people were settling down, and clashes between left and right were few. There was hope of an industrial revival.

Soon, however, these dreams were shattered when, in March 1920, the whole of the Ruhr district began to erupt under the Kapp-putsch. Kapp, himself a Prussian politician of the right, tried to overthrow the Government of the Reich. Civil war had broken out, discharged soldiers still having a flair for shooting, which they had acquired during the great combat.

This was the signal for the Spartacist masses. A fully equipped army, dressed in dirty and ragged civilian clothes, they swarmed over the Ruhr district in their hordes, scaring the wits out of their compatriots. Like an avalanche they rolled through Bender's hometown on lorries, others following behind on foot. They were a noisy lot. From their vehicles they would shout, "Close your windows, or we shoot!" Some of their machine guns were in action, their light artillery drilling holes through the tower of the near-by town hall, while others were at the ready. All day long, they fought their way through the town and its suburbs, spreading havoc wherever they went.

In the evening, back they came, bringing with them some of their political prisoners. What happened to these poor chaps, no one ever knew.

During the night, the market-place of Ronsdorf was turned into one large bivouac, where the ruffians distributed their ill-gotten booty. The leader was a tall, local chap, dressed in a badly-fitting suit and trilby hat, with a long cavalry sabre dangling from his tight belt.

Kapp's effort to overthrow the Government was soon quelled by the Spartacist armies who left a lot of rubble in their wake. Through Bender's place of employment they roamed, forcing the doors during night-shift, and throwing coils of barbed wire into the running motors with the object of destroying anything belonging to Capitalist employers.

However, once more, peace reigned over Germany — at least for a year or two — and life settled down. Then, like a malignant growth, the financial rot set in. Prices began to rise at a fantastic rate, while wages, on the whole, remained static. Like so many others, Theo Bender worked hard at his job in an endeavour to save money for a rainy day, only to find in the end that it was to no avail.

Money became cheap and was spent as quickly as it was earned. Places of amusement, such as dance-halls, etc., did a rewarding trade during the 'Roaring Twenties'. People were light-hearted, adopting the attitude that they could not care less. The youth enjoyed themselves, dancing the exciting Charlston, just as hysterically as the twisters and rockers of today.

From 1922 onwards prices no longer tallied with the money earned, the spiral of inflation rising skywards like a rocket. Like everyone else, Bender was always up against time. When he received his pay-packet, it was useless depositing the money in the bank, or putting it in an old stocking, for within a fortnight, it would be valueless. Bank notes had to be exchanged into merchandise as quickly as possible.

The inflation was so great that, by 1922, Bender had contributed no less than 29,600 marks monthly, towards his stamps for health, unemployment and pension. An equivalent, in 1914 values, of £1,480.

Firms were no longer able to obtain the necessary notes through their banks, as the printing machines could not cope with the demand. Consequently, as employees had to be paid, the Government finally sanctioned the pressing of notes by local printing firms, with the result that everybody soon began printing money. Some of these notes were very fine specimens indeed but of little, or no, value.

It was farcical to pay salaries weekly or monthly, and daily payments had to be made. A race from factory to shop, in order to purchase the merchandise before the value of the money ran out, became the pattern of shopping.

Still, the rising spiral had not reached its limit, and it was nothing unusual for Bender to pay the fantastic price of 1,000,000 marks for just one glass of beer, being equal to £50,000, according to pre-war rate of exchange. Some of his pals became so extravagant in throwing their money about, that they would buy scores of bottles of champagne, just for the sake of washing their faces in it. There was no longer any point in saving money, even for the following day.

Deep into the abyss the German money-market had sunk with no signs of recovery. This was the time for foreign tourists to visit Germany and take advantage of such cheap holidays, when for either £1 or a dollar they could obtain billions of marks. The story goes that, at this time, a foreigner, missing the last connection on the Rhine, bought a motor-boat, including the captain, for a couple of dollars. On reaching his destination, he sold the lot for a few cents, still making it a cheap journey.

Every German individual was affected. Many were worried about their savings, which they visualized would dwindle away. How many older people, hoping for a comfortable retirement, saw their dreams shattered, their money valueless?

Josua Bender, the draper, possessing no capital, belonged to a different category. His business was ruined through the war years, and his stocks were depleted. But he held one trump card; his large three-storey building in the centre of the town. Believing that this would make him rich, he sold at the peak of the inflation. Obtaining billions of paper marks for his property, he liquidated his mortgages and so legally deprived his creditors of the real value. He then deposited the remainder of the money into his bank, only to discover a month later that he had exchanged his property for no more than the price of a pair of boots. Had he only kept the house for another year, no matter what the cost, he would have saved his only asset.

Josua now found himself poorer than ever. He was without a job, and with his family, he had to look for a small flat. No longer could he afford the extravagances of the past, when he was able to supervise his own staff or pay for domestic help.

The whole family were still together, everyone in relatively good health, with the exception of Magdalena. The war years, the loss of her home and financial backing, coupled with the death of Luise, her eldest daughter, had taken their toll. Her anxiety about the future did not improve matters. Fortunately, Josua was able to find something to do. He took over a tiny branch of a dry-cleaning firm at a ridiculously low wage, but this was all he could expect at his age. The years ahead were nothing but a hard, financial struggle. Theodor contributed his part, while Heinrich, in a good plumbing job, financed the rest. Lydia assisted her mother in the running of the flat.

1923 proved to be an eventful year. The inflation sapped the will-power of the German people. Many were aggravated by the strong terms of the Treaty of Versailles, according to which, quantities of coal and steel had to be supplied to the Allies. The miners and steel workers of the Ruhr became more and more reluctant to work, finally stopping altogether, thereby forcing the Allies to intervene. During their occupation of the Ruhr district the Allies once more brought home to the German people that they had lost the war and, under the supervision of rifles and bayonets, production recommenced.

On the surface and to an outsider Germany looked calm, but, here and there one could observe Germans on the march again. Militarism was not dead after all. When strolling through the countryside, one could encounter marching columns in civilian dress. Grouped in exact formation, they carried a broomstick in front of them to which the flag of the

Swastika was attached. Behaving like soldiers they would sing revolutionary songs, the prohibited war medals glittering on some of their chests. Occasionally loud commands would rend the air, and right arms were raised in unison when they bellowed, "Heil Hitler!" To the ordinary man in the street, this was something new and at the time, people took little notice of these so-called idiots.

The reverse side of the picture was represented by other human formations marching with the same military exactness, but without war medals. They behaved louder and wilder than the disciples of Hitler, carrying their banner before them with the Hammer and Sickle as their symbol. Occasionally they would raise their clenched right fists high into the air as they enthusiastically sang *The Red Flag*.

Germany was now confronted with two new and different aspects of politics. The Nazis and Communists began openly to make their impact upon the public. Though very small at the beginning, both parties grew faster than anyone had imagined, and as time went on, head-on clashes between the two rival formations became more and more frequent. Then political arguments were fought with bare fists and knuckle-dusters in the streets of the towns. Bender often wondered where all this would lead. He disliked the arrogant marching of the Nazis. They were full of fighting spirit, and people like this would go through anything if the right leader called upon them. Often, he would openly discuss this with his intimate friends, expressing his own view that the spirit of 1914 was dead, and that Germany could not, and never would, be ruled again by the Kaiser and his monarchy. What if one day a man was to arise who was a strong union leader, in contact with the working masses? If that day came, anything could happen and, once again, the fury of the militant youth of Germany would be roused.

That man was already there! Even those who knew, would not admit it. Hitler was busy enough at his headquarters in Munich, soon drawing the attention of the German people to himself when, in November 1923, he and his staff felt strong enough to overthrow the German Government. However, this first attempt on the part of the Nazis failed, landing Hitler in jail for a term of five years.

Only twelve months later he was released and, from then on, was able to build up his party properly. In Hitler, the German hierarchy of high finance recognized the coming leader. Germany's rise to power started again, and who would have thought then, that a painter and decorator — a casual labourer — would one day be the Führer of a new Germany?

1924 brought the end of the inflation when, overnight Hjalmar Schacht, the financial wizard, introduced the Renten Mark, a new currency backed by the produce grown and taken from the soil of the German Republic, i.e. one Renten Mark in exchange for one billion paper marks.

From now on, it meant toil and hard work for the whole nation. The people had something to work for, and the money they earned as a result of their labours was real, an incentive to German thrift.

The years flew by and Germany revived, the lavish spending of readily given foreign loans soon altering everything. No longer was Germany a poor nation. New buildings shot up, and modernization took place everywhere. Germany began to prosper on borrowed money.

In the company of his many friends and acquaintances, Bender enjoyed this spell of life. He liked people! His chief interest was in his job, in which he steadily made headway. Of his recreations, swimming came first, football second, and occasionally one would find him on the stage, entertaining large audiences with wit and humour. His organizing capacity in business and sports took him far beyond the boundaries of Ronsdorf, and his was a well-known figure in many places.

Despite all this however, he still felt unsettled, and he had not forgotten the dreadful experiences of the war. Some of his friends were already talking about the new Nazi movement, and their formations appeared more and more frequently in the streets of the towns. Clad in some kind of a uniform, with jackboots, belt, brown shirt and a new kind of peaked cap, they looked more like soldiers. People began to respect these brown-shirts as the marching soldiers of the future. Could it be possible, Bender thought, that these fellows would one day march again, as those in 1914 had done?

Such thoughts were always on his mind, and after considering the strict discipline and the manifesto of the Nazi party, he came to the conclusion that Germany would not be a very pleasant place in which to live should she unleash her soldiers against her victors. It was too early yet, to take such matters seriously but, nevertheless, Bender was always looking for an opportunity to work abroad.

His first chance came in 1925 when a textile buying agent from New York approached him. Bender seemed to be the right man for an executive job at Haledon, near New York, but not only did the agent want Bender, but weavers as well. These could be found in abundance in the surrounds of Ronsdorf, and Bender soon found many young men who were willing to go. He obtained everything the agent wanted. To Bender it was just a simple matter of leaving his home and going to America and he refrained from discussing it with his parents until the day of departure drew near. When finally he put his cards on the table, his mother was very upset, and that was the end of his dream. Unable to withstand his ailing mother's pleas, he gave in, and the party of weavers left without him.

Shortly afterwards, Bender had two more chances to emigrate, one to Roumania, the other to Austria. These, again, he turned down owing to his mother. He stayed at home and carried on in his job, enlarging his knowledge in anticipation of an opportunity at some later date.

When 1926 came his mother's health began to fail. Josua made a last effort to send her to a sanatorium on National Assistance, which he could never repay, but even this did not improve matters. Still happy and content, Magdalena lingered on. On Christmas Day, the whole family sat around her in the local hospital. It was to be the last family reunion in which their mother would take part. She remained cheerful looking forward to the coming spring when she hoped to be home again.

On Boxing Day, all the members of the family looked sad and depressed. Theodor could not stand the sorrowful atmosphere any longer and, packing his boots and skates, he made for the near-by lake which was frozen over with a thin layer of crystal clear ice. What a treat it was to be in the open air. He knew that he could not help his mother and, trying to forget his troubles, he cut his figures-of-eight into the ice, which was just strong enough to support a solitary skater. Theo had not been there long when his girl friend called him to come home as his mother had died that same morning. He and his brother walked to the hospital expecting to find their mother devoutly laid out on a hospital bed. However, they were mistaken. She had already been removed to the mortuary and all he and his brother could see of her, were two pathetically cold feet peeping out from one end of the shroud.

At the age of sixty, life was over for Magdalena. On the whole it had been good, though the later years had proved hard. With her funeral another chapter in the history of Josua's family ended.

The years from 1927 to 1930 passed with the Nazi party's intent becoming clearer every day. Bender felt that, one day, this new force would unfold itself in the brutal suppression of anything democratic, and nobody would be allowed to express his own opinion. Many of his old friends had already joined the party or the brown-shirts. The moment this happened, friends were no longer friends as long as the other one remained in the opposite political camp. He became more and more convinced that in such a Germany there was no room for him to live.

Opportunities for emigrating grew less and, at the age of thirty-one, his thoughts turned more and more to marriage. His brother was already married, and filled Josua's little flat to the brim.

Theodor Bender had always had a liking for girls. He had flirted with many, but the memory of Paula, his first love, always stayed in his mind, though she was now happily married, and had given birth to triplets, much to the surprise of herself and her husband.

One day, while strolling through the near-by city looking in the shop windows, he came across a photographer's. Stopping to admire the work of a real craftsman in the many beautiful portraits exhibited, his eyes became rivetted on one particular portrait in the very middle. For a long time he gazed, as though hypnotized, into the frank eyes which looked back at him from the picture. Somewhere, he had seen that face before. On the spur of the moment he went into the shop to buy it. However, without the consent of the person concerned, this was not possible. Eventually, he obtained the girl's address, and went round to meet her. Although she was only seventeen, the attraction was mutual.

Marianne's father did not approve of the association, as he considered Bender to be far too old for his daughter. Theo's friends could not believe that the romance would last but, to everyone's surprise, it did.

As the months went by and their relationship strengthened, Bender began to see a new horizon. He had forgotten all about politics and thoughts of emigration, so absorbed was he with his young sweetheart. Together they planned for the future, money could now be saved without it losing its value and, surely, here was something worth saving for!

When he went to the rectory to acquaint the eccentric parson with his intention to marry, he knew that this would not be an easy interview. In the past, he had failed to please the parson, who had a good memory. Not only had Bender failed to attend church regularly but, worst of all, he intended to marry a member of the Lutherian church which was against all the principles of the Reformists.

With this on his mind he rang the bell and entered the parson's study. The interview turned out as he had expected, short and brisk, without any feeling of joy at a forthcoming wedding. The parson was reckoned to be a God-fearing man and Bender could not understand why he should consider it wrong to marry a Reformist to a Lutherian.

The atmosphere between the two men remained cool and formal during the interview until, finally, they stood in the hall of the rectory talking about minor things. After Bender had taken his leave of the parson, he left the rectory. He knew that the actual church ceremony was bound to be a cold and gloomy one, but visions of his dear bride-to-be drove these dismal thoughts from his head. The deep love he and Marianne felt for one another was surely right, and he was certain that a greater power than any on earth would not frown upon their marriage, regardless of their respective denominations.

When the wedding ceremony took place, it was a small gathering of the couple's relations and close friends. In the high dome of the huge church, the feeble singing of the tiny congregation was lost. The ceremony was short and matter-of-fact, and it was a disappointed gathering that filed out of the church to make their way quickly towards the near-by reception hall. Here they were greeted by a gramophone, in full blast, blaring out the 'Wedding March'.

Soon the atmosphere in the church was forgotten. Theo and Marianne enjoyed their day and when evening came, they made their way to their new home. Although only two rooms in all, it was large enough for this blissfully happy couple. Their financial resources did not stretch to a honeymoon, but what a pleasure it was to sit together in the evenings, just the two of them, and discuss the future.

Theo spoke to his wife of his fears for the future of Germany. Explaining to her the Nazi regime he told her of his plans to emigrate. As young as she was Marianne had sense beyond her years, and did not seem perturbed at the thought of leaving the country of her birth, but said she would go wherever he went. They planned and planned, so as to be quite ready when the opportunity to emigrate arose.

The months rolled by and Bender concentrated even more on his career. He now had the qualifications for a really good job, and, despite political danger, the future had a rosy aspect.

To Theo's joy, one day Marianne told him he was to become a father. He was so excited at the news that he could hardly refrain from standing on his head.

As the time for Marianne's confinement drew near, she was transferred to the hospital. One Sunday morning, a neighbour rang the bell to tell Theo that his wife had given birth to a daughter, and both were quite well. Getting up, he washed and dressed, and set out for the hospital. Calling at a near-by nursery, he purchased a huge bunch of flowers, and, as proud as a peacock, wended his way to the maternity ward. There, he found his young wife, only nineteen, looking as rosy as ever in spite of the ordeal. However, never having seen a newly-born child before, Bender's first reaction was real disappointment when he realized that the thin, frail, blue-looking baby, with the jet-black hair, was actually his daughter. He was sorely afraid that it would not survive.

Marianne and baby Luise soon came home from hospital,

and what a difference it made to the routine of the flat. If he had to, Bender would sit up all night just for the sake of the baby. Probably he was no more crazy than many other fathers.

The first discord to strike the happy family was when Bender's best friend, a baker, delivered the usual morning rolls and bread. It was during the parliamentary elections in September 1930, when Otto, a staunch supporter of the Nazis, noticed the baby's drinking cup, adorned with the national colours of Germany, standing on the sideboard. This was sufficient to arouse his temper. Picking up the cup, he exclaimed that there was no place for the national colours in the house of people who were voting against the coming regime. So ended, through Otto's political affront, a friendship which had lasted for many years.

The whole world was in a state of chaos, not only politically but, also, from the financial viewpoint. The Wall Street crash in America in 1929 had started the rot, and there were masses of unemployed everywhere. The British Cabinet was doing its utmost to keep the wheels of industry turning until, finally, in September 1931, came the devaluation of the pound. This decision became of great importance in Bender's life. The firm by which he was employed, carried on a substantial trade with their English customers and friends, and with a stroke of the pen, the British Government had wiped out the whole profits on the firm's books. All goods were sold on the basis of pound sterling, which they lawfully obtained from English customers when the goods were delivered. From then on, however, through the depreciation of the value, foreign suppliers received 20% less, which, in many cases, represented a trade loss. Worse was to come when the pound began to fluctuate on the world market. In the end, no manufacturer knew how much he would get for the goods supplied unless quoted in gold or Swiss francs to English customers.

Automatically, Continental firms became aware of the financial situation, their only alternative being to start manufacturing in England. The industrial exodus began — probably the object of British politics. There was no doubt as Bender, with his knowledge of the textile trade, concluded, that the Lancashire cotton industry had grown stale over the years. Something had to be done to revive it. At one time this industry represented an enormous asset, grown up through the ingenuity of the British, fostered by the natural moist climate of Lancashire and Yorkshire. Through its own expansion over the years the pattern had changed, and the industry had been partly developed by other countries, Japan in particular. In addition, the moist and foggy Lancashire conditions could now be artificially created in any factory in the world, so that by the end of the twenties the art of spinning and weaving was practised everywhere. The English had gradually brought into being a competition against their own trade.

There was no doubt that, to counteract this growing loss, new industries had to be attracted to the British Isles. The shrewd move to devalue the pound was a lever of attraction, and so it proved in later years when many foreign firms settled down amongst the British, creating a new impetus to industry.

At that time there was great activity within the industrial establishments of the little town of Ronsdorf, where ribbon-weaving of special articles had been centred for many years. As a substantial part of the exports were destined for Great Britain, it now became necessary for all these firms to decide whether to sacrifice the British market or to start manufacturing in England. This call came to many factories and, with the persuasion of English friends in the trade, the exodus of the Ronsdorf industry began. One firm after another opened branches in St. Albans, Stockport, Colne and other places, whilst established English firms in the ribbon-weaving industry called for key men from Western Germany. Weavers packed their bags, making for places like Luton, Croydon and Middleton. Little Ronsdorf became full of unemployed people, watching the exportation of their own industry from under their very noses.

The day arrived when Bender's chance came. He was summoned to the firm's boardroom, where the plans of a new factory in Hyde, Cheshire, were laid before him. Being appointed as Director and Secretary he accepted with alacrity. The directors were amazed at their employee's quick decision, without having even consulted his wife. They were not to know that this had been discussed, and settled, some time ago.

Before his move to another country could be accomplished, Bender had another task to perform. He had to purchase the whole of the machinery and auxiliaries, secondhand, as cheaply as possible. As the industry was at its lowest ebb, these were easily obtainable. By this time a nervous tension had set in amongst the population. Most other firms' machinery had already been transported to England. People stood around in groups while Bender supervised the packing of the train-ferry wagons. Things had to be done quickly, as there were signs that some enraged extremist elements would interfere with the wagons. They would have smashed the lot if they had not been too late, but the consignment was already on its way to the English Channel.

On the 30th January, 1932, Bender spent his last night in his German home. His bag was packed, ready for his departure the following morning. He had to travel alone to England, his wife and child following later. In his conversation with Marianne, he turned over the leaves of the last few years. There was no doubt that, inside Germany, the political position was nearing its climax. For some time, now, it was highly dangerous to leave the house after dark. It was common practice for Communists to lie in ambush behind hedges or thickets, just for the purpose of sniping at a lone Nazi, whilst the same happened in reverse. Living, as Bender did, on the outskirts of a town, one could expect stray bullets. Political murders became more frequent, people just disappearing without a trace.

All this ran through Bender's mind. He was glad to be leaving his own country. Whilst he was away, the Germans could fight it out between themselves, probably one day returning to a true democracy.

At 6 a.m. the next morning Bender set off. It was bitterly cold, with the roads covered with a thick layer of black ice. There seemed no earthly chance of reaching the tram stop, half a mile away, and so, without saying good-bye to his wife, he thought he would just make an effort to see how far he could go on the slippery ice. Reaching the top of the steeply sloping street, using his large leather suitcase as a sledge, he shot down the half-mile gradient at top speed. It landed him near the tram stop where his pal Paul, a loom engineer, was waiting for him. Would the tram be able to negotiate the ice and take them to the city? Both thought not, but were mistaken. When an hour later the express rattled towards England, Bender was very upset at not having kissed his Marianne good-bye.

## THE COUNTRY OF ADOPTION

When stepping aboard a ship for the first time, a landlubber usually experiences a peculiar sensation at the thought of crossing the sea. Bender, who had never been on anything larger than a paddle-steamer on the Rhine, was no exception. The passage was a rough one, and he positioned himself in the middle of the ship, near the main mast, where the rocking was less pronounced. His thoughts passed to and fro between Marianne and the baby, and the unknown shores of England. What did he expect of this strange land? How would he get on with the language, which he had not practised for years? All this was on his mind when approaching the Harwich coastline — not unlike the one he had just left at Flushing.

Stepping ashore, Theo and Paul found their luggage being whisked away by a couple of men from amongst the hordes swarming around the passengers. They all looked the same in their dark smudgy suits, cloth-caps and mufflers. Lacking a proper uniform, it did not make a good impression. Had this happened on the Continent, Bender would certainly never have seen his belongings again. However, he soon discovered that this was the common practice in England and that, in spite of their doubtful appearance, these men could be trusted.

When approaching the platform large advertisements caught his eye: ' Sheffield for Steel, Lancashire for Textiles '. A sure way of drawing the attention of incoming businessmen.

Bender soon realized that his English left a lot to be desired.

A foreign language can play tricks, and it did not necessarily apply that one could translate one's own language literally into English. Walking along the platform, studying the London-bound train he noticed on many of the carriages the word ' Smoking '. In a German dictionary, the definition of the noun smoking means an evening-dress suit and, for the life of him, he could not deduce why all these compartments should be reserved for people in evening-dress. Nevertheless, he was quick to learn.

The train took Paul and Theo to London. For many years the two had known each other. Paul was a broad-shouldered, easy-going chap, with a liking for a good glass of German schnapps. Both of them were unmistakeably typical countryfolk. How would they fit into the large City of London they were fast approaching? When they eventually walked out of Liverpool Street Station, they were full of expectation.

This huge Metropolis is a fascinating place and makes quite an impression on any newcomer. In horror, they watched the traffic speeding past them, expecting an accident any minute. Large double-decker buses the like of which they had never seen before, rolled through a sea of little cars like so many match-box toys.

On leaving the train, Bender's luggage had disappeared, once more, amongst the crowd. Needless to say, he was very relieved when a smart porter turned up with it just in time for the taxi. At an unbelievable speed they raced through the dense traffic with only inches to spare, expecting a bump any moment. It always has been a great revelation for any foreign visitor to see and explore the great City of London. On this occasion there was no time to explore the Capital, as business had to come first.

After a hectic and tiring day, the two travellers eventually settled into their hotel at High Holborn. After a good meal, they sat down in the lounge to chat over a glass of beer. One beer became two, then three, four and five, until Paul remarked that the waiter must be deaf. The mistake was theirs in not knowing the English language. In the Continental fashion, they answered "thank you" to the waiter's request. Had they replied "no thank you" their beer drinking would have finished sooner.

Early the next morning, the train took them northwards to Manchester. Their breakfast on the train consisted of grapefruit or tomato juice, porridge, fried haddock, bacon and egg, bread, jam and tea, sufficient to fill a man for the whole day. What a contrast from the simple German breakfast of rolls, bread, butter, jam and black coffee.

There was plenty to study during the journey. The train, the waiters, people in general, and the gents in bowler hats with rolled-up umbrellas, the living image of the English businessmen Bender had seen typified in cartoons in German newspapers. When putting their luggage on the racks, he was horrified to see that some of these men stood with their dirty shoes on the expensive upholstery of the seats.

Outside the landscape rolled by. Although it was winter, the grass in the meadows still showed a full sappy green, unknown on the Continent at this time of the year. The weather was typically English, with brilliant sunshine in some places interspersed with patches of thick fog, turning yellowish when approaching big towns. Compared with continental standards, these places looked dirty with their chimneys belching out smoke from the rich tarry coal.

They finished their journey in comfort, the train coming to a halt at London Road Station. Bender jumped out first, taking his suitcase with him this time. Making for the first taxi, he now had an opportunity to try his English. "The best hotel in Denton," he said, and off they went. Through many main and side streets they careered, the figures on the meter climbing higher and higher.

It was a Sunday afternoon when Bender and Paul were deposited outside the Denton Hotel which was nothing more than an ordinary public house. How quiet it was compared with those at home. There was not a soul around, and the doors were closed. Why is it that English people are not allowed to drink when they like? Bender banged hard with the knocker, and the door was eventually opened by a white-haired lady. "What is it you want?" she asked. "Where do you come from?"

"Lodging — Germany," Bender replied, which was all the vocabulary he could produce.

The old lady could not make sense of what they were trying

to say, but she let them in. Nevertheless this was to become their domicile for many weeks.

As evening came the pub began to fill. The news had spread around that two Germans had arrived. In a small English town, only fourteen years after a world war, this was enough to fill the house for many days. To the proprietor's delight, everyone was eager to see the two strange men. Theo and Paul felt rather like monkeys in a cage at the zoo. They were offered gallons of beer, far more than they could possibly drink, and what had been intended to be an early night, turned out to be a late one.

Every morning they made their way to the factory, just across the border to Hyde, where, in a compound behind high walls, they found the empty derelict buildings of a typical old cotton mill. Everything was in the course of demolition except for a few small structures, and a larger weaving shed which was earmarked for the enterprise Bender had to manage. The shed was old and damp with half the windows in its saw-tooth roof missing. It had not been used for years, and it was not going to be an easy task to convert such an old shed into a factory. There was no office on the whole of the premises and, apart from the rough and tough Lancashire and Yorkshire demolition workers, there was no one with whom the new director could talk.

When Bender tentatively approached these chaps, he soon found out that he would have to learn real English the hard way. There was no resemblance whatsoever between the English these fellows spoke and that which he had learnt at school. In fact Bender was doubtful whether these chaps spoke English at all. Quite obviously, therefore, the language he acquired there was not the standard at which to aim, and there were sure to be repercussions later on.

In the early thirties, Hyde was a dreary place, with much unemployment and, as a result, many poor people. When walking around the town hall, men in caps and scarves, who had not worked for years, could be seen sitting around in their dozens.

Rumours of a new factory had spread like wildfire. Every morning Bender found the queue growing longer and longer. These people were in dire need of work, some even offering

## The Country of Adoption

their services free for the first three months so long as they could get in.

By then, the weaving machinery, which had escaped the Nazis, had arrived from Germany, and the building up of the new premises went according to plan. Bender had been in England two months when he travelled down to Harwich to meet his wife and daughter, together with the ten keymen from Germany. The journey back to Hyde was a miserable one. In those days, the L.N.E.R. trains did not look very respectable, neither did the stations. The dismal weather did not offer any encouragement to the newcomers at all. As they passed the Woodhead tunnel, he informed them that they were nearly home. There is no pleasant view travelling through the Derbyshire moorlands on a drizzling misty day. No wonder Marianne shed a few tears when she heard that this was where she had to make her home.

They reached their destination, and the family settled down in a small flat in Dukinfield, whilst the men lodged with various English folk. What an invasion this was for little Hyde, and how the people stared when they saw all these new arrivals from Germany. It did not take long before the shuttles began to click and weaving started. Customers soon began to call, and, whether English or German, the employees soon became one big, happy family.

It was at this juncture that Bender slipped up badly with the English he had learnt from the toughs. One morning the office bell rang and his secretary ushered a potential customer into the director's domain. The conversation in broken English started behind closed doors. Then, the bell rang a second time, the girl announcing another customer. On the spur of the moment, and quite innocently, Bender instructed his secretary in the presence of his first client, to — "Please tell the ———— to wait!" This was plain English — in fact, too plain. The new director was well reprimanded by his business friend and told on no account to use such language again.

For the next seven years the experiences of these Germans were too numerous to catalogue here, but many highlights were not without significance especially in the political field.

From a social point of view these aliens were soon absorbed into the community. The English are a sporting lot and once a war is over they do not bear malice. They are grand folk in Cheshire and Lancashire and, if ever there is hospitality, it can be found in these two counties. Bender had ample time over the years to study this aspect and often he would draw comparisons between the north and the south. Travelling in the north was a pleasant affair, and one's travelling companions do not hide behind newspapers as they do in the Metropolis, where one has difficulty in making conversation with one's neighbour. Particularly in Lancashire, there is a certain joviality. People are frank with one another and their houses are open at any time, even to foreigners.

Most of these Germans soon lost their homesickness, the younger men taking out girls, the older ones taking part in all kinds of social activities. In a free democracy, week-ends became a real relaxation. Although Hyde itself is a typical industrial town, the surrounding countryside is very beautiful, and Bender enjoyed many a long walk at the week-end. Climbing up the steep slope of Werneth Low, he would make either for Romiley, or turn further west towards Glossop and into the Derbyshire hills which, on a fine summer's day, are delightful.

In the evenings he took pleasure in visiting a country pub with its jovial, smoky atmosphere. Once he was able to talk the local lingo, he would mix with people and enjoy their company. He was not so fond of the English beer, however, which was far stronger than, and lacked the sparkle of, the light lager in Germany. His English friends were always curious to learn more about his native country and how it was possible for a man like Hitler to rise to the top. Here he could talk freely without the fear of being overheard by the Nazis.

The years ahead promised to be nothing but pleasant. He loved his work, the factory was doing well and was employing about fifty people. His home life was happy and there were many friends. This could have gone on indefinitely, had it not been for the political development inside Germany.

During 1932/33 there was nothing to mar the pleasure of this small German colony. Bender had anticipated that the Nazis would, one day, take charge of Germany, and therefore was not surprised when Hitler took over, in January 1933, as Chancellor of the Reich. So far these few Germans were safe in England, but all were worried as to how long it would last. Permits for work were difficult to come by, depending on the importance of the work foreigners were doing. They all had to rely on the goodwill of the British Home Office and so far, Bender had been lucky for year after year his permit arrived.

This was not the case with his key men. The number soon diminished, as it was of the greatest importance that British labour should be employed. Bender made a mistake, at that time, when making a statement to one of the inquisitive newspaper reporters of a national paper. Elaborating on the skill of the local textile workers, he remarked that half the key men had been sent home. In England, this would have been a harmless report, but somehow the newspaper found its way to the Foreign Office in Berlin and Bender was promptly reprimanded by the Nazis.

The political change in Germany was beginning to have its effect on Germans abroad. It was not enough that the eighty million people in Germany were roped in by the new regime. Every national by birth, wherever he was, had to be drafted into the movement. Up until then, these weavers from Ronsdorf (and there were sixty of them in and around Manchester) had occasionally held meetings amongst themselves, with the sole aim of getting together and having a chat. There was nothing wrong with this but, as time went on, the propaganda from Berlin began to spread far and wide. The first signs became visible when harmless looking gentlemen from London or Liverpool began to comb the country gathering their sheep into the melting pot of the German Third Reich. At first, on the surface, it all looked quite innocent. The meetings were normally held in the form of Harvest Thanksgiving or Christmas parties. Bender had nothing against this so long as it kept that way. So far, there were no signs of National Socialist propaganda or the appearance of the Swastika, and these gatherings were no more than seemingly harmless-looking national affairs.

Parallel to this ran another doctrine. Every German abroad was informed about the disbandment of all labour unions, which were replaced by the only, and compulsory, national union — ' The German Labour Front '.

Bender and his men wondered how long the Home Office

would allow them to stay in England. At the same time, German firms were informing their key men abroad that it was imperative to join the Labour Front or else they would find themselves in difficulties when returning home. There was no alternative and reluctantly, as a matter of form, they paid their monthly subscriptions.

In the meantime, the now organized, monthly gatherings of Germans went on in every town and city in England, and all over the world.

The time was not far removed before a leader would have to be found for every group abroad. When an approach was made to the Stockport group, the man in question, a red-hot Nazi by the name of Wuster, was already earmarked from London.

He was rejected by most men, who wanted Bender to carry on with their meetings in the old beer-drinking fashion. The votes were cast and Bender found himself with a majority decision in the embarrassing position of being leader of the Stockport group of the German Labour Front. Without upsetting the London officials, he could not say a word against it.

From now on the tempo began to increase. Hitler was in full power. Once again the boots were marching in Germany, and Goebbel's propaganda was spreading to the far ends of the globe. The meetings of the group grew more frequent. Lecturers arrived from London, spreading the Swastika flags over the walls of the meeting halls.

The harmless Easter and Christmas parties no longer had any connection with what they represented. They became highly political, the fists of the speakers pounding the desk. In those days, it was not unusual to encounter, in any city in England, the official meetings of the German Labour Front, with the Swastikas blatantly fluttering in the hall. Everybody was invited. 'Bring your English friends!' was the motto. Many accepted the invitations, so opening wide the doors to Scotland Yard, whose plain-clothes officers, unbeknown, frequently mingled with the crowds at the meetings.

Throughout this time, Bender had watched this development with awe. At first he was unable to do anything against it, but when the Home Office allowed him to stay in England indefinitely, he began to pursue his own politics.

The literature, which he received from headquarters in the early days was harmless, but as the tempo increased, the Nazi arrogance, brutality and race-hatred became prominent. ' Down with the Jews — Down with Communists and Socialists ' became the slogans printed in bold headlines.

When distributing pamphlets and brochures to his fellow countrymen (as he was instructed to do) Bender would first of all go through the lot, sorting out the good from the evil. Anything of a political nature went into the fire, the remainder was distributed.

Sooner or later, he knew he would be found out. When that day did come, he was officially sacked. In no uncertain terms he was informed that he was not a good leader but, as an ordinary member, he was still compelled to attend the meetings.

From now on Bender was on his own. As a lone wolf, he swam against the Nazi regime. As early as 1936, he wrote to the Home Office for naturalization papers but, unfortunately four years residence in England were not sufficient to make him eligible. He had to wait another year.

When Hitler occupied the Rhineland, Bender had expected the Allies to forestall this event, but nothing was done. What a tragedy it was for the people of the world when the Nazis' first bluff paid dividends. Had they been chased back the Second World War might have been avoided.

During this period, Bender tried to convince his English friends of the aggressiveness of the Hitler regime, pointing out the danger of a coming conflagration, if other nations lulled themselves into complacency. Having lived through one war, like many others, he wanted peace. He did his utmost to make his opinion felt, but what could he do — a lone foreigner in another country?

In February 1937 Bender lodged his application for naturalization and hoped for the best. A month later he joined the Rotary Club, an organization with high ideals, their main one being — 'To encourage and foster the advancement of international understanding, goodwill and peace through a world fellowship of business and professional men in the ideal of service.'

Here, he could at least do something. But, as a German national, by joining the organization, in applying for British citizenship and through helping German Jews financially, he had put himself into the greatest jeopardy with Nazi Germany. Rotary was strictly prohibited, so were the other issues and in taking these steps Bender was liable to be put in prison.

In spite of this, he travelled to Germany in July, when called to the bedside of his ailing father. The journey was a nightmare. The Gestapo heard of his visit and were soon hot on his trail. For several nights he slept uneasily with his passport under his pillow, ready to flee at a moment's notice. Tipped off, he dodged his way to Kaldenkirchen, slipping across the border into Holland, just in the nick of time. He did not know then that for the next decade he would not see Germany again.

Back in Cheshire he became more active than ever. Here at least it was possible to talk as he liked. From the platform Bender made public speeches enlightening the English as to "How Hitler obtained power". Now he was really in the swim but against the current. In England, the German Labour Front meetings still took place, but without him. All their persuasions to make him pay subscriptions did not help to bring back the lost sheep.

Bender had not long to wait before repercussions came from across the Channel. To the embarrassment of his Company Chairman in Germany, the steps he had taken had a far-reaching effect. The only way this gentleman could forewarn his co-director in England, was by slipping into Holland to post an uncensored letter.

It was to inform Bender that the Foreign Office in Berlin had approached the Chamber of Commerce in Wuppertal in connection with the political behaviour of a certain Herr Bender in England. In due course the chairman was told:
1. That his partner in Hyde no longer attended the meetings of the Labour Front, neither did he provide transport for his key men for this purpose.
2. That he had joined Rotary, which was prohibited.
3. That he was making attempts to become a British subject, which, under the circumstances, had to be

p evented, and
4. That he was showing distinct British tendencies in walking about with a Union Jack in his breast-pocket (a red, white and blue handkerchief given to him by an employee during the coronation).

So the Foreign Office in Berlin knew it all. But Bender did not know the person who had spied on him. However, there was more to come when a newspaper cutting found its way to Berlin, relating, in detail, his public address — "How Hitler obtained power". Another cutting landed in Ronsdorf where the Gestapo summoned his poor sister, Lydia, to headquarters and informed her that her brother was causing considerable political bother in England and that the family would learn much more unpleasantness about him.

Now, Bender knew exactly where he stood, being aware that behind every German abroad was someone to do the official spying. Obviously, a return to Germany while the Nazis were in command, was now impossible.

In the meantime, he had heard from London that his first application for naturalization could not be entertained and that he should try again in twelve months' time. It is not easy to become a British subject and, when discussing it with a friend in the know, he was told that it was easier to go to Heaven than to become British. In spite of this Bender persevered, sending another application in October 1938.

The international barometer now pointed towards war when, in the same year, Hitler annexed Austria, soon afterwards incorporating Sudetenland. Everything mounted towards a crisis when Prime Minister Neville Chamberlain met Hitler, during the famous gathering of statesmen at Munich, in a last effort to secure peace. What a relief when the Prime Minister returned, waving his piece of paper ' Peace in our Time '.

This political tension had not helped Bender in his application for naturalization, and he was told to try yet again in twelve months' time.

Hitler was not to be trusted. The little note which Neville Chamberlain brought home meant nothing, as the Nazis carried on just as they pleased. They were out for nothing less than world domination.

Bender's job was still flourishing and a few of his German key men were still with him. Some had married English girls and, in spite of all the political turmoil, they were quite at home in England. If there was to be a war most of them would stay and put their full trust in the justice of British democracy.

By 1939, the German war machine had rolled on into Czechoslovakia and, with the attack on Poland, the world became engulfed in another bloody war.

During the last days of August, London Road Station in Manchester was packed with Germans making their exit. Bender and his wife accompanied some of their acquaintances to say good-bye. The very last train was full, the people standing crammed together. When the Station-master's flag went up, everyone shouted at the two lone figures on the platform, "Come in, or you'll miss the train." And with that, the carriages rolled out of the station. Herr and Frau Bender waved, until it was out of sight. Their last connection with Germany had gone.

Only a few days of peace were left. On Sunday, the 3rd September, the Benders sat listening, with tears in their eyes, to the morning broadcast: "We are at war with Germany!"

## THE WAR TO END ALL WARS

The time ahead was one of expectation. At the outbreak of war there were many enemy aliens left in England. Most of them were German and Austrian Jewish refugees. The rest were Aryans who, on account of their opposition to the Nazis, had no alternative but to stay in England. Others, although tainted with the colours of the German Labour Front, took their chance and hoped for the best, only to find themselves behind barbed wire as soon as the war started.

In their own community, well known to everyone, the Benders continued to live their lives just as if nothing had happened. The English showed no animosity towards the few enemy aliens in their midst. The German branch of the textile firm carried on as usual and when standing amongst his English employees, Bender often wondered whether such a thing would have been possible, at that juncture, inside Germany.

In spite of the war, the social season was still in full swing. Quite unperturbed, the Benders continued to attend the official functions and dances, feeling that they were accepted along with the rest of the community.

After a hard day's work, Bender would take Bruce, his dog, for his evening walk. The black-out was in force and, with a candle-lit jam jar carried on a string, he would enjoy the quaintness around Gee Cross, his walk culminating with a nightcap at the *Grapes*.

This went on with nothing to break the daily routine, until

9th October, when the few Germans remaining in the area were called to appear before a tribunal in Chester. Without the slightest foreboding, Bender and his family went along. By the evening he was home again, his passport stamped with the words: 'Exempt from internment until further notice '

For a short while life continued peacefully until, on 14th October, the first friction occurred. It happened one evening when Theo and Frank, a neighbour of his, were out walking. The two men had been good friends for some time. Frank was a stockily-built fellow, short and weighty with a reddish, healthy-looking square face, the complete opposite of Theo, who was tall and lean, his face more oval. Both were in high spirits, ready for a joke. Anyone seeing the two would have judged Frank to have been the German and Theo the Englishman; and so it was when they made their way to the *Grapes* for the usual.

They were sitting in a corner, enjoying their glasses of ale, when hectic arguments filled the room. That day, H.M.S. *Royal Oak* had been sunk by a German submarine. The people at the bar were swearing about the ——— Germans, glancing over their shoulders in the direction of Frank and Theo. Frank took up the challenge and admonished them, only making matters worse. The whole abuse was directed towards Frank, and it nearly came to blows. It seemed strange that not a word was cast in Bender's direction, who stood quietly by amongst the furious crowd. To avoid further discomfort the two made for home. His face still pale, Frank could not understand why they had all turned on him. The answer was obvious, with his square head, Frank had given them the impression that he was a German living in the district.

From then on Bender avoided pubs, keeping amongst people he knew. If only he could obtain British nationality, matters would be much easier for him. Seeing his solicitor, he lodged his third application in February 1940.

In the meantime, the phoney war carried on. As yet, not much had happened in the west. In the east, in a short space of time, Hitler had tramped through Poland. Things began to hot-up when, to everyone's surprise, in April 1940 German troops occupied Denmark without a fight, followed by the landing of troops along the Norwegian coast as far north as Narvik. In spite of Allied counter measures, Hitler, assisted by Norwegian Quislings, had a relatively easy task in occupying the whole of the country.

If dangerous Quislings were able to assist the enemy in Norway, the same could apply in England. And so the round-up of every German and Austrian started, bringing them before another tribunal.

Bender's turn was not far off. With a clear conscience, on the 27th April, he appeared at Manchester. Again, he was certain that English justice would prevail. Never previously having been before a court, he wondered what a cross-examination would be like. While waiting for his call, he saw one German after the other being marched off to an internment camp. Finally, the door opened for him. In he went and sat down facing a row of distinguished ladies and gentlemen behind a long table, the principal judge sat in the centre.

After confirming all personal data, the cross-examination started in a fashion Bender had not expected.

Judge: You have a daughter?
Bender: Yes, sir!
Judge: How old is your daughter?
Bender: Nine years, sir!
Judge: Your daughter is fond of kite-flying, isn't she?
Bender: Yes sir, and so am I!
Judge: What kind of kites did you fly?
Bender: They were made of sticks and paper!
Judge: How large were they?
Bender: Any size, sir!
Judge: How high could they fly?
Bender: It depends on the length of the string, sir! (By that time Bender was agitated and the judge apparently irritated).
Judge: Can you fasten a lamp to the kite?
Bender: Yes, sir!
Judge: Did you fasten a lamp to the kite?
Bender: Yes sir, in order to amuse the youngsters!
Judge: A lamp could be seen far away in the dark?
Bender: Yes, sir!

| | |
|---|---|
| Judge: | You have been flying these kites in wartime? |
| Bender: | No, I would not dare to, sir! |
| Judge: | We have it from authority that you have. |
| Bender: | No, sir. Only in peacetime for the benefit of the other children and my daughter! |
| Judge: | The police confiscated two road maps at your house! |
| Bender: | No, I gave them voluntarily to the officers, sir! |
| Judge: | On the road maps there is a line drawn in ink stretching from Cheshire to the English Channel, continuing on the Continent from the Channel to the Siegfried Line. Your intentions are quite clear; you were flying kites in the dark, near your home and, with a lamp attached, you made signals to the enemy planes. |
| Bender: | (At this stage Bender became really agitated. Here he stood, in the eyes of the judge, a German spy). In a trembling voice he replied: No sir, I have an explanation for this! |
| Judge: | There are crosses inserted in ink in various places along the line exactly where our aerodromes are. |
| Bender: | I agree there are crosses, but they have nothing to do with aerodromes, sir. These maps were supplied to me a long time ago by the R.A.C. when it was my intention to motor to the Continent. The R.A.C. marked the route on the map, the crosses coinciding with the itinerary showing places of interest such as castles and cathedrals. |
| Judge: | Are you a member of the German Labour Front? |
| Bender: | *No,* sir! |
| Judge: | Have you ever been a member? |
| Bender: | Yes, sir. I was forced to join but resigned a long time ago. |

And so on and on it went. The factory was mentioned and Bender's position in the concern. Finally, his English friends were brought into the court room to give their testimonials in his favour. When all the evidence had been heard, Bender expected this to be the end of the case.

"We are prepared to give you a fair trial," the judge said. And with that, the hammer came down — "Case adjourned!"

Bender went home, to be recalled for a second grilling on the 2nd May. This time the procedure was short. The door to the free world closed when two police officers led him out of the building to his car.

Both officers knew the prisoner well, he had enjoyed many an outing with some of the force. With one of the members he was in closer friendship, at one time enjoying a joint continental holiday trip. Socially, these two had much in common, and their young daughters both attended the same school. Clifford, a sturdy six-footer, with huge muscles and strong wrists, was a typical policeman, and could hold any offender at bay.

Accompanied by two policemen, Bender was permitted to drive himself and his wife home. As he drove through the City he was in a complete daze, knowing that the outcome of all this would be a prison cell. Thoughts of suicide flashed through his mind, making him feel like driving the car, policemen, his wife, the lot, straight into the next lamp standard.

Slowly, however, common sense prevailed. Looking at the facts squarely, he came to the conclusion that there was a war on, and many people would have to suffer — what did it matter if he was one of them!

## THE INTERNEE

The car drew up outside the police station, and in the four went. It all looked so harmless. There were no handcuffs shackling Bender to a policeman.

Edgar, one of his key men, was already inside. A young German, he was going to join Bender on his way to internment. The two other fellows from the factory, married to British wives, had not yet been interned, but no doubt, their turn would come later.

And so these two endeavoured to make themselves comfortable in one of the large police offices. They could not concentrate enough to pass the time by reading, and so they wandered about investigating. Their bedroom for the night was situated behind thick iron bars. And what a bed it was. A gently sloping wooden platform without any sort of covering. Apart from this, the room was empty, a hole in the wall covered with bars representing a window. What a humiliation! That he, who had been liked and respected in the community, had brought employment to a hundred people for the last seven years and worked amicably with British labour without friction, should be brought to this.

The thought of his arrest filled him with revulsion. He saw no reason why he should be expected to sleep on wooden planks, and so he complained. The friendly officers understood, and Frau Bender was sent home forthwith, to return later with sheets, pillows and blankets.

During the afternoon the internment news had spread

through the district, bringing a number of people to the police station to bid farewell to the two unfortunate men. More and more came, one policeman remarking that the station had never received so many visitors at once. In the evening the room was practically full, one woman shouting about ——— British democracy and justice. This brought the proceedings to an end, and the room was cleared, leaving Theo and Edgar alone once more.

To Bender's surprise, he was granted one more privilege. With two officers sitting in the back seat of his car, he was allowed to drive home and pack what he needed for his long journey. Needless to say, he was very grateful for this gesture.

The evening was long and weary, with policemen coming and going. The air in the room was blue. Never had Bender smoked so much in one day. When it was time to settle down for the night, Marianne and Luise left for home. The two prisoners walked through the iron gate into their cell and, with a clang, it swung to behind them, the key rasping in the lock.

Wild animals in the zoo have a habit of walking to and fro behind the iron bars — probably a sign of restlessness at being shut in. Bender did not differ much from them during the evening. He walked and walked up and down the cell, occasionally sitting down at the small table near the gate. Here he sat and brooded until he was shaken out of his reverie by the rattling of keys. It was the superintendent with one of Bender's business friends who wished to pay a farewell visit.

The officer apologized about the predicament. "It's war," he said. "We don't like having to do this, but it's our duty. Try to get some sleep and forget about everything."

He meant well, but Bender knew he could not sleep after all the excitement of the day. If only he could obtain a few bottles of beer to drown his sorrows and help him to sleep. With this thought in mind, he bluntly asked the superintendent for a favour. "All right," came the reply. "I'll see you later." the *au revoir* party was over.

By now it was really late and the police-guard on duty had changed. A young policeman was now watching the cells. Seeing Bender sitting at the small table with his head in his hands, the guard ordered him to go to bed.

"I am not going to bed," was the retort. "I'm waiting for some bottles of beer!"

With a laugh, the policeman replied: "That *would* be the limit. It would be the first time in this establishment that a prisoner has been served with beer." This remark annoyed Bender intensely.

"I am not a prisoner," he shouted.

Soon the keys rattled again. It was the superintendent with two bottles of heavy stout. This made the internee feel better. Thank God there were still some kind-hearted people in the world.

The young policeman watched as Bender emptied the bottles. It was the best beer he had tasted for a long time. Getting up from the stool, he smiled through the grille at the young policeman, as though to say, "I told you so," and got into his sloping bed.

The next morning brought Bender face to face with a new life. Before he and Edgar were taken to the waiting ambulance, (the Black Maria would have been the last straw) Bender was paid a visit by the company's solicitor and accountant, and the last technical details about the firm's future prospects were discussed. The meeting was cold, and impersonal — typically English — making the internee feel like a corpse in a coffin who, still conscious, was listening to his funeral oration.

The deliberations over, two soldiers with rifles took charge of the men. There was quite a crowd outside, and, after a last farewell from his wife and child, office girls and friends, the ambulance, occupied by some more policemen set off for Manchester Exchange Station. From here on Bender and Edgar became unknown persons, marked with a number allotted to them from the War Office. Guards and internees disappeared into the station and Bender, forgetting for the moment that he was now a prisoner, made for the nearest newspaper stall. He was immediately brought back to reality by a shout from the corporal, "Come here you ———!" On the platform, a third internee, by the name of Otto joined them.

In the train the three had much to talk about. Bender had known Edgar Mann for many years. A young, sturdy, healthy-looking fellow, he would have made a fine middleweight boxer or a smart soldier for Hitler's army. Otto Trusberg, the new arrival, was a strongly-built quiet kind of chap, and it took some time to draw him into conversation. He was worried about his English wife and the child he had left behind in Manchester. He was unable to write in English, and as his wife could not read a word of German, he did not know how on earth he was going to communicate with her. However, Bender put his mind somewhat at rest by promising to help him when the time came.

The train pulled into York where a jeep with army officers was waiting for them. They all made for the internment camp, situated on the race course. As he walked in, Bender could see in the distance, the Rowntree factory where, only a short time ago, he had called for an order for chocolate ribbons. How times had changed since then.

Intelligence soon took charge of the three, Otto being the first to face a line of high-ranking officers, whilst Edgar and Bender sat at the far end of the room. The interrogation was short, after which Otto had to listen to the chairman's final remark, "When you enter this camp, I would like to advise you to lift your right arm and shout loudly 'Heil Hitler'."

Bender thought this was the limit and stood up to lodge a complaint to the officers. He was soon calmed in true military fashion, making him realize that, in some way, he was in a kind of army. When his turn came, he knew exactly what to say. In his case, the procedure was the same, with the final remark to shout "Heil Hitler".

The following question and answer game took place,

Bender: I'm not going to do this, sir. I have never done it before and shall not attempt it here.
Officer: You have to do it!
Bender: I shall not, and would like to know what kind of Germans are in this camp.
Officer: About seven hundred enemy aliens, merchant seamen picked up from German ships.
Bender: They are seamen. We are civilians. Only yesterday, we held prominent positions in British industry. They are Nazis. We are not. You cannot mix the two categories, sir!

Officer: You have been sent to us by the War Office, and we have no other alternative.

Bender: If we enter that camp without lifting our arms and shouting "Heil Hitler", there will be trouble for you and us. *You* may have bloodshed on your hands. If, on the other hand, we do what you tell us and mix with the inmates, the War Office will soon stamp us as Nazis, and this we do not want.

There followed a short conversation amongst the officers who, realizing their predicament, brought a German from the camp to talk with Bender.

The two met and, introducing himself, the man bowed and clicked his heels, saying: "Friedrich!" He then went on to explain, in Northern German, that he was a ship's captain. Bender, having learnt the English method of introduction, replied, "Bender!"

Friedrich continued: "I can understand your feelings Herr Bender. You have been living in England for some time and have not yet been touched by the spirit of the German Third Reich. When you come into our midst, we will all of us make you welcome."

Bender, looking at the mediator with contempt, answered loud and clear, "No, I am sorry. It will not work!"

The conversation ended, and the officers held a further consultation. Somewhere, they had to find alternative accommodation for the three men. Realizing their difficulty, they decided to house them for the first night in their small hospital, containing only a few Germans. Bender, Edgar and Otto knew that they had no choice but to comply and, in due course, a private took them to their new quarters. On the way, Bender was thinking, 'Did the officers really expect Nazi seamen to be in harmony with three English-inclined civilians?' If they did they were mistaken!

In lounge suits and homburg hats, their leather cases in their hands, the civilians walked in to where eight sturdy North German sailors, in rough seamen's jerseys, stared at them in amazement.

In camp, it was a great event when newcomers arrived, and conversation started immediately. Looking the well-dressed men up and down, the sailors walked all around them.

"Where do you come from?" came the first question, from the chief spokesman.

"Near Manchester," was the reply. The three arrivals behaved very casually, surveying their new surroundings and looking for their beds, the inquisitive questioning continued.

"From Manchester? What were you doing in Manchester at this time?" the sailor countered. "There's a war on. You must be German spies. Hard luck you were caught."

"Look here," Bender replied. "We are not spies. We *worked* in England."

"You worked in England?" came the incredulous reply. "For the British, in wartime? That's treason!" Then, heatedly, "Wait until you get back to Germany, they'll hang you for that." (One fellow muttered the word "schweinhunde.")

"For a long time, now, we have been living in England with our wives and families," Bender went on. "I had just had a new house built, and could not leave friends and property behind."

"You wait and see." Then, airily, "In any case the war will be over by September; we've just had news from Hamburg to that effect. The British are down and out. They've no food and are starving. Our submarines will see to it that ships will no longer get to British ports. They are lost!"

"The English starving? You're not in the picture. Only two days ago we walked through local shopping centres, and the shops are full of goods — meat, butter, bread, tomatoes, oranges, lemons, bananas, and the rest. I can tell you, the war will not be over by September. It will last another three, four or even five years!"

The sailors did not like these outspoken remarks. They were not prepared to stay in an internment camp for that length of time. In his enthusiasm, Bender kept on talking, which angered the sailors even more. Some grew aggressive, shaking their fists at the three civilians, and the atmosphere became electric.

At the first signs of a fight, Bender hurried outside and intercepted the guard on duty. "Look here," he said to the private. "There's going to be a fight inside any minute. Get me an officer as quickly as possible." When the Commanding

Officer arrived, Bender related the political tension inside the hospital. "Please do something about it, or there'll be bloodshed." Telling the internee to keep calm in the meantime, the Commanding Officer promised to see the Commandant.

Making his way back into the hospital, Bender decided it was wiser to keep his mouth shut. The three outcasts began to make up their beds in the far corner of the huge room, leaving a large empty space between them and the sailors.

It was quiet now, and Bender did not say any more to the sailors. Everyone was on the verge of dropping off to sleep when, unexpectedly, the guard came in calling Bender outside, where he met the Camp Commandant, a high ranking British officer.

"Look, Herr Bender," he began, "I have good news for you. I wired the War Office about the three of you and have just received a reply. You have to be ready by 8 a.m. tomorrow, your luggage packed. You will then be transferred to a new destination."

Deeply grateful, Bender said, "Thank you, sir!"

That night, the three musketeers slept well and next morning, promptly at 8 a.m., they left the building, the German sailors staring after the departing figures.

They made for the square in the compound where an officer handed them over to two immaculately dressed Tommies in khaki, with rifles. A jeep transported them to York Station, where they had not long to wait for the train to the south.

The carriages rolled in, the five watching until a train window with the blinds pulled down and a 'Reserved' label attached, hove into view. Reaching the compartment, they made themselves comfortable, the three internees on one side and the two soldiers on the other. Throwing their rifles underneath the seat, the soldiers pulled the blinds up. Here they sat, like five ordinary passengers.

When the train set off, Bender handed around cigarettes, and conversation started. "Now then," said one of the Tommies, "we are taking you to London. Our Commandant picked us specially and told us that you fellows are all right, and that we are to treat you like gentlemen."

The journey was most pleasant. They smoked, read papers,

played cards and talked about the fake war. Soon the waiter arrived announcing first lunch.

"Here," said Bender, "come along with us, and I'll stand you your lunch." And so, the two soldiers and the three internees made themselves inconspicuously comfortable in the dining-car, the two rifles still resting under the seat in the compartment. The journey turned into an unusual incident, not only to the three civilians but also to the two soldiers.

King's Cross was the end of the journey. A short ride took them through the City and through the gate of the Oratory Central School, S.W.3.

The soldiers handed over their human consignment to the officer in charge. There were no farewell handshakes, which would have looked too familiar, but Bender and his mates still waved when their excellent companions departed.

What kind of a place had the three entered now? After short preliminaries with the Commanding Officer, they mixed with the crowd inside the establishment. There were folk milling around everywhere, speaking in all the dialects of the German tongue. Many were agitated, probably fresh internees, who complained bitterly about the injustice of being locked up.

The three made their way to the bedroom, which had rather a low ceiling. The place was crammed full with treble bunks, leaving just enough space for the top man to creep into bed. He could not lift his head without hitting the concrete above. How long would they have to stay here? It could not be for long, as they had learnt that this was only a transit camp.

They were right. Next morning the journey continued, and they were driven further south to an unknown destination. When the trip came to an end they found themselves on another race course, this time at Lingfield in Surrey. This camp made a most pleasant impression. Surrounded by wonderful country, it was a place at which they hoped to stay, provided, of course, that the German inmates were all right. By now, Bender was travel-weary. For five successive nights he had slept in different beds in various places. It was time to settle down and write to his wife and child.

The first few days were full of newness and excitement. It was a glorious May and, even under these adverse circumstances, one could accept this camp as a kind of health resort; better here than in the stuffy atmosphere of smoke-laden Cheshire. Soon Bender and the other two settled down to a new routine of camp life.

The composition of the Lingfield camp, as far as the inmates were concerned, differed from the set up at York. Lingfield showed more variety in the form of three main groups of people, each one biased by their own political opinion, according to their upbringing. The first and smallest group represented the Jews (some of whom had already been behind wire in Germany because of their denomination). The second, larger group, consisted of merchant sailors, the third and largest one of all being the civilians. What a cosmopolitan mixture these people were. On the one hand, there were the Jews, who would always keep together, more particularly so during these days of war when the very existence of their whole race was being threatened by the marching masses of their adversaries, the Nazis. On the other, were the merchant sailors who, filled with Nazi propaganda, and believing in it, hated the Jews as their Minister of Propaganda, Goebbels, had taught them to do. It was difficult to understand why these two extremes had to live under the same roof.

The third class, the civilians, were an agitated and frustrated set. Most of them talked in the same strain to the effect that they had never had anything to do with National Socialism; they had done a lot towards British industry and the country; they had been obedient to the British Crown and therefore, it was an injustice to be put behind wire. Pleading letters were despatched to the Home Office, the Custodian of Enemy Property and to Members of Parliament, stating all the above facts. Only a few isolated cases were lucky enough to be sent home as being valuable to British industry, the majority receiving the brief reply: 'Interned for the duration of the war.' Such an answer had a most demoralizing effect (probably desired) on those concerned, and was a good way of testing their political stability. Soon, the wheat and the tares began to sort themselves out, many of these staunch businessmen falling by the roadside. Hurt by the injustice meted out to them they swung to the extreme, preferring to become red-hot Nazis, than to wait for British justice. Others steered the middle course. On hearing of the great successes of Hitler's army, they supported the Nazis. The next day they became anti-Nazi, especially in the latter days of the war when the going was not so good.

Only the more steadfast amongst them kept to their convictions. Bender was one of them, Otto was another, but Edgar was nearer the middle course. The best attitude to adopt in a camp of such nature was to leave politics alone, which did not hinder Bender from mixing freely with the more decent men in the camp.

During this period he came across some very interesting types. According to their passports, they were all Germans. Nevertheless, their outlook on life, political and social opinions, were so vastly different that they could well have come from different nations. From a national point of view, one section was in favour of Germany winning the war, while the other wished them to lose it, and the sooner the better.

There were many good brains amongst the Jews and in the civilian section, there were several people from the upper structure of industrial life. One who impressed Bender most was a tall, elderly gentleman, with broad shoulders and a large intelligent-looking head. During the summer evenings he would play the old piano under the grandstand, just below the spot where kings and queens had stood on many occasions in the past. Putzi was often taken out of the camp by British Intelligence for interrogation in London. He was something of a genius and had an amazingly extensive general knowledge. From the very beginning he had worked in close association with Adolf Hitler, becoming the Foreign Press Chief of the Nazi party when the Third Reich started. But he escaped from Germany in 1937.

Often to be seen in Putzi's company, was another elderly gentleman, rather short and broad, with a wise-looking face. His pure white hair was always immaculately dressed. On most occasions he wore his commodore's uniform and peaked cap, some of the few souvenirs he had salvaged from his sinking ship. At one time he had been a man of some importance plying the large liner *Europa* from Hamburg to New York. When war broke out he was living in retirement, but still Hitler put him in command of a little tramp ship, with dockers and navvies as his crew, to help in the invasion of Norway. The English sank his ship and captured the captain. Even old men had to follow the Nazi discipline.

Bender sometimes joined the two in conversation, thereby learning more about Putzi. A well-seasoned traveller, his mother was American and he had lived in the U.S.A., even during the First World War. Educated at Harvard College, which he joined in 1905, he counted Theodore Roosevelt as one of his acquaintances. As a Hitler strongman he had met many world-famous people. He liked to talk about his meeting in a Munich hotel with Winston Churchill and his family in the company of Lord Camrose, Professor Lindemann and Randolph Churchill. Having worked as Hitler's right-hand man, he knew the whole of the Nazi hierarchy from Hitler, Goering, and Goebbels, down to the lesser known ones.

Our three internees had now been living in the camp for some three weeks. They were pleased with their camp-beds on the glass-covered terrace which overlooked the whole race course. And so the routine life rolled on, the letters from home being the only break from monotony. Only poor Otto had received no news from his wife. Unable to write to her himself, looking very miserable, he approached Bender, asking him to write a letter for him. On a piece of censored notepaper Bender translated into English the words dictated to him in German. When it was finished, Otto signed his name at the bottom of the page. The first letter was intercepted by an intelligence officer, who cross-examined Otto on the spot. The poor fellow had to explain and Bender was called in. The whole matter looked innocent enough, but was against the rules. Devising a new method, Bender re-wrote the letter, this time in bold English capital letters. All Otto had to do was to copy it.

On the grandstand there were many interesting people, most of whom were quibbling about their internment. Referring back to their tribunals, they wondered how the C.I.D. were so well-informed. Many had said "No" when asked about their membership of the German Labour Front. However, the judge had known better. One fellow was told that he had belonged to this organization while working in Holland, and that when he moved to England, he had paid his subscription up to the last day of peace.

Under the circumstances, Bender felt reasonably happy. At home, his wife had set the wheels in motion to secure his release. Fresh testimonials by the dozen had come in from English friends, backing up her application. So far, however, nothing had matured, for at the end of May, a police officer had called at Mrs Bender's home, and the following short conversation ensued:

Police Officer: Good morning, madam. I trust you know what I've come for?
Mrs Bender: Do you need the keys to the office?
Police Officer: No. I'm afraid not.
Mrs Bender: You haven't come to fetch me?

That was just what he had come for, and Mrs Bender was taken away forthwith. Luise, then only ten, had the option of staying with friends, but she preferred to be with her mother. The same evening found them in the most deplorable quarters at a seaman's home in Liverpool. A few days later they were transferred, along with masses of other German women, to an internment camp at Port Erin. The Benders' home was then locked up.

By this time, practically every German and Austrian was behind bars, the last two key men from the factory amongst them. The British method was a good one. They had learnt from the Quisling disaster in Norway that it was far better to lock up the lot and sort it out later.

Bender had resigned himself to his fate when, on 28th of May, the War Office informed him: 'Not sufficient grounds for ordering your release.' This was better worded than most of the replies. 'For the duration of the war' was not mentioned, so there remained a very faint hope.

The camp provided plenty of recreation. Organized walks in the surrounding country were arranged. Tough football matches took place outside and, at the age of forty-three, Bender tried his hand at goal-keeper again. The German spectators came out of the camp by the score to support their teams. Inside was a good canteen and as long as there was money to spend, one could buy almost anything, as rationing had not yet come into force. The food from the kitchen was relatively good, though margarine replaced the butter.

Concert parties flourished, at which Bender was often to be found on the stage, soon becoming well known as a comedian.

And so it went on, but only for a short while. The battle in France was in full swing, the phoney war was over, and the guns from across the English Channel could be heard as far afield as Lingfield. Restrictions in the camp became more severe, and newspapers were stopped. Every night, orderlies would arrive with large empty sacks and collect all the shoes from the internees. Most likely the British administrators expected German parachutists to drop near the camp in force, with a supply of arms, pistols and ammunition for the internees, as had happened in Norway. An army without shoes in such a situation would have been no good at all.

After this, life in the camp became very dreary as, with the exception of letters, they were completely cut off from the outside world. Italy's declaration of war on 10th of June brought a change in the monotony and on the 11th and 12th, a large number of Italian internees arrived. Rumour had it that there was something in the air — but what? On the 19th everyone was ordered to pack. The inmates of Lingfield camp were leaving — destination unknown.

On the morning of the 20th, headed by the sailors, the large column set in motion towards the railway station in a sort of military formation. Feeling a sense of freedom out in the open, at the tops of their voices, the sailors sang in Nazi fashion, *"Denn Wir Fahren Gegen England."* Even the cows in the fields turned their heads to see what all the noise was about.

The internees boarded a normal, extra long, passenger train, chalked all over with slogans and cartoons — ' Greetings from down under '; ' Down with Hitler — hang him ', and so forth. Obviously the train had just been used for transporting the Aussies from one place to another.

The train pulled out of the station in a northerly direction. They travelled through fine countryside to the Midlands. Wherever the train passed or stopped, farmers and town-dwellers would wave and cheer, mistaking them for the Aussies. This went on and on without suspicion until the train stopped dead on an open stretch in the heart of Liverpool. Again the English folk waved and cheered until someone realized that Australian soldiers do not dress in civilian clothes. The sailors were aggressively singing their Nazi songs, while others exchanged words with the public outside. Nasty remarks were passed, and then stones started flying through carriage windows. Everyone inside the train ducked, as they came in one side and out the other. Slowly the train moved off, out of the danger zone and once again, people waved as they passed until Liverpool Station was reached.

From now on it was a different picture. Tall men in khaki lined the platform, their rifles at the ready. The flood of internees left the train and lined up in rows of four. A military "Quick March!" thundered through the station, and the columns moved. Complacently at first, the sailors took the lead, but as the rhythm of their marching feet sounded, their song rang out abusively. *"Horst Wessel"* could be heard outside the station. The tall guards were on the alert, and rifle-butts were pushed here and there into the ribs of some of the more insolent fellows.

From one subway to another, the whole formation marched, everyone believing their destination to be the Isle of Man. Bender was at the back when, on turning another corner, he nearly passed out. There, clearly on a signpost, were the words, ' To Gladstone Docks '. "Good gracious me," he shouted. "D'you fellows know where we're going? It's not the Isle of Man — they're shipping us to Canada!" Some became annoyed when Bender said this, and raised their fists, threateningly.

"Shut up you ——— fool!" others retorted. "What do *you* know about Canada?"

The former company director knew full well. He had shipped far too many textile cases to Gladstone Docks, not to know their ultimate destination. The fellows around him had not long to wait for confirmation. Turning another corner, they were confronted by the large liner, *The Duchess of York.* Anchored not far away was the ill-fated *Arandora Star,* reserved for further internees to be shipped overseas.

## A FREE TRIP TO CANADA

Like cattle, the internees were herded up the narrow gang-plank. On board the ship, most of the passages were restricted, some with barbed wire. Bender and his group found themselves facing a large square surrounded by cabins, where, in spite of the menacing bayonets, Theo soon found berths for his crowd.

Everything was organized just as if they were wealthy people taking a holiday cruise. Even the pink berthing tickets were not forgotten. Bender carried his in his hand and knew its details by heart: 'Canadian Pacific Berthing Section A/1, Gents Berth No 717 — Passengers retain card to show at embarkation.'

Picking up their blankets, they settled down in the double bunks, the guard bolting the door behind them. They were obviously to be locked in until the ship had put to sea. The whole boarding manoeuvre did not take long, and soon the ship sailed away on its voyage to Canada.

Not much could be seen from inside the cabin, which had only one porthole. Everyone was hoping to catch a glimpse of something, and about a dozen heads strained to see through it at once. The *Duchess of York* sailed the high sea alone, with not a single warship for protection.

The *Arandora Star,* leaving unexpectedly a few days later, was doomed when a German Submarine Commander spotted her through his telescope. Down she went in a trice, leaving the survivors struggling in the rough sea. In all, there were

1,673 persons on board, of which 805 were drowned, mostly Germans and Italians. Unknowingly, some Nazi submarine hero had killed his own men.

After a while cabin doors were opened, and the prisoners in the *Duchess of York* were allowed to come out. They milled around in the small space, stretching their legs. As soon as Bender came out, he began to explore the layout of the ship. A rough type of soldier was in charge of them and, when Bender attempted to chat with him, he swore at him fiercely. Leading off from the small space in which they were standing, was a broad passage. Wondering where it led, Bender walked slowly in that direction. He was out of sight of the first guard, when another chased him back with pointed bayonet. Apart from meals which were taken under guard in a large hall it was obvious they were not to be allowed anywhere else on the ship. Bender kept on prodding the reluctant guard, whose dialect pointed towards Liverpool, and occasionally the two exchanged a few sentences, but that was all. Eventually they retired for the night.

The sea grew rough and most of the passengers, whether soldiers or civilians, had never been to sea before, the majority turning violently sick. In Bender's cabin, no one could sleep properly owing to the frequent rushes to the toilet, people were vomiting all over the place. At about 2 a.m. Bender paid a normal visit to the W.C. where he found the guard from Liverpool hopelessly bundled up on the floor in front of his cabin. The chap really was sick. Hoping that in adversity people will help one another, he made an effort to get the sick man to his feet. As he spoke to him, the other swore back. "This is no good," Bender said. "We're all human beings, I'm trying to help you. Look, go into the next toilet and put your finger down your throat and get rid of the stuff." Realizing that the internee was right, the guard allowed himself to be steered to the toilet, leaving his rifle against the cabin wall. What a situation Bender found himself in. Dressed in pyjamas, he took hold of the loaded rifle and positioned himself on guard over all the internees whilst the real guard sat behind the door of the W.C. If a British officer had arrived at that moment, it would have needed some hard explaining.

When morning came, the ship was still rolling. Getting

dressed, Bender decided he was going to explore. Walking up the passage, he was again challenged by the second guard. "Look here, young man," Bender said to the private. "I have to see a doctor. I'm sure there is one on board this ship." The guard, deciding the internee looked trustworthy enough, told him to go down the passage to the last door on the right. Bender walked a long way before he saw a queue of soldiers and sailors standing in front of the surgery door. Joining the end of it he awaited his turn.

When it was Bender's turn, he walked in to confront a most astonished looking doctor. "Where do you come from?" he asked.

"From my cabin," Bender replied.

"How did you get here?" was the next question.

"I walked down the passage," Bender said. "I'm not too well. I haven't been to the toilet for five days."

With a smile, the doctor turned to his assistant, saying, "Give him five pills — the strong ones. They'll cure him."

Holding the pills in his hand Bender said, "Thank you," and made for the door.

"Oh, no, not so fast," the doctor shouted after him. "You take those pills here, in my presence, otherwise they may not work." The internee opened his mouth and popped in the pills, much to the doctor's apparent satisfaction. Once out of sight up the corridor, however, Bender spat them out, putting them into an empty matchbox ready for another occasion. Although it had looked as if he had swallowed them, he had not done so at all.

He had no intention of going straight back to his cabin, but intended to explore further. Coming to a narrow ladder, leading to the lower deck, he quickly ran down it. At the bottom was a door which, on opening, led him into the back room of the kitchen. There he was confronted by another internee. It was Hans Gutwald, a German ace motor cyclist. Known from the Manx races, he, too, had been interned along with all the others. Hans already had a job on the ship, that of peeling spuds and cleaning vegetables for the kitchen. "Is there any good coffee here?" Bender asked.

"If you bring a large tin you can have some boiling water," Hans replied.

So Bender went back to his quarters, making for another cabin where the chaps from the Lingfield canteen lodged. Finding an old toffee tin, he made a handle for it out of a piece of wire and partly filling it with ground coffee, wended his way back to Hans. This time, no guard challenged him, for by now, he was well known. That day the internees enjoyed the best coffee they had had for some time.

The rest of the day passed uneventfully but during the evening, there was a surprise. For the first time, they were all herded out into a large opening at the stern of the ship, where everyone could enjoy the fresh air and the sea. What a mixture of people one could find here! Not only did they come from Lingfield, but many other camps as well. There were also chaps in Nazi uniforms, some wearing flying boots. They talked excitedly to the German sailors of their experiences in Holland and France. Apparently, some of them had been dropped by parachute during the invasion of Holland. Bender could hardly believe his eyes when he saw these fellows. Now, not only was he amongst internees but Prisoners of War as well, who were, seemingly, the cream of the German Army. One officer of a high rank, tried to impress upon the youngsters around him how far Germany had advanced on the battle-fields, *"Wir Schlagen Alles Kaputt!"* he said. (The Allies haven't got a chance).

How on earth did these chaps come to be on the ship? Bender made a mental note to avoid them like the plague. The interval of fresh air exercise soon came to an end when a British officer informed the assembly that it was time to return to their cabins. Reluctantly, they started to move, the more arrogant hot-heads looking challengingly at the officer. Consequently the Commanding Officer adopted sterner measures, ordering his soldiers to hustle the men through the steel exit. Still they did not move quickly enough, some Germans asking for trouble by employing delaying tactics. Bender had already disappeared from the deck when he heard shots ring out. The Commanding Officer, whose patience had snapped, had ordered his men to fire. The deck soon cleared, save for one dead German and several wounded. The wounded were taken to the ship's hospital, and the following day, the dead man was put on a slide and slithered over the ship's stern into the sea. It was the first funeral Bender had witnessed at sea.

This incident did not improve the relationship between the British and the prisoners. The atmosphere on board was aggressive and amongst the internees, every faculty of sea-faring man was represented. A well-planned mutiny could put them in command of the ship and sail her straight to Hamburg; in fact, some of the sailors even spoke in that strain. But the British knew what was in their minds and held the reins tightly, imposing severe restrictions on the internees.

The morning of the 24th June was clear, the ocean was calmer, but a fair swell remained. Seppl, the Bavarian in Bender's cabin, was the first one to peep through the porthole. Awakening the others, they all peered through the thick glass. Now, one could see the surface of the water, the ship following the curvature of the waves in a gentle up and down movement. Their cabin was not far above the water-line but, so long as the swell remained even, only occasionally did the water rise to the level of the porthole. It was stuffy inside the cabin and everyone longed for fresh air. Seppl, having been a donkey-man on German trawlers, knew something about ships and had an idea. Finding a large spanner, he tinkered around at the porthole for a few seconds and, the next thing anyone knew, it was open, admitting a rush of pure sea air. By lunch time the open porthole had been forgotten. Whilst the others were lying on their bunks, Seppl, his pipe in his mouth, stood enjoying a view of the vast ocean. The ship still rocked gently up and down, with the same rhythmic motion. Whether the wind had strengthened, or another liner some distance away had caused additional velocity, no one knew, but for some unknown reason, the *Duchess of York* suddenly sank into a deep trough, bringing the porthole well below the water-line. The ferocity of the sudden gush of sea water, knocked Seppl over like a matchstick, soaking all the others to the skin. In a second, the cabin was waist-deep in water. The ship lifted again and, for the moment, the danger was over. For some time, however, water seeped through the nicks in the door alarming the ship's personnel, who, with a stream of invective, locked the porthole and took the spanner away.

After three days of sailing, life on board became very

monotonous for the internees. There was nothing to do but talk, and always it was on the same topic. Their boredom was aggrevated by the shortage of cigarettes and tobacco. Although there was plenty of these commodities in the ship's canteen, it was only for British sailors and soldiers. None of the prisoners had anticipated as long a journey as this and consequently, had not stocked up with smokes. Even the few who had could not reach them, for their luggage was securely locked in the ship's hold. It is far easier to control a thousand contented men, than a mass of irritable, highly-strung nervous individuals, which, without their usual quota of cigarettes and tobacco, was what these men were becoming.

Nothing could be done in this respect, however, and Bender, himself an inveterate smoker, had not yet devised a means to overcome the dilemma. There was not a smoke to be had anywhere, and it would have been futile to approach a British soldier.

In this frame of mind, Bender strolled along the same corridor he had explored before but this time, branching off along another one he had not yet investigated. At the end of it, his way was barred by two Tommies. He made no move to approach them but stood some ten yards away, casually glancing through the porthole. Here, he was able to listen to their conversation, and understand every word. After a short while, he ascertained that the taller one of the two was speaking in a north Cheshire dialect. Trying his luck, Bender called over to him, "Dust cum from Hayde?" The response was immediate.

"What dust knaa aboot Hayde?"

Eager to talk, Bender quickly replied, "An awful lot. I can tell you about the whole layout of the town. Let us start at Broomstair bridge, walk up the slope behind Kingston Mills, then along the street towards Hyde Junction into Dukinfield. Or, go the other way, up Dowson Road, pass Gee Cross and climb up Werneth Low." A short silence followed his words.

"He knows the lot," the tall soldier said to his mate. Then, turning to Bender — "I cannot tell you where I come from but I'll give you a tip. My nephew played in the Hyde United team."

"As what?" Bender asked.

"Outside-right!" came the reply.

"That's Richards, and I can tell you more that will surprise you! If Richards is your nephew then Joan his sister, is your niece. She typed for me in my office for quite a long time."

"He's right, you know," the soldier remarked to his mate. "There's no doubt about that!"

Once the ice was broken, Bender became more talkative. "Look," he said, "can you get me some cigarettes?"

"Have you got any money?" came the reply. "If you have, stuff it behind the door where you're standing."

Bender was off like a shot. Officially, the internees were not permitted to have money with them but, if a pound note was to be found anywhere, it could only be on the side of the interned businessmen. The lack of smokes was a most tempting bait to extract money and Bender was sure that someone would have a few pound notes hidden away somewhere. A little later, with a twinkle in his eye, he came out of one of the cabins, with a pound note in his pocket. Reaching the appointed spot, he put the note, as instructed, behind the door.

Sure enough, when the time came, there was a large parcel of genuine Players behind that door. Hugging it close, he shouted his thanks to the soldiers, and made for his own cabin. Everyone's eyes stared unbelievingly, when they saw Bender counting out packet after packet of cigarettes. Owing to the fact that they were duty free, there were twice as many as could be purchased on the mainland for the same money. Dividing the cigarettes in half, he kept one portion for himself, and took the other to his financier.

Back in his cabin once more, he shared the Players amongst his fellows, and soon the cabin was blue with smoke. They now had sufficient to last them until they landed in Canada.

By the time they approached the western hemisphere, restrictions had been somewhat relaxed, and on 26th June, many internees were allowed out into the open air on a reserved part of the deck. It was a beautiful day and as far as the eye could see, there was nothing but the wide expanse of the North Atlantic, glistening in the sunshine. In the distance, could be seen tiny white specks, dotted around in the water.

As the ship furrowed through the waves, these specks grew

larger and larger until the liner was surrounded by a multitude of rugged and gigantic icebergs. It was an impressive sight to see the ice sparkling and glittering like diamonds. The men clung to the railing, absorbing the spectacle. More was to come when two huge whales swam into sight, keeping up with the speed of the ship. Up and down they went, spurting fountains of water into the air with every movement. Despite the fact that they were interned, to the passengers this was worth watching. The war momentarily forgotten, the clement weather, plus the breathtaking beauty of the scene, caused the trip to take on the aspect of a cruise. During these few hours of relative freedom, the internees had settled down considerably. Out came the accordions and guitars, the fresh sea breezes carrying the melodic sound of the German folk-songs to every corner of the ship.

The 28th June marked the end of the voyage. Passing Belle Isle along the rough coast of Labrador into the Gulf of St Lawrence, the majestic *Duchess of York* finally came to anchor at Quebec. How different was their arrival from pre-war days. There were no waving crowds, no relations or friends waiting to meet the passengers. Busy dockers rushed to and fro and there were Canadian soldiers standing by. Circling the liner were a number of police patrol boats, the sight of which drove any thought of slipping through a porthole from the minds of any would-be escaper.

By dawn on the 29th, the soldiers on board were already assembling the internees into groups near the exits. Bender, who was still in his cabin, was very worried as to how he could let his wife, in the Isle of Man, know of his whereabouts. Taking three of his business cards, on the back of each he wrote a different address of some of his friends in England. When the guards came to fetch him, he passed them to the men in the hope that the message would get through.

Now they were all up on the quay, surrounded by armed soldiers, who lined up to form a very narrow channel, not more than three yards wide. Facing inwards, their bayonets pointing towards the middle of the lane, their fingers on the live triggers, one behind the other the prisoners moved down the avenue of grim faces. These soldiers looked even tougher than the ones they had left behind, and would have shot anyone who did not behave. When Bender reached the end of the quay he noticed the internees' trunks and suitcases strewn all over the place. Peeping through the soldiers' legs he tried to catch sight of his own belongings, which contained a large bag of tobacco. The smokes he had acquired on the ship were exhausted. If only he could get hold of that bag of tobacco for the long journey that lay ahead. Whilst dawdling along he suddenly caught sight of his own suitcase, just behind the feet of a sturdy Canadian. On an impulse he shot between a pair of khaki-clad legs and flung himself upon his case. Several rifles were trained upon him but, thankfully, no shot was fired. The move was so quick that, by the time two soldiers grabbed him, the bag of tobacco was his; he had sufficient to last the rest of the journey.

At the end of the quay, a long train was waiting. Before boarding it, they each filed past a food depot, and received a large paper carrier-bag. Inside the train there was not the usual clamouring for seats, instead each man was told where to sit, and to remain there. During the whole journey, only one man was allowed out of his seat at a time.

As the train pulled away on the start of its journey, the occupants began examining the contents of their food bags. From the amount each contained, it looked as though the journey would last many days. Another interesting feature was the interior of the carriage. It was very old-fashioned, probably from the days when the first trains rolled west. The inside of the carriage had an open aspect, with an ancient coal burner standing at the far end, its flue-pipe leading through the roof. Four internees at a time sat in each cubicle with a type of pull-out contraption above them. A heave on the handle brought down a complete bed, hinged on one side and hanging on bicycle chains at the other. Everything was provided — two could sleep below and the other two above.

The train had gathered speed on its way towards Montreal. For a solid forty hours, it went on and on, passing through Ottawa, Mattava, Sudbury, Dalton, Nipigon, and arriving eventually at the tiniest of all places Red Rock, on the shore of Lake Superior. They passed through magnificent country. Bender had seen the Black Forest, the Alps, Norway and Scotland, but here, everything was rolled into one on a gigantic scale, distances without end. His face glued to the carriage window, he followed the kaleidoscope where lake followed lake, and pine trees, as straight as candles, grew in their millions. Here was the country Bender had read about in his boyhood. Red Indian stories, such as Winnetou or Old Waverley. Every moment he expected a Red Indian to pop up from somewhere.

During the long journey, the boys killed time playing cards, eating more than they could digest, or sleeping.

In Bender's party, an occasional whiff of smoke could be seen from the tobacco he had requisitioned at Quebec. Dog-ends were in great demand, and passed from man to man until the very last puff had been drawn.

At dawn on July 1st, the train slowed down, to stop finally in an open field. As it was only 4 a.m. the early morning mist had not yet lifted. Bender was one of the first to wake, due to the screeching of brakes and, wiping the moisture from the window, he peered out. He could see nothing but an expanse of country with a large misty lake in the far background. He expected to see a railway station, but there was nothing, neither in the way of a house, nor any other sign of life.

The guards took up their positions outside, and the internees were informed that they had reached their destination. One by one they left the train, forming accurate columns in the field. Handling more than one thousand enemy aliens in open country was no mean operation. The guards had to be firm, but many showed it more than was necessary. The Canadians were hard and their commands harsh. After all, were they not dealing with explosive material — 'German parachutists caught in Holland.' This seemed to be the general impression amongst the soldiers with whom Bender had managed to exchange a few words. He and his mates were aware that since landing in Canada, their status of internee had changed to that of Prisoner of War.

The masses of well-dressed civilians, flanked on either side by the khaki-clad guards, made a strange spectacle as the long line snaked from the empty train towards the far-away shore of the lake. In the early morning sun, which was now breaking through, the soldiers' bayonets sparkled and glittered.

On and on they walked until turning a corner, the column

came to the only road, from where the land sloped down to Lake Superior. What resembled a factory, surrounded by numerous wooden huts, appeared on the horizon. This was to be Bender's new address for the next twelve months — R. Camp, Red Rock, Ontario.

It is amazing how quickly large numbers of human beings can be organized. The factory, a wood-pulp mill, was empty, as were the huts. Apparently, the place had not been used for years. It also looked as if these internees had arrived far sooner than had been expected, as there was nothing in existence that one could call a camp. Granted, the empty wooden barracks were there, but the barbed wire fencing was only partly completed.

First of all, the internees had to be put under lock and key, and about sixty at a time were ushered into each hut, until the whole lot had disappeared. Whilst gangs of Canadians slung barbed wire from post to post, armed soldiers filled the gap until the job was completed. A risk of escape at that time was great, and the instructions came accordingly. Nobody was allowed even to show a head at a hut window. "Pop your heads out and we shoot!" was the order, in no uncertain terms. When some of the more hot-headed sailors ignored instructions and showed a head here and there, it was followed immediately by the crack of a rifle, and the splintering of wood as the bullet hit the hut near the window.

As the canteen was not yet ready, for the first day, the men still lived on the iron rations they had received at Quebec. It was an unpleasant situation to say the least. With sixty inmates in each of the relatively small huts, devoid of any furniture or beds, the men just walked about in circles, stood around in groups, or sat on the floor. When evening came, they bedded down on the wooden boards with no blankets for cover. On the floor they were cramped like sardines, and when one moved during the night, the rest had to follow suit.

By morning, men working overtime had completed miles of barbed wire fencing to make the camp secure. The doors of the huts were unlocked and for the first time, the prisoners were able to stretch their legs properly. Although there were none in the compound, there was a plentiful supply of Canadian guards outside.

Automatically, an exchange and barter trade commenced immediately. Although still suspicious about these paratroopers, the guards could not ignore the German wrist-watches, fountain pens and other valuables. On the other hand, all the internees were interested in was tobacco. Watch after watch whirled over the high barbed wire fence into the Canadian compound, whilst packets of tobacco flew in the opposite direction. Articles were sold dirt cheap. A watch costing £20 would be bartered for a few packets of tobacco.

The internees' luggage had not yet arrived inside the compound. Hundreds of valuable trunks and leather cases were piled up, as though ready for a bonfire, on open ground. Fortunately, the weather remained dry, as this cargo was left outside for some days.

During the very first days in camp, there was a shortage of everything. Meals were served in some of the larger huts and apart from tables and plates, no other implements were provided. The internees sat around the tables in the order in which they came in, there being no distinction between them. The food was handed out on large plates, one serving four men. In the absence of knives and forks, they all had to resort to using their fingers. However, it is amazing how soon one learns to adapt oneself to prevailing conditions.

There were, of course, those who complained bitterly. One in particular was a middle-aged German who challenged a Canadian about the appalling conditions. A heated argument ensued which resulted in the guard pointing his bayonet at the other fellow. This did not frighten the German sailor at all, however, and ripping open his jacket and shirt to reveal a broad, hairy chest, shouted — "Here! Just try and put that bayonet through my chest!" The men near by were worried that the worst would happen, but fortunately tempers abated.

On the third day, there was a marked change in the attitude of the Canadian guards towards their charges. Their aggressiveness had disappeared, and they became approachable, even mingling with the internees inside the compound. Whether orders to that effect had been received from headquarters, nobody knew, but it certainly appeared so.

Within a week or so the camp was properly established, the

large square then being surrounded by several layers of high barbed wire fences. Observation towers, each housing a machine gun manned by a guard, had been erected at the corners.

It was not long before the internees settled down in their surroundings. Every day new equipment arrived, so that in a short while, reasonable living quarters were provided. The arrival at such short notice, of masses of enemy aliens, must have caused the Canadian Government quite a headache at the time, and one can only admire the speedy organization which created a well-run Prisoner of War camp out of nothing in such a short time.

Conditions became more pleasant, and as soon as Bender had found his feet, he started to survey the business prospects. With Otto, his friend, he walked through the compound, but was finally convinced that no kind of profitable transactions could be organized from the material available. There was nothing but clay, grass, stones and the odd chipmunk showing its nose from underneath the huts.

No tools were available and when the luggage was distributed to the men, the tools were not allowed into their possession. From his experience in Lingfield, Bender knew that many a potential craftsman existed in the camp but without tools, they were useless. The first break came when a quantity of knives and forks arrived for the canteen, a third of which disappeared immediately into the pockets of the internees.

By this time, a few men had permits which enabled them to leave the camp during the day for odd jobs. Under cover, they brought in a long piece of iron rail which provided the material for the necessary anvil. Others sacrificed an old accordion, the bellows of which were used for a small smithy. When the iron works started production, the knives and forks from the canteen were turned into all kinds of tools. Then the men began making anything, and everything; replicas of the *Graf Spee,* destroyers, submarines and aeroplanes. With the arrival of string and bottles came ships in bottles, and belts were rolled off the assembly line.

As usual, Bender was wide awake directing trade into his own channel. His quarters were in the hut nearest to the main entrance, and owing to the various political opinions inside, it was called the 'rubber' hut. As an organizer, he became responsible for all the inmates, which brought him into contact with the administration outside. He would not allow any political trouble from the chaps with the Nazi outlook who were amongst them, and they had to keep their views to themselves. Until the termination of the war, all had to make up their minds to sink their own personal opinions and live together as amicably as possible.

Bender had not yet started up business on his own account. Being short of tobacco he had done a foolish thing by parting with his golden watch-chain for ten packets of tobacco. One of the German seamen working outside had purchased it, and it now dangled ostentatiously from his waistcoat.

One of the packets of tobacco bought Bender a hair-clipping machine and although he had never cut hair before, he soon learnt. However, the profit was small, only one cigarette for each hair-cut.

In Bender's hut were many interesting fellows, one of whom was a jolly fine chap who occupied a double bunk near by. He was a very talented fashion designer, and came from a good family, but had no idea how to make his craft pay in the camp. One day, Bender said to Joachim Von Quillberg — "Look here, you're a clever fellow. Can you paint anything in water-colours or oils, put something on paper? Try drawing a few cartoons — you know, near the border-line. The chaps outside will buy anything."

And so Joachim started his first collection of pictures. Bender had no doubt that they would be just the thing for the Canadian soldiers. He proved correct for immediately the soldiers saw them, they went like hot cakes, and were paid for with Canadian money, which was not allowed in the possession of the internees. Joachim produced more and more of the pictures until he was doing a flourishing trade.

Then came the requests for larger portraits to be copied to send to Canadian wives and sweethearts. Many an evening Bender entered the compound after a day's work with scores of soldiers' passes in his pockets. Joachim tried his skill at drawing enlarged pictures from the small military pass-photos with success. What an unusual occurrence for an internee to be in possession of Canadian money and military passes. Had he been able to procure a soldier's uniform, he could have walked out of the camp to the nearest railway station without being noticed. The portraits were now in great demand by officers as well as privates.

Business began to prosper without any liquid capital to start with. When the money arrived which internees had deposited in England, whilst at Lingfield, catalogues from a Canadian chain store were circulated, and everyone was allowed to buy through the camp's accountancy office.

All took advantage of this facility, being eager to purchase cigarettes, cigars or tobacco. Bender had too much of this stuff already, but had other ideas in mind when ordering pounds of window-putty, oil paints in various colours and cocktail-sticks. When Otto and Edgar saw Bender's order-sheet they thought him daft, but Bender just told them to wait and see . . . .

The goods soon arrived, and were loaded on to the table in each hut. Sorting out his own purchases, Bender busied himself rolling small lumps of putty into the size of golf balls and tinting them with various colours. He then stuck a notice on the window of the hut, 'Putty and paint for sale for those wishing to make ships in bottles. Apply within!' Every sailor was able to make a ship in a bottle, and every Canadian would buy one. Bender was well aware of this, and had not long to wait before a stream of customers began to arrive.

Business grew and, after a few weeks, Bender ran into the fellow to whom he had sold his gold watch-chain. In exchange for the hair-clippers, plus three packets of tobacco, he got it back — not a bad deal.

The number of little workshops began to multiply, and the quantity of fine merchandise grew. In the meantime, Bender had made a new acquaintance in the form of Sergeant Mac from Winnipeg, who was responsible for the organization of work-gangs amongst the internees. The two were on very good terms with one another. The sergeant was a jovial fellow, and liked his bottle of beer. This indulgence strained his pay-packet to the limit, and he could never last out to the next pay-day. Aware of this predicament, Bender was always willing to give financial support and ultimately became not only money lender to Sergeant Mac but to other Canadians as well. Bender was not the least concerned to whom he loaned his money, provided it was paid back, with interest.

Bender was really in the swim, and enjoying camp life. There was never a dull moment. Hardly a day passed without Sergeant Mac visiting the hut for a chat with Bender about trade in general and the potentials of working gangs for work outside. On such an occasion, Mac put forward a new proposal, demanding eight sturdy men, with Bender in charge, to cut firewood for the cook-sergeant in the Officers' Mess. This was the sort of job for which the boys had been waiting, and how they enjoyed it out in the fresh air near Lake Superior, the coastline of America visible across the lake. Although they received no wages, it was good healthy work, and the extra delicacies thrown in by the appreciative cook-sergeant made it worthwhile.

By now, business had become so plentiful, that Bender had to engage other people. His first shop was inside his hut where, with Edgar in charge, an array of articles was placed for immediate sale below the ceiling, on long boards. A second shop was set up outside the 'rubber' hut, in full view of the adjacent highway. Aeroplanes, ships, destroyers and cotton belts dangled in the wind, to be seen by any passing Canadian or American traveller. With a young internee in charge, this shop did well and made a good profit. Whenever a vehicle passed the camp, the tourists could not help stopping to question the guard on duty about the peculiar merchandise fluttering in the wind. Business procedure was always the same. Someone would call for Bender to come to the gate. Sergeant-Major Kimberley would then emerge with pencil and paper and supervise the sales, jotting down the amount of money which would be duly transferred, and credited, to Bender's account in the accountancy office. From an internee's point of view this kind of business was most stimulating, as many interesting people were met in this way.

During the wonderful summer of 1940, most internees had their hands full. There was no idleness or boredom. It was a healthy life, and the food was good. In fact, so plentiful was it, that a deputation was sent to the Canadian Commandant with the object of curtailing the food rations in the canteen.

Meanwhile, the job of cutting logs all day in the fresh air was one of the finest exercises, and kept the men in good trim. In between supervising the work, Bender was on the look-out for other business. After a while, he hit upon a further opportunity for the expansion of his trade. Near the Officers' Mess was the latrine. Here, he could set up a fine shop and serve a larger number of customers. On investigating the inside, it meant the closing down of four of the twelve lavatory lids, so establishing a platform on which goods could be displayed. The remaining seats, he thought, could still be used for the real purpose.

As usual, early next morning his gang left the camp, their lumber-jackets stuffed full with all kinds of saleable articles. Whilst the gang went to work, Bender tastefully displayed his goods at the far end of the lavatory.

He had not long to wait for his first customer, a sturdy Canadian, not yet fully awake. It was getting-up-time when more soldiers started the first short morning walk towards the latrine, wearing only vests and khaki trousers, their braces hanging down at the back. Normally the early hours were cold, and out of the waves of mist which rolled in from Lake Superior, the soldiers' silhouettes would emerge, to disappear inside the latrine.

On entering, the men's first reactions were of amazement at seeing the salesman in one corner attending to his handicraft shop. His wares could have competed with any establishment in a major city. What a strange sight it was to see eight hefty Canadians sitting on the bench while Bender, acting as salesman, offered his goods. As soon as these customers realized what kind of bargains they could buy, a brisk trade started. Soon news travelled on the 'grapevine' from hut to hut. Never before had the latrine received so many visitors in one day.

To Bender's satisfaction, by evening he had completely sold out. Dollars, nickels and dimes jingled in his pockets as he entered the camp, whilst on his back, he carried a sack full of tobacco. Day after day this performance was repeated. The craftsmen in the camp were now kept busy producing goods galore for Bender, the agent.

Camp life was now well-established. As in Lingfield, there

were the three main groups — sailors, civilian internees and the Jewish section. In all, more than a thousand men were housed in Red Rock. The paratroopers from the *Duchess of York* had apparently been shipped to another destination in Canada.

The sailors, who were in the majority, were confined to one part of the camp where they lived in adjacent huts. Near by, were the civilians, whilst the Jewish internees occupied the remaining barracks. Bender's was the only hut representing a mixture of all three. Sailors, civilians and Jews, they all liked one another and did not trouble their heads over politics.

Everybody was of the opinion, with the exception of the sailors, that the war would be a drawn-out affair and, to avoid growing stale, most of the men concentrated on some kind of work which made time pass fairly quickly and life as pleasant as possible. The camp, as a whole, was well organized, the Canadian authorities not neglecting to provide amenities for recreation.

The first effort was to convert a rough piece of ground outside into a football pitch, where weekly matches were played in open country amongst the rival groups of internees. It was always a big day when the teams, clad in their respective jerseys, were allowed out of the camp, flanked by dozens of bayonets. Then followed the crowd, even more heavily guarded. It was a strange, though exciting spectacle, to witness one of these football matches played on a soft and very bumpy ground, with the players often disappearing in clouds of dust. Honours were at stake, just as amongst the first division teams of the Football Association, and they went all out to win. The spectators shared their enthusiasm, whilst the Canadians were kept running to and fro with rifles and machine guns, watching all the time that nobody disappeared into the near-by jungle.

Second to football came swimming in Lake Superior — a treat to everyone during the sunny days of 1940. Again, the danger of escape put an unusual aspect on an otherwise hilarious and healthy exercise. A great circle of water had to be framed in by all kinds of obstacles, with boats and guns in the background. On land, several heavy machine guns covered the whole area, making the enterprise relatively secure. Everyone turned up to the swimming galas. In their hundreds they came running down the slope, plunging into the cool water in their birthday suits, oblivious of the rifles and machine guns around them.

A third recreation was walking in the country. These outings, however, proved a flop, as it became monotonous walking up and down the only lane in the district in tight groups. Here again, they were under rigid surveillance, although here, the risk of escape was negligible, as the surrounding country was so thickly wooded that no one would have dared to run far owing to the risk of starvation in the vastness of Canada's open spaces.

Facilities inside the camp were second to none. The canteen and food were excellent, and there was an abundance of washrooms and shower-baths, all kept impeccably clean. The hospital inside the compound was exceedingly well managed by German staff, with prominent Jewish doctors in charge.

It was mainly left to the sailors to run the sports section for the many juveniles amongst the internees, the outstanding feature being boxing. In a relatively short time, a team of pugilists was trained to such a high standard that it became a joy to go down to the small improvised stadium on a Saturday afternoon, and watch the bouts. In a specially provided boxing-ring one could see fights from the lightest to the heaviest weights. On such occasions, the ranks of spectators were filled to capacity, whilst on the other side of the fence, the Canadians watched from any kind of vantage point, including barrack roofs. The standard of fighting was high, but fierce with frequent knock outs. Everything was provided, right down to the boxers' outfits, which were kindly donated by the Red Cross.

Although the camp was officially administered by the Canadian authorities, within its perimeter, the Germans organized their own affairs. A leader, supported by a committee, represented a link between the War Office and the internee. Naturally, on account of the majority of Nazis inside the camp, the men chosen for this council, were ardent supporters of National Socialism, and were ignorant of the plight of Jews and those internees who, for many years, had lived and worked in England.

From the very beginning, Bender had made up his mind to return to England at the earliest opportunity. The problem was, how could he lodge an application of this nature and present it to the only official source inside the compound? It would never reach the British liaison officer outside the camp, as the Nazi link in the chain of communication would stop such an attempt forthwith. A German camp leader would not understand a request from a German to go back and work for the English in time of war. To a Nazi this was high treason, for which the applicant deserved a good hiding, and which could easily be meted out by a heavy-weight boxer in the shadows of night.

Bender had to devise his own method for forcing his way through to the British officer. Carefully he wrote two applications. The first was a harmless request to see the Commanding Officer with regard to his wife and child in the Isle of Man. This he posted to the Nazi camp leader. The second was entirely different, and read:

Sir,

Re: The separation of those supporting the Axis Powers, from those opposing the Dictators.

As it is my only desire, as expressed on several occasions, to be separated from the Nazi supporters, I kindly beg to ask you to grant me an interview with regard to the above.

Yours respectfully,

. . . . . .

This second application Bender kept in his pocket until the day came when a Canadian guard took him to the British liaison officer.

The Commanding Officer opened the conversation. "Please tell me, Mr Bender, what do you think I can do for your wife and child in the Isle of Man?"

"I suppose nothing, sir," Bender stammered in reply. "My sole reason for lodging this harmless application was to enable me to see you personally." By this time Bender had pulled the second application out of his pocket. Handing it over to the officer, he continued: "This, sir, is the application I want to present to you and when you read it, you will agree that it would never have passed the German camp leader, owing to its contents being anti-Nazi. My one desire is to get out of this camp, and go back to England." Bender had succeeded in by-passing the Nazi link and, knowing the Commanding Officer to be an understanding man, there was now hope of a return to England.

The remaining months of 1940 passed quickly. It seems rather surprising that internees could busy themselves behind wire, absorbed in social and other activities, forgetting altogether that there was a war on. Nothing much of great importance happened, but the incidents which did occur were magnified in the eyes of the internees, as life as a whole still had its limitations. The majority of people were content, but there were still a few who had set their hearts on liberty, regardless of the cost, and escape through the secure fences.

In the early morning of 30th July, the first man was away and, fortunately for him, the escape was not noticed until ten hours later, thereby affording him a good start. This getaway was simple enough. Joining a gang of internees in the charge of a soldier, who were going for their usual shower-bath at the far end inside the compound, his bathing-bag was packed full of food instead of clothing. Being the last man in the group, he was able to slip unnoticed into a narrow niche between two huts from where, shielded by high grass, he made his bid for freedom. Lucky enough to negotiate Lake Superior in a rowing boat, he turned up, a few days later, in America. In spite of the U.S.A.'s neutrality at the time, the fellow was soon caught as an unwanted visitor, and given the option to return to Germany. However, owing to his communistic activities in the Spanish war, he did not relish the idea of going back to a Nazi Germany and so, after a few months, he returned to his mates in the internment camp at Red Rock.

A second man escaped on 19th August, as a result of a pre-arranged break-out. Late in the evening, when the camp cinema was emptying, a lot of noise was made by those in the know, attracting the attention of the guard on the watchtower. The latter was more interested in the fracas made by the men to notice the escaper wriggling through the wire on his stomach. Nevertheless, he was apprehended after only a short spell of freedom.

Soon after this incident, a third internee, together with a

Part view of the wood-pulp factory, Lake Superior and the U.S.A. in background.

The 'rubber' hut 63A, first on left.

*Winter 1941, the cooks' quarters.*

*Canadian winter, part view of camp.*

*Part view of camp — ice-rink in background.*

*Part view of the camp.*

The work gang, showing latrine (Bender's shop) in the background.

*Some members of the work gang.*

Joachim's cartoon of morning roll-call.

Full view of R. Camp, Red Rock, Ontario.

very young seaman, ran away from a gang working outside. They both got lost in the thick undergrowth of the near-by bush. Such an incident was always an event for the prisoners as well as the Canadians. The latter were furious, as not only had they to do their daily routine duty but also spend hours tracing the escaped men in difficult country. Swearing amongst themselves the Canadians hacked away the undergrowth with their bayonets, whilst the rifles were at the ready. Smoke issuing from the chimney of an empty lumber hut finally gave away the men's hide-out, with the result that a few rifle shots were fired, one fatally wounding the older chap. Accompanied by the Canadians and the frightened young internee, a covered stretcher was brought back to the camp.

During the winter, the first tunnel had been completed and, instead of tunnelling away from the Canadian quarters, they drove the escape shaft straight amongst the Canadian huts occupied by many soldiers. The bluff paid off and, in the middle of the night, two men broke surface to escape over the ice of Lake Superior, making for the near-by towns of Port Arthur and Fort William. Again this escapade came quickly to an end. In a couple of days the two fellows were back, having been caught by the Canadian Mounted Police.

It was quite obvious that the Canadians did not like these break-outs. They were well-planned, with plenty of food supplies but, most of all, it was the ample supply of money that puzzled the Canadians. How this money got into the camp was the main question.

At this period all internees were still wearing their own civilian clothes, making it relatively easy for them to get away, provided they could speak good English, which most of them did. Obviously drastic action had to be taken. Firstly, to curtail the influx of cash into the camp, secondly, to dress the internees in some kind of a uniform which could be seen from far away and, thirdly, to take everyone's finger-prints.

In due course, a large consignment of uniforms arrived. It became compulsory, from then on for gangs working outside to wear the new and comical looking outfits. Not resembling a soldier's dress, they were nearer in comparison to the uniform worn by jailbirds condemned to hard labour. The jacket, which was made of a strong twilled serge material, was light blue in colour, with a sixteen-inch diameter scarlet red spot inserted at the back, which could be observed from a great distance. To make the outfit even more distinctive, one of the trouser legs was adorned with a two-inch wide bright red stripe running from hip to toe, and which tended to give the wearer the appearance of a general. The cap crowned the lot. Again in blue with plenty of red on the top, it had a fairly long shield protruding at the front, similar to the caps worn by engine drivers. On the whole, the uniforms looked ludicrous, but were most effective for the purpose. With the greatest reluctance the internees had to fall in with the course of the law, and whether they liked it or not, the garments had to be worn.

Soon after the distribution of the uniforms, Sergeant Mac called at Bender's office inside the 'rubber' hut. To obtain more privacy, a section of their double bunks had been screened off so that all negotiations of a delicate nature could be held in greater secrecy. In spite of it being a Sunday, Mac had an immediate job to be done outside.

In their brand-new uniforms, everyone smiling at each other in amusement, a group of six men climbed into an open lorry, accompanied by two Canadian guards. On and on through the wilds of Canada they drove, nobody knowing, with the exception of the guards, where they were going. This was quite an adventure for the six men, who had never been so far away from the camp before. Ultimately, the lorry stopped in front of a large building, the headquarters of the Canadian formation. They all trooped into a well-equipped canteen where, at the far end, a Wurlitzer organ blared its music through the large hall. Evidently, this organ had to be transported to another unknown destination, and they had been allotted the job.

Giving his men instructions to shift the instrument on to the lorry, Bender busied himself examining the well-stocked counter of the canteen. With the canteen manager watching him curiously, he picked up article after article — pocket-knives, scissors, pipes, soap, toothpaste and many other commodities. At the end of his perusal, like any ordinary customer, Bender told the manager to wrap everything up, and asked the price. So far the puzzled salesman had not uttered a word, but leaning over the counter, he inquisitively asked Bender how he was going to pay for the goods when internees were not allowed to possess any money. In any case, the man went on, he did not think that internees could buy articles like knives or scissors. The manager's complacency soon vanished when Bender dropped a ten-dollar note upon the counter. There was nothing wrong with this transaction. The goods were there and so was the money and, without further ado, the sale was completed, just in time for Bender to catch up with his mates and the Wurlitzer organ.

The lorry branched off the main road, along a narrower one, finally running on tracks between the bush, barely wide enough for the large vehicle. Nobody knew where this thicket would finish or what to expect at the end. To their astonishment, out of the dark of this huge forest, the lorry finally drove into a large cultivated clearing, completely unexpected in a spot such as this. A magnificent mansion had been erected on top of this elevation, with one of the finest views over the whole of the lake. This grand summer residence, architecturally assimilated to an outsize Canadian blockhouse, dominated the beautiful gardens surrounding it.

The lorry jerked to a halt, and the Wurlitzer organ was carried through two large glass doors into one of the most splendid halls the boys had seen. Rolling the instrument over the smooth parquet floor, they entered a huge, impressive-looking room. It was obvious from the decor, that there was either a dance or a party in the offing. There was no one about, apart from a couple of gentlemen in dress-suits, whom Bender approached regarding the instrument. Having put the organ in its right place, there was nothing more for the gang to do but to go back to camp. Whilst hesitating, some more people entered the hall from various doors, the ladies dressed in most expensive evening gowns. What a contrast they made with the internees, in their cheap, serge uniforms.

Bender had not yet made a move to return to the lorry, but instead, he approached the proprietor, shyly asking him a favour. "Look, sir," he said, "it is not our fault that we are interned; we are entirely cut off from the whole world. Such things like these we do not see any more. Although in delivering the organ we were merely carrying out orders, we would be more than happy if you could play for us one of the famous waltzes of Johann Strauss." The kind proprietor immediately obliged; starting the instrument and turning up the volume to full, the music penetrated every corner of the hall.

At the sound more ladies and gentlemen entered the room, and soon the internees were chatting with some of the guests. Trays of peaches were handed round, and the prisoners were asked to fill their pockets. The two Canadians still stood on guard at the far end of the room, watching the strange scene.

Bender studied the wonderful layout of the magnificent hall, with its high walls made up of horizontal layers of thick, smooth, but natural, pine stems with a highly varnished glossy surface. The fireplace was of such dimensions as to enable it to accommodate wooden logs four feet in length, and it represented a most unusual and decorative addition to the whole room.

The music had just reached a crescendo when, suddenly, both glass doors flew open to reveal the figure of a high-ranking officer. With his legs spread wide and his stick under his arm, he stood surveying the unusual situation, not quite sure whether to shout at the guards and the internees, in true military fashion. Realizing the delicacy of the situation, he winked one eye at the guards, who disappeared outside, whilst he approached the party guests in a gentlemanly fashion. Weighing up the situation, Bender thanked the proprietor for his hospitality, and led the other internees away from that unforgettable incident. With this pleasant memory in their minds, they started the journey back to camp.

Back at Red Rock, the goods from the canteen were soon sold to the internees at a handsome profit and when, a couple of days later, the Wurlitzer organ had to be transported back to the canteen, Bender was well prepared for another big shopping expedition.

And so the routine of life in captivity went on and on. Work in the morning, work in the afternoon, monotonously cutting logs for the mess. Bender's shops were still doing well, in particular the latrine branch. Nobody had yet interfered with

## A Free Trip to Canada

his sales, but the writing was on the wall, and the influx of money into the camp would have to be stopped sooner or later. The authorities could not afford to make future get-aways too easy.

So it happened that one day, two privates entered the latrine and, throwing everything on to a large groundsheet, including the cash-box full of money, they confiscated the lot, whilst two Canadian officers watched from a distance. Not a word was said when the merchandise was taken away. Bender was wild, with nothing to show for a day's sale, for he had to pay all his craftsmen for the confiscated goods.

Rumours soon spread, Sergeant Mac being the first one to see his internee about the incident Sergeant-Major Kimberley then came to warn Bender about the consequences and when, finally, the Canadian interpreter expressed his pleasure about the confiscation, Bender blew up. He knew he could be punished for these cash sales but he alone was not responsible. Everyone was in it, from Commanding Officer to private; in spite of the prohibition, they had all bought and paid cash. If it should com to a hearing of the case, Bender was prepared to tell the whole story whether the Canadians liked it or not. Mac and the interpretor were aware of these intentions and fearing the worst, tried their best to avoid a scandal. For several days nothing transpired, Bender still bemoaning the loss of the shop and goods. However, common sense prevailed after all. One day two privates appeared in the 'rubber' hut to dump the fully-packed ground-sheet at Bender's feet. Everything had been returned including the cash-box. Not a dime was missing, and the following morning saw the latrine shop thriving again.

People living in free and organized communities can have no idea what it is like to be fenced in for months and years, especially with only one class of sex represented. In Red Rock more than a thousand men did their utmost to keep up the harmony amongst three, politically opposed, groups of people. In each of the barracks each group lived its separate life of which that in the 'rubber' hut, 63A, was a typical example. For many months the inmates had been living together, each day more or less the same as the rest. They were packed together so closely that each could not help but know his neighbour almost as well as he knew himself. The composition of intelligence amongst the occupants ranged from the very highest to the very lowest level and consequently it was ridiculous to imagine that an illiterate man could win an argument over a highly intelligent chap. However, such was the case, the uneducated stubbornly bullying the other fellow into submission.

Here they were, thirty-four men in all, occupying hut 63A. Consisting of a cross-section of the community, they represented able-seamen, ships' engineers, captains, circus artists, head waiters, foremen, factory workers, doctors, scientists and delegates from the German Consulate in Iceland.

The inmates of hut 63A were usually rudely awakened by a thump, as Merchant Seaman Hankel jumped from his top bunk on to the wooden floor. Instead of morning prayers, the result would be cursing and swearing from some of the occupants of the other bunks. Hankel, a chap of diminutive stature, was a seaman who had for years travelled the seven seas. Apart from being fully conversant in geography, his knowledge was limited. He was very proud of the snakes and darted hearts which were tattooed all over his broad chest. One masterpiece was a ship depicted in various colours. His face was devoid of all intelligence, his rather flat, silky flaxen hair giving him a feminine appearance.

Once out of bed he would strip off his Asiatic pyjama-jacket to reveal his colourful chest and putting on wooden-soled slippers with a loud *clack, clack, clack*, he would make his way to the wash-room at the far end of the barrack. Everyone was awake by that time, getting ready for the morning roll-call. The latter was an event in itself. The far door would open with a loud "Attention!" from the Commanding Officer as he entered, followed by Sergeant Mac and the ex-commodore of the liner *Europa*, still wearing his captain's uniform and peaked cap. The internees would fall into line from one end of the barrack to the other, waiting to be counted. What an assembly of men; tall ones and short ones, fat and thin, some dressed properly, others half naked, some awake, others still half asleep and unkempt. The picture was well worthy of the cartoon Joachim drew, and sold by the hundred.

The morning and evening roll-calls were just a precaution taken to ensure that no one was missing. This was the only military drill to which the internees were subjected. Apart from this they were free and easy, and could do what they liked. Some read books from the library, others played Monopoly or cards, whilst the circus artists kept up their training, walking on their hands or swinging about on improvised circus gadgets. Many did work outside without pay, whereas the majority, reluctant to support their Canadian enemies, stuck it out in the stuffy atmosphere of the hut, or walked round and round the compound like so many lions in a zoo.

In the evenings all were together again, the early curfews keeping the men confined to the few square yards in the wooden structure. On many an evening, in the dim light, Bender would start the ball rolling by unravelling stories of the past. Others would follow suit until, gradually, they all dropped off to sleep.

Everyone was permitted a restricted amount of correspondence on censored notepaper. At the outset, Bender had waited three months before the first news from his wife came through. Eventually however, correspondence was flowing regularly. After the sinking of the *Arandora Star*, Marianne had had a hard time on the Isle of Man. Suspecting that her husband had been shipped abroad, she studied the lists of casualties at her camp post office day after day, expecting to see his name. Other women did the same, many collapsing on reading of their bereavement.

Through correspondence, Bender endeavoured to make all kinds of contacts, especially with Rotary clubs in Canada, but in vain. War had altered the structure of international understanding. Even from his own club in Cheshire, he heard very little, except from a few true friends. One in particular, wrote that it was difficult for the average Englishman to distinguish between the German who bombed English cities and the German who had done his best to swim against the stream of Nazi brutality. Resigned to his fate though he was, Bender was still determined to go back to England at the earliest opportunity. A letter from the Inland Revenue, demanding that the sum of £74.1.8d. for income tax should be paid, did not serve to alter this opinion. At first Bender kept quiet about this, but when the news did leak out, he was accused of all manner of things. This note represented a proper lever for the Nazis and their propaganda. Here was a chap, they said, who had been put into a concentration camp by the English, yet these same people had the effrontery to demand payment of a huge sum from a prisoner. Nobody expected Bender to pay, but he thought differently. Knowing that he owed the tax, and being conversant with ethical business procedure, he paid promptly, regardless of what the Nazis thought.

Although winter was not far off, the internees were enjoying a typical Canadian Indian summer, which acted as an added incentive to open-air life. The days were very warm, the nights cold, and during their slumbers, the internees were stung by large mosquitoes. With winter near and in anticipation of wet weather, Bender approached Captain Bradbeer with a request that some type of shelter should be erected for his gang. "Don't worry about that," the Captain replied. "You don't need a shelter, as it will not rain from November to April!" How right he was, but instead the snow came down in unbelievable quantities.

The first October marked one of the incidents which can only happen under a totalitarian regime. As usual, Bender and his men had started work near the lake. It was a peaceful morning until, at 11 a.m., rifle bullets started to fly all over the place, and the machine guns could be heard rattling in the distance. Bender's gang knew nothing of the cause until they were shepherded back into the compound, the doors of hut 63A closing behind them. No one in any of the barracks was allowed to go out, and scores of Canadians marched into the camp to restore order.

The reason for this war-like manoeuvre had been an attack on the hospital by the Nazis. There had been friction days before. Previously, it was an accepted fact that some Jewish doctors and staff should administer the well-run German hospital, but when later a further Jewish doctor was added, action had to be taken. The Nazis just did not like the Jews, and so the best heavy-weight boxers had been chosen by the

German administrators to put matters right in their own way, resulting in a most brutal attack. Doctors, and some members of the staff, were lying unconscious on the floor and not satisfied with this, assailants had ransacked the place, throwing correspondence, documents and equipment through the windows. Some people yelled, others screamed, setting off the machine guns. When eventually order had been restored, no one knew who was responsible.

It will be difficult for an Englishman to understand such Nazi psychology. The explanation is simple. English Prisoners of War or internees held in enemy camps, fell into one class only, and that was Englishmen, their only difference being whether they were Tory, Liberal or Labour. Not so with Germans. They were either Nazi or anti-Nazi, and woe betide those who did not rally around the Swastika.

The episode had far-reaching consequences. Identity parades, supervised by the Canadian Commandant, took place but in spite of his perseverance backed up by hundreds of soldiers, the culprits were never found. Finally, a stern ultimatum was issued to the German camp leader, holding him responsible for the tracing of the offenders.

The eventful day over, camp life moved back into its normal channels. Men went in and out of the leader's hut trying to find a formula for a reasonable reply to the Canadian Commandant. When agreement was reached, the leader of each hut was called to the office where a draft of a long-winded statement was read out to them. The contents were to the effect that every hut leader was responsible for the brutal assault on the hospital. It was the Nazis' intention that this should be endorsed by everyone of them. Bender sneaked out of the office and made his way to the Sergeants' Mess. By the time he returned in the evening, the important document had already been delivered to the Commandant, duly signed by every hut leader, with the exception of Bender. He got into very great trouble with some of the occupants of his hut. Nevertheless, he had achieved his object by avoiding to surrender by compulsion, to a lie. Quite obviously, this statement was unacceptable to the Canadians and despite their efforts, the real culprits were never found.

As the year 1940 came to a close, the real Canadian winter

had set in with a vengeance. Hardly a day passed without a fall of snow, which was already lying deep. The days were cold, but dry, and still the internees kept up their outdoor exercises, mainly on a man-made ice rink in the compound. Bender enjoyed skating to his heart's content, often in temperatures of forty degrees of frost The air was crisp and healthy, the weather being so severe that it froze the perspiration from his body. Lake Superior was covered with ice approximately three feet thick, and it was here that the Canadians played their ice-hockey matches. Not only was the ice on the lake used for sport, it also had its uses commercially. A specially devised lorry, carrying a large circular-saw, criss-crossed over the ice, the saw cutting it into cubes three feet thick. These were then heaved out and placed in a specially built storeroom near by, where it was stacked to the level of the roof, freezing together into one massive block. Even when the spring sun came out, it hardly had any effect on the mass of ice which represented a long-lasting supply for all kinds of commercial and industrial uses.

The wooden huts gave inadequate protection against the freezing nights, and the internees' best clothing, which hung on the walls, turned green with mildew. To keep the boys warm in bed the very large stove in the middle of the barrack, had to be kept alight all night on a rota system. On the whole, the stokers were reliable, but there were those who did not know how to handle a stove, or even fell asleep, letting the fire go out in the middle of the night. When this happened, bedlam was let loose, with fellows jumping out of bed and performing vigorous exercises in the cold air to keep themselves warm, all the while swearing at the chap on duty. A good night's sleep was spoilt, as it took some time to heat the place again. On other occasions, fellows on stoking duty would keep the fire going all right, but would exaggerate the noise made when refuelling, just for the fun of disturbing the slumbers of the other fellows.

The severe frost, which covered the whole landscape, had jeopardized the camp's water supply, which was drawn from the bottom of the lake, well away from the shore, and pumped through a pipe into the water-tower on the top of the hill. Parallel to this water system ran the camp sewer, which deposited its contents near the shore. Nobody was aware that the ice had cracked the intake pipe, and instead of fresh water being pumped into the tower the filth from the lavatories went in. This occurrence was not traced until the taps in the barracks became contaminated, causing quite an outbreak of illness amongst the soldiers and internees. The whole water supply was cut off, and motorized water lorries brought in fresh supplies until the whole system had been cleared.

In spite of the cold, Bender's gang still enjoyed their work, stepping up the output of logs in order to keep warm. Near the water's edge, where they were working, it really was severe. They adopted half-hourly shifts, and at the first sign of ears or noses turning white, they had to run into the warm cook-house to avoid frost-bite.

In a mantle of crisp white snow, the landscape looked magnificent, even the cook-house looked a picture with icicles a yard long hanging from the roof. The latrine, half embedded in snow, was still in use, for the soldiers as well as Bender's shop. The change to winter demanded other forms of transport, and the gang built a large sledge which carried the goods each day to the shop. No soldier ever searched the sledge, which was covered by many lumber-jackets, the merchandise hidden beneath.

On one of these cold, bright mornings Bender found time to explore the neighbourhood. Whilst strolling along the frozen water's edge his progress was brought to a halt by a fence. Behind it, some distance from where he stood, he could detect a small detached villa. Wondering whether it belonged to the cook-house personnel, he decided that, as there might be an opportunity to explore further, he would find out. Making his way back to the Sergeants' Mess, he asked the cook sergeant. As he had expected, the villa did, indeed, belong to the sergeant and his staff.

Suggesting that he should take a quantity of firewood to the house, Bender was told by a delighted sergeant, to carry on. The sledge was packed full with a few hundredweights, and pulled in the direction of the lake. A long distance was covered before Bender and another fellow finally reached the villa, which was well out of bounds, and away from everything. In they went to find some of the cooks, who were off duty, asleep.

Whilst the other internee stacked the firewood in a convenient place, Bender nosed around, finding piles of up-to-date American journals, an unknown commodity in the camp. One of the cooks permitted him to take the lot, including a stack of the latest uncensored newspapers of highly potential value to internees. That same evening it had all arrived safe and sound in hut 63A without anyone having discovered the secret cargo beneath the lumber-jackets, piled upon the sledge.

In an improvised office, assisted by Otto and Edgar, Bender sorted out the valuable treasure. Monthly journals, such as *Esquire, Life* and *Vogue,* went to the German camp café to be hired out at a small charge, from which Bender drew his commission. The newspapers were retained and studied for several days. Although most newspapers were sent to the camp officially these were of no great value to the internees, as the most important items were blacked out by the censor. The supply from the cook-house was different. Here, Bender found all the news he wanted, and came across some encouraging articles on debates in the House of Commons — in particular, those that concerned internees. Fierce arguments had taken place regarding this problem, some M.P.s having challenged the Government about the German Jews who had been imprisoned in Buchenwald and Belsen and, after seeking refuge in the British Isles, were now faced with the dilemma of being transported, by the British, to camps in Canada or Australia.

Another bone of contention was with regard to the civilian internees many of whom, having lived in England and supported British industry for a long time, had never been in contact with National Socialism. Many had sons fighting in the British Army, somewhere in Europe. From these newspaper items it was apparent that something would be done to ease the plight of these internees, the Government having consented that a special representative should visit Canada and Australia with the object of shipping some of them back to England, and releasing them from internment. This was the finest news Bender had read for a long time. The day could not be far off before his return to England. Keeping the stack of newspapers, he hired them out, at five cents a time, to news-hungry internees.

On account of the severe restrictions at that time, it had become rather difficult to obtain cash from the Canadians for goods sold. Some of them still paid, one fellow buying a ship in a bottle for one dollar. On producing a fifty-dollar note, he was very surprised when, without batting an eyelid, Bender changed it on the spot. However, new means for barter had to be found and when one of the Canadian cooks produced a series of photographs of the camp taken from all angles, Bender knew the answer. With his goods, he paid for hundreds of photos to be sold in the camp against the special camp-money. There was always a way of making a profit.

Christmas, the time of peace on earth, had come. How would the festive season be spent behind barbed wire? The first thing Bender did was to have a word with Captain Bradbeer about Christmas morning. Explaining that he and the gang would like to go for a stroll through the beautiful snow-clad pine forests instead of their normal wood-chopping job, the captain readily gave his consent.

Christmas Eve brought many surprises. In such an adverse situation, no one had anticipated any festive celebrations. Contrary to their expectations, however, at a given time, the large recreation hall was opened, where they duly took their seats. Then, the merrymaking began. Putzi, who was still amongst them, played Christmas carols on the piano. Everyone sang, capturing the spirit of the festive season, whilst Father Christmas handed out a substantial parcel to every internee in the camp. On opening them, they were filled with surprised delight at the contents — eighty cigarettes, four packets of tobacco, toilet soap, gloves, a bag of toffees, one comb, half-a-pound of chocolate, a tin of sardines, one bag of hazelnuts, another of figs, a Christmas cake, one other cake, a bag of peppermints and a handkerchief. For a while, the men forgot they were internees, giving themselves over to the full enjoyment of the occasion. Whether Red Cross or Canadian Government, someone had brought untold happiness to those far away from their own folk, making them realize that they were not completely forgotten by the outside world.

On Christmas morning, Bender and the gang rose early. Reporting at the main gate leading out of the camp, two soldiers were waiting to accompany them on the proposed walk. In astonishment, the internees stared at the two Canadians, who were immaculately dressed in new khaki uniforms, with not a rifle, bayonet or revolver to be seen. Bender's thoughts flew to Captain Bradbeer, thinking what a fine man he was to make this stroll befitting for such a bright, sunny and holy Christmas morning. To the Canadians, as well as to the internees this two-hour walk would remain in their memories for a long time to come. Chatting amicably together and exchanging cigarettes, they covered quite a distance through the thickly-wooded forest and the countryside, deep in snow. They visited spots they had never seen before, all behaving towards one another as though there was no war on. Arriving back at camp, they went their separate ways, the Canadians to their barracks, the Germans through the large compound gate. Back to reality though they were, no barbed wire encirclement could erase those happy hours of Christmas morning, 1940.

In war or peace, religious people will pray and even this aspect was not neglected by the Canadian authorities in this camp in the wilderness. With the morning's walk still fresh in his mind, Bender, along with many others, wended his way to the tiny improvised chapel. Standing in front of the plain wooden cross, singing carols and listening to the simple, sincere words of the German pastor, they were all able to worship in their own way, finding solace in this tiny retreat, while outside the machine guns still pointed downwards from the watch-towers. Of the many Christmases Bender had celebrated in the past, none had been of such unforgettable magnitude as the one spent in 'R' Camp, Red Rock, Canada.

\* \* \* \* \*

The first two months of 1941 passed without any major incident, the persistent frost and bitterly cold weather having an adverse effect on the internees' morale. Even Bender was affected when he wrote in his diary one day: ' Time is dragging on slowly. It is not that I am ill, but the uncertainty of the future causes one more and more distress. It is not the body that suffers but the soul. If only this war would finish soon. '

He was still awaiting signs of an eventual release, but, on

weighing up the facts, he came to the conclusion that, taking into account the vast number of Nazis in 'R' camp, it seemed highly unlikely that the representative from the Home Office would call just for the purpose of releasing the few chaps who merited a return journey to England. Many other internment camps which contained no Nazis whatsoever were spread all over Canada and unless he could contrive to get himself transferred to one of these, he had not a chance.

Patiently he waited for the impossible to happen and, behold, on the 10th March, the British liaison officer entered the compound. Chatting informally to one of the Jewish internees he suddenly came out with the intriguing question — "Are there still chaps in this camp who want to go back to England?" For the moment, Baumann, who had a great chance of being released, was stunned.

"Of course!" he replied. "There are a few of us who want to get out of here, and as quickly as possible!"

"Very well then," said the officer. "Here are a few forms to fill in. I am relying entirely on your good judgement as to the men you pick."

In the greatest secrecy, Baumann chose a couple of internees, making sure that those chosen were one hundred per cent anti-Nazi; Bender was one of them. Getting together, they made a list of potentials, only to scrap it and make another one, always discovering that they had far too many names. To propose a long list of probables would have been folly, as the whole scheme might then collapse. Finally they reached a definite decision of thirteen men only. Bender had proposed Otto Trusberg on whom, politically, he could fully rely. Edgar Mann however, was a different proposition and, although Bender had known him for many years and would have liked to have included him, this was no time for sentiment. Steadfast anti-Nazis were required and, therefore Edgar had to be ruled out. Another one Bender had included was Arthur Rahmann, a staunch Socialist and foreman weaver from Bender's German hometown. Before the war, Arthur had worked in Colne, Lancashire, and was married to an English girl.

That day, a lot of undercover work went on amongst this small group of thirteen men. Sacrificing their meal, they met, secretly, in a small hut during the lunch hour. They all signed their forms, breaking off any future connection with their native Germany and by evening, these documents were on their way to headquarters. Outwardly there were no signs in the camp that anything had happened. This time for a welcome change, the authorities worked fast, as by March 12th, the thirteen men received word from the Commanding Officer to be ready for release on the 17th. In spite of the good news, the lucky men had to suppress their hilarious excitement, for they still had to keep everything quiet. When the news did eventually leak out from a different channel, it became most interesting to study the attitude of fellow prisoners who had missed their chance. Needless to say, Edgar was furious, as were many others, and those Nazis who did not want release heaped every abuse imaginable on the thirteen fellows, accusing them of all manner of crimes including high treason.

What with the atrocious weather and the strained atmosphere, the few remaining days were most unpleasant for the thirteen men. By March 16th, a bad blizzard set in; the worst experienced for sixteen years. The same day, troops arrived who had marched through blinding snowstorms, their frost-bitten ears nearly dropping off.

The 17th, the day of departure, was no better. Instead of the dense snow falling vertically, owing to the force of the howling gale, it drove past horizontally. Whilst the thirteen men stood outside the compound ready to leave, the bulk of internees clung to the fence like monkeys, some shouting distasteful language at the fortunate ones.

Setting off in the direction of the railway station, the only road in this wild territory was covered by a sheet of treacherous and glassy ice. Although the soldiers endeavoured to keep the prisoners together, the blizzard hampered their efforts. Whirled about by the wind, they were all spread out, but the soldiers were not unduly worried. The natural elements alone were sufficient to stop any attempt at escape. A long irregular string of soldiers and prisoners finally covered the icy street; everyone for himself was the motto. Bender, his two heavy suitcases dragging him down, had dropped out of the column altogether. Far behind, he was frozen stiff in his thin serge uniform. As he struggled along, trying to catch up, he saw a fellow approaching him through the whirling snow. He proved to be none other than the German camp leader, the commodore from the *Europa*. Here, for the first time, they could talk freely without the risk of being overheard by the Nazis.

"Well," said the ship's captain, shaking Bender by the hand. "I don't blame you for going home, Herr Bender. After all, your family is in the British Isles. I wish you the best of luck." Then with tears streaming down his face, he abruptly turned in the direction of his provisional home, the camp which he so detested. Watching him disappear in the blizzard, Bender felt compassion for the elderly gentleman, who, through Hitler's folly, was temporarily confined to the wilds of Canada.

On meeting up at the station, the internees and their guards boarded a cosily-heated train, where they received rations in a quantity which indicated a long journey. For thirty-four hours they travelled, their only stop and change being at Montreal. Passing Phillippe and Versailles, they finally stopped at the small station of Farnham, their destination.

Their new abode was a camp not much different from the one they had left behind, though the living conditions were better. However, the rules were stricter, as became apparent the moment they entered, when a sixteen-stone sergeant-major, a tall, stout chap of Irish descent with a Yul Brynner head, bullied them into order.

Within a couple of days, the newcomers had settled down amongst the other men, who had been there for some time. It was a good camp, with well-built, much warmer barracks. The security wire was far more substantial than at Red Rock, a high fence, similar to that of a tennis court, surrounded the compound. After about ten yards of open ground, came another similar type of fence, with very high watch-towers erected at each corner. To stop any attempt at tunnelling, the sergeant-major ordered that a ten-ton lorry should be driven between the two fences, at intervals, in order to crack any tunnel under construction.

The population, from a political point of view, was more to Bender's liking, as the majority of people were anti-Nazi and, in due course, the privileges granted were far greater. What a treat it was to be able to listen to the radio and read uncensored newspapers once again. Recreation and social facilities included movies and sports. An up-to-date wood-working factory provided facilities for work at twenty cents a day, and produced tool-boxes for the Allied Forces.

After a week in the camp, Bender received his first surprise call to appear before the representative from the Home Office. Taking a seat in the waiting-room he started counting his fingers, saying to himself, "Will I go back to England — will I not?" And, when the V.I.P.'s door opened, the last finger indicated — "I will!" Feeling this to be a good omen, he sat down on the chair facing his judge.

The conversation was most cordial, but short. There was no need for Bender to say anything, as the file in front of his superior apparently contained all details. After studying them for a while, the envoy lifted his head and looking at his charge with a fatherly smile, said, "Herr Bender, I am sending my recommendation to London for your transfer to England." Bender was so overcome that he could hardly refrain from jumping over the office table and embracing the elderly gentleman. However, containing his feelings, he muttered a grateful, "Thank you."

Out of the office he went, full of glee, broadcasting his good news to everyone he knew. He was not the only one, as many others had had the same good fortune. It was now only a matter of time before the return journey to England.

All thirteen men from Red Rock were on the transfer list, besides many others from various camps. A new list had to be issued after a week, however, as a good proportion of the transfer internees had refused to travel, being afraid of crossing the German submarine-infested Atlantic. Many of these men remained in Canada for the duration of the war, as did the thousand or more in Red Rock. The few lucky ones to go back to England were Bender and five others, including Otto Trusberg and Arthur Rahmann.

The other internees had made a grave mistake in refusing, as they should have realized that the British Government expects every British soldier and civilian to do his duty and, likewise, a pro-Allied German.

The snow was still lying deep, but beginning to melt. Where this process was not sufficiently rapid, the sergeant-major revelled in putting every man to work with shovels to clear the slush. When some of the men objected, their supper was stopped. He was a very strict disciplinarian. The weather was relatively warm for the time of year and for this type of job, the men turned out in bathing trunks. Owing to the additional rays from the sun reflected by the snow, some of them had already acquired a tan. By the third week in April, the temperature had reached the unusual height of eighty-five degrees.

Life became a matter of routine. In the barracks, where political opinions ran roughly along the same lines, one soon got to know one's neighbours. Whereas in Red Rock the majority were in favour of Germany winning the war, in the Farnham camp, this privilege was granted to the Allies. Here, the greater part were civilians, Jewish and Christian alike. The sprinkling of Communists, whom it suited to be pro-Allied for the time being, cherished quite different aspirations for the future. In general, conversation was of an intelligent nature, but in spite of this, some fellows got on each others' nerves; the root of the trouble being that there were far too many men in a confined space. Some devoted their time to study, whilst others whiled away the hours playing games. To the annoyance of others, some liked to play the crackling gramophone — a present from the Red Cross.

Time passed quickly and with the spring came the chance for internees to work in the fields, outside the camp, planting potatoes. Bender enjoyed this occupation far more than working amongst the sawdust of the factory. April and May passed without incident, and those on the transfer list heard nothing further regarding their plight. Not until 17th June were the lads told to pack their bags in preparation for the long return journey.

## THE RETURN JOURNEY

About midnight on the 18th, scores of internees boarded a train in a near-by station, thinking they were practically free. They soon discovered their mistake. The first request to wear civilian clothes was turned down by the Commanding Officer, and they had to cross the Atlantic in their shabby blue and red uniforms. The second surprise came when, during the journey to Halifax, another set of French-Canadians took control. These were rough chaps, each equipped with hand-cuffs which they bandied about ostentatiously and which, at the slightest provocation, would have had no hesitation in using. There was too much at stake for the internees to give offence and all through the long journey to the coast, they were very much on their best behaviour.

The fine weather and the beautiful countryside were sufficient reasons to make the men gaze through the large carriage windows, watching the changing scene, as the wonderful landscape of New Brunswick and Nova Scotia flew past. The most impressive thing about Canada is its vastness; here, there is room to breathe, and people do not live close together as they do in the British Isles. The train thundered past forests and lakes with, here and there, tiny specks of distant houses indicating the presence of people. It took thirty-four hours to complete the journey, touching upon only a relatively small proportion of this huge country.

Bender had enjoyed the journey, but was wondering what to expect on reaching Halifax. For practically a year now, he had heard nothing but propaganda from German merchant seamen in Red Rock. According to them, the British were down and out; the German submarines had played havoc with the British Navy, and there was hardly a ship left. It was, therefore, with some misgivings that he approached the destination.

After being herded together like sheep, the Canadian guards marched them in the direction of the docks. Turning the last corner, they were suddenly confronted with a view of the whole harbour basin. And what a sight it was. In amazement he stared, unbelievingly, at the number of ships lying at anchor there. Large, small, from the biggest battle-cruiser down to the tiny tramp-steamer. Here was the British Navy, still in its full glory; the war was by no means over — the German merchant seamen in Red Rock were in for a long wait before being sent home

On the prisoners marched towards another dock, where one of the largest convoys awaited them. Five large liners, filled to capacity with newly-trained Commonwealth aircraft personnel and soldiers, were ready for the Atlantic crossing. The Canadian officer brought his column of men to a halt. The prisoners relaxed slightly as they surveyed the large strong-looking hull of the *Indrapoera,* the ship that was to carry them home.

Out of the grip of the French-Canadians, one after the other, they climbed the steep gangplank to land on the deck of the ship amongst the British Army, Navy and Air Force. Still in their conspicuous uniforms, no one knew quite what to make of the newcomers, or exactly what kind of folk they were.

Bender had been one of the last men to reach the deck but, as his head popped over the railing, he heard someone calling to him. "Hello, Bender." Hardly able to believe his own ears, he looked around in an endeavour to see who it was that had known him by name. Suddenly, he saw a figure pushing his way through the crowd of soldiers in an effort to reach him. It was one of the guards from Red Rock, to whom Bender had sold many an article. They greeted one another like old friends, patting each other on the back and shaking hands warmly. The soldiers and airmen standing around were inquisitive to know more about the history of these chaps in the flamboyant attire, and questioned the sergeant until he enlightened them.

The sergeant and Bender had much to talk about, recounting their different experiences at Red Rock. "How is business nowadays?" asked the sergeant.

"Very good," replied Bender. "As a matter of fact, I've brought a lot with me. My cases are full of battleships, and all kinds of other things."

"Come here," retorted the Canadian. "What are we waiting for? Get your cases and let's pay a visit to the officers. When they see them, they'll buy the lot!"

In no time at all both were entering the luxurious quarters of the officers, and whilst the sergeant introduced his acquaintance, Bender exhibited his articles, displaying them all over the place. Just as at Red Rock, the goods were too tempting to be refused, and in a short time, everything was sold.

As he left the cabin, Bender thought what a fine start it was to the journey, and thanked his pal for the good deed. On that they parted, as Bender had to rejoin his companions who had already gone down into the ship. He found them on the lowest deck, where they were endeavouring to make themselves comfortable against the steel walls. There was no available cabin this time, and they had to make do with hammocks in an otherwise empty store-room. It was a veritable trap, out of which no one could escape should a torpedo pierce the outer skin of the vessel.

When they had all settled down, they split up and explored the ship. A slender, graceful-looking Dutch liner, she had been used in peacetime for crossing the Pacific. Otto, Arthur and Bender grouped together and, for the first time, felt like free men. They could go all over the ship, just as they pleased. It was wonderful being able to mix with the army in their quarters, and despite their incongruous uniforms, be allowed to buy cigarettes and most of all, a cool drink of beer, the like of which they had not tasted for over a year. More than satisfied, the internees turned in for the night, sleeping peacefully, in the calm of the harbour.

They were roused from their slumbers on 21st June, by the

clanging of chains and the hooting of ships' sirens. The day of departure had arrived. Soon everyone was up on top deck. As far as the eye could see, there was nothing but ships. What a majestic sight, they made, their sheer lines enhanced by the sombre grey of their war-paint.

By 11 a.m. the transportation of troops was under way. The convoy moved along in calm seas, the ocean liners in the centre, framed squarely by a dozen destroyers, and some anti-aircraft vessels, whilst in the distance, were two battle-cruisers. Overhead, they were covered by an umbrella of Canadian planes. Every protection, humanly possible, was afforded this valuable cargo.

Up until the second day, the internees had enjoyed their freedom. However, as usually happens, some had taken advantage of this, and had been discovered snooping in prohibited quarters. The result was new restrictions lasting a couple of days.

When the internees were summoned to one of the large halls, they received all the accumulated Canadian credits. Paid out in hard cash, down to the last cent, Bender came in for quite a tidy sum.

Apart from a few depth charges on the third day, the whole journey passed uneventfully. Onward the ships sailed in a zig-zag, northerly route with not a German submarine to be seen. Sometimes the sea was calm, but at others, it would roll furiously, rocking the internees' hammocks like swings in a fairground. Bender had never slept in such a contraption before, and rather enjoyed the sensation. Baumann, an elderly chap, who occupied the next hammock was a man of experience, having sailed as an officer in many of the Zeppelins. He took the precaution of hanging a long thick rope from his hammock, down to the floor. Never without this rope, he reckoned it could be invaluable to a survivor, should the ship go down.

Land was sighted on the ninth day of the journey and after cruising through the longish swell of the Irish Sea, the ships finally sailed up the Clyde, coming to anchor in the middle of a large loch. For some of the luckier internees, their day of freedom had already arrived, and they were taken off the boat. The majority left the following day, by steamer, in the direction of the Isle of Man.

On the 2nd July, 1941, a new world opened up for the prisoners when they stepped on the quay at Douglas to be received like human beings. In a quick march, they crossed the town, only a few unarmed soldiers accompanying them. Their new domicile was Hutchinson Camp. Situated in the centre of the city, it was a camp completely different from those occupied in the past. They entered a large square surrounded by boarding houses, all of which had been requisitioned for the accommodation of internees. Here, at last, was a proper home, nothing remaining to remind them of the days they had spent behind wire.

On arrival a roll-call was taken, the Commanding Officer addressing the new arrivals in something after the following terms:

"You lucky chaps have come from Canada where you have had far too much to eat and too many cigarettes to smoke. Now you are in the British Isles, where we have all had to tighten our belts. We are rationed. You, who were not, have, I am sure, brought a lot of merchandise with you — food, smokes, drinks, and other items. For the time being, your belongings will be confiscated. You can settle down in your rooms, but the luggage will be examined in your presence, and then locked up. I now appeal to your generosity and charity. The chaps here have had a lean time and so, all that you have brought with you, will be shared out amongst all the inmates, including yourselves. All I want is a fair deal, and I hope that all of you understand."

After the Commanding Officer had departed, there were some discontented murmurings, but the majority were content with the arrangements.

Sure enough, on the following day, all the luggage was stacked in the large hall. As it was taken in alphabetical order, Bender was amongst the first batch to enter. He had a lot of stuff in his suitcases, apart from a large wooden box specially made for the purpose. There were pounds of butter, fat, ham, jam, marmalade, thousands of cigarettes, packets of tobacco and many more items. Readily, along with many others, he handed over the various commodities to a sturdy sergeant.

## The Return Journey

Everyone soon settled down in the houses provided, which they found infinitely more draught free than the flimsy huts of Canada. Bender had gleaned information of a married quarter in the Isle of Man, and he was not prepared to stay where he was for long. Submitting applications for transfer, all married men were taken forthwith to visit their wives at the women's camp. What a joy it was to see his wife and child again after all these months, and to learn that they were well cared for.

On returning to his quarters, he waited eagerly for his transfer to come through. There was little point in starting work at this juncture, so he whiled away the time mixing with the other men, and making new contacts. There was always plenty to talk about, and the days passed fairly quickly.

The hospital was the cosiest of places. Attending it one day for a minor ailment, he was surprised to come across an old school pal from his native Ronsdorf in charge of the administration. Adolf Baumer, a company director of a firm in the south of England was another who had not escaped the net of British Intelligence. His naturalization had not come through before the outbreak of war and, as a result, he went the same way as so many others. Many a happy evening they spent together in one of the furnished hospital rooms in the company of the doctors, where they could chat intelligently and privately over a bottle of beer.

The main subject for discussion was their release, which Bender did not anticipate in the near future. Adolf was better placed, however, probably because, apart from being a genuine anti-Nazi, he had never belonged to the German Labour Front. Secondly, being a staunch Socialist, he had a stronger chance in the eyes of the British adjudication. Both exchanged many views on this subject, which induced Bender to lodge a new application for release. Not long after this Adolf said good-bye, handing over the hospital administration to his old school friend.

This new, and welcome, job enabled Bender to occupy his time during the otherwise boring days. In his new office he was able to concentrate, taking up more correspondence in his spare time, receiving letters from many a friend. In the eyes of the outside world, it made all the difference being in the Isle of

Man, as internees there had not the same stigma as those Nazi-tainted ones in Canada or Australia.

One morning, he received a ray of hope in the form of a letter from the chairman of a large English textile concern, asking after the internee's well-being. Until then, Bender had not given much thought to the future. His own factory in Hyde, had been amalgamated with another firm for the duration of war. There seemed little chance of him being able to continue work where he left off on the day of his internment.

On the strength of this new contact, Bender made plans for the future. If he could not return to his old firm, no one could prevent him joining another, after his release. The chairman of this company had many projects, the chief one of which was the opening of a new factory in New Zealand. Here was an opportunity for Bender to furnish all financial data and layout for a new concern abroad. Already he was doing some practical work instead of selling ships in bottles.

At the beginning of September, Bender received his longed for call to take up married quarters. After a separation of seventeen months, this was really worth a celebration. In a furnished flat they could be together again, and endeavour to return to a normal life.

The British behaved very generously towards the alien prisoners when it came to housing them during war. It is doubtful whether anywhere else in the world the same amenities would be given by any of the belligerent nations. Port St Mary, in the Isle of Man, is in itself, well known to those who seek holiday happiness during the summer vacation. The internees had all these facilities at their disposal, the only exception being that it was up to them to keep the boarding houses clean and to prepare the vegetables, whilst the Manx landladies and hotel proprietors supervised the whole business.

The Benders, with many other families, had found accommodation with the Maddocks, a charming family who made their lodgers feel very welcome, living together as if there was no war on. The boarding house was well situated at the top end of the promenade, overlooking the picturesque bay, and the distant Irish Sea. The alien occupants were hand-picked, and the whole atmosphere and social intercourse in this camp was completely different from anything they had experienced before.

Families were still enjoying the autumn sunshine without a break but after a time, even there halcyon days can pall. Many did no job of work at all, though others worked on farms at a rate of nine shillings a week. No barbed wire surrounded the camp, except for a fence marking the boundary. There was no need for greater security, as the vast sea around the island was a deterrent to any would-be escaper. Twice a week the main gate was opened, and the internees could enjoy local shopping, or go to the cinema.

Bender was far from content with the money he earned on the farm, and one day his real chance of improvement came when a heavy sea washed up a quantity of fine drift-wood on to the beach. A plan already forming in his brain, he picked it all up and with the help of some mates, carried it to a sheltered place for drying. For many days he sat at the drawing-board designing a weaving loom, a machine far advanced from the old-fashioned hand-loom the crofters used in the Hebrides. The new design developed from a highly automatic factory loom into a semi-automatic machine, on which a length of cloth, sufficient for a costume or an overcoat, could be woven within a day. The plans completed, the drift-wood was carried to the local joiner, to be cut up according to instructions. Very soon the weaving machine began to take shape, old friends in Lancashire supplying the special equipment, such as healds and reeds. With a good supply of wool available from Manx mills in Sulby and St Johns, Bender's little factory started.

First of all he transferred his banking account from the mainland to the camp accountancy department, enabling him to settle his commitments in England and the Isle of Man directly. During the bleak winter months, there was little to do outside, and the business steadily built up. Weaving the finest multi-coloured and plain designs, many customers arrived, amongst them the Camp Commandant, delegates from the Swiss Red Cross, officials from the Home Office in London, the Manx police and many of the landladies. Cloth was in great demand and furthermore, at that time, Bender was probably the only manufacturer in the British Isles legally selling without coupons. When he got into deep water about this with the local Chamber of Trade, he defended his own case, making it plain that anyone could purchase wool yarn without coupons as long as it contained oil. He went on to point out that any person could twist the threads, with the aid of knitting needles, into a garment. As he was twisting the yarn into a piece of cloth with the help of his machine, the final result was the same, and to this, the local Chamber had to agree.

The business carried on without interruption. Bender wove most of the day, whilst Marianne supervised the finishing department.

Many people did nothing at all, but just waited, day after day for the end of the war, studying newspapers to try and find a clue as to when this would happen. Some showed vexation at the lack of headway the Allies appeared to be making in bringing about Hitler's downfall, and although the camp, from a political aspect, was usually calm, the quiet was disturbed when, on the 15th February, 1942, the Japs occupied Singapore. In spite of professing to be anti-Nazis, some of the inmates suddenly switched their opinion, and fancying that Hitler, after all, could win the war, they walked along the promenade in a small procession, proclaiming their joy at the Japanese victory. This certainly did not do these fellows any good, as one cannot be on the British side one day and on the German side the next, and get away with it. British Intelligence was always on the alert, watching incidents of this kind and it was more than likely that these types would have no chance of remaining in England after the war.

The months of 1942 passed. Bender received the news that he could not be released yet, even though many of his English friends had written to the Home Office, giving him their backing. There was nothing for it but to continue with his weaving. The only major change came in August, when the whole population of the camp was transferred to Port Erin. Once more they packed their bags, the Benders requiring a wagon to transport the machine and stocks.

A new boarding house, situated on the top of a cliff overlooking the fine bay, was opened for them. They joined a typical Manx family, the Hendersons, who did all they could to make these aliens comfortable in their home. In internment, one cannot choose one's neighbours who, in this case, varied in opinion as chalk from cheese. There were about a dozen of them in the house, of various religious denominations. The Salvation Army represented the largest contingent, from colonel down to captain. Next in line came the Jehovah's Witnesses in the form of a couple from Vienna. Then there was a husband and wife from Bavaria, whose sympathies were with the Quakers and, lastly, numerous Methodists. In general, they aimed at the same target which was to reach heaven, their methods to achieve this varying considerably.

Normally, they lived apart, each party occupying their own flat, but whether they liked it or not, they had to meet at meal times in the small dining-room. The Salvation Army and the Benders (Reformists) occupied one large table, pleasantly chatting together for a start. However, after the meal, when Bender opened a bottle of ale and lit a cigarette, the curtain came down, the stout Major and Frau Bunse heaping abuse on the poor victim.

The atmosphere was none too pleasant, and Bender was not a man who cared to be spoken to in that strain. Accordingly, he went in search of new digs, which he found higher up the hill in a much larger boarding house, which also had a beautiful view over the whole of the bay. During his hours of recreation he explored the camp. He could go where he pleased, and would go walking with his wife and daughter through the fine gardens of Bradda Glen, half-way towards Bradda Head, amongst a profusion of fuchsia hedges. They clambered over the rocks bordering the bay, and would sit watching the sea, the seaweed swaying to and fro. Twice a week when the main gate opened, one could explore the whole of Port Erin down to the station and harbour. In general, it was an easy life and although Bender still longed for his release, he knew such ideal conditions could not be found at home, in Hyde.

To begin with there was the well furnished boarding house, with a pleasant landlady and family. The people were more cosmopolitan and broad-minded. Bender enjoyed a chat with Mr Muir, his landlord, and Henry, his son. Often father and son would go down to the rocks and fish. One day Bender accompanied them on the expedition, and successfully hooked a fish at the first attempt. From that day Bender became an angler for life, and apart from his work, he now had a hobby as well.

The house was surrounded by large gardens, with a recreation hall at one end. Part of this was used for the weaving, an ideal spot for work-and-store-room. So busy was he with the weaving, that Bender had to obtain permission to use the place after curfew, making his working day much longer. Everything was available on the premises, including a large wash-house where, with the help of an interned chemist, they started dyeing the material exclusive shades, unobtainable at the mills. The range of designs grew, bringing in orders from as far away as Manchester. In order to fit everything in, Bender's day had to follow a strict routine. Fishing required bait, and there was no time available to dig worms. Going down to the nearby women's camp, Bender advertised in the window of the Labour Exchange: 'Worm-digger required — ½d. per worm.' Immediately a muscular Polish girl applied for the job, and was taught the art of digging. From now on, the daily programme was complete. Part of the day for work, the rest for fishing. At the appropriate time, an hour before high tide, the bait would be placed at the main gate. How Bender enjoyed this sport, the size of the fish he caught growing from day to day, many a five-pounder amongst them. Young Henry Muir often accompanied him. Although only a schoolboy, in spite of the difference in ages, they enjoyed one another's company, catching big fish and small, with, one day, a record of a six foot conger eel which nearly landed them in the water.

Week in, week out, the programme was the same, only changing when Bender found a rusty, but perfect, miniature lathe in a scrapyard. Polishing it he surveyed its potentials. Sitting down, he turned tops and whips, candlesticks, wooden bowls and dolls, but being short of time, he had to find labour to do this extra work. His best pal in the camp was Herbert Warner, a taxi driver from London, who willingly took over the new wood-working department on a commission basis. One of the industrious fellows amongst the internees, he enjoyed his work, especially in his main occupation, that of administering the camp café in the nineteenth hole of the Golf Club.

The weaving shop became busier than ever. People came and went, many visiting out of curiosity to see the loom in action. One day a delegation of Manx teachers called and made up their minds to purchase some of the looms for the schools. This was a tall and expensive order which, again, Bender could not execute himself. However, on talking the matter over with Gustav Gruber, a circus artist, they came upon a solution. Gustav was clever with his hands, and could also read a drawing. All it meant was getting more wood and opening the loom building department, which Gustav was prepared to take over at an hourly wage.

It was well into 1943, and the war was still in full swing, although hardly noticeable in the Isle of Man. Bender's three departments were still going, but when Herbert received a letter from London summoning him to appear before Intelligence for interrogation, for the time being, the dolls' department had to cease production, leaving the Benders in a quandary as to whether they should run the camp café as well. In spite of their business, they took on this additional job, serving about eighty customers on the first Saturday. They shared out their work. The new proprietress in the kitchen, whilst the proprietor himself, became counter-attendant and waiter. How the cups of coffee rattled in his hands when serving his first customers. They soon got into their stride, enjoying the new occupation. On shopping day, they bought provisions — bread, lettuce, tomatoes, etcetera, all the essentials which were required. Geese, ducks and chickens, bought by wealthy internees arrived at the café to be roasted in the only stove large enough for the purpose. The charge was 2/6d. a bird, which the proprietress cooked, keeping the dripping to be used for the German speciality of toast with dripping, salt and tomatoes. The fun of running the café did not last too long. Herbert returned, bringing the whole business back to the old routine.

Over the years, many a yard of cloth had been manufactured without a hitch in the supply of yarn. Unfortunately the source was now drying up and when supplies ran out, there were signs that the little factory would have to close. Taking the initiative, Bender went to the Commandant's office. A Scotland Yard officer, he had a great understanding for the internees.

"Look, sir," Bender said, after sitting down in the proffered chair, "would it be possible for me to journey all over the island, accompanied by one of your policemen of course, as I have run out of yarn and would like to visit the local mills to procure fresh supplies?"

The officer's face grew grave. "No!" he said to the internee. "I'm afraid that is too tall an order, and which, under no circumstances can I allow. If I can help you in another way, however, I will do so. Give me the names of some of these firms, and I will contact them for you."

The Commandant proved most helpful and, sure enough, a few days later a hundredweight bale of the finest yarn at a ridiculously low price, arrived at the camp. Bender was delighted, and thanking his chief profusely, he paid his bill and pulled the load on a hand-cart to his weaving shed.

It was not uncommon to find many other enterprises in the camp similar to that of weaving. Many people were not content to work on farms at the rate of 9/- a week, and the more skilled amongst them, rather liked to use it to their own advantage by opening up all kinds of little factories. It was something of an eye-opener to visit an exhibition at the Hydro Hotel, to find so many articles such as shoes, sandals, cloth, knitwear, baskets and many others produced solely by internees under primitive conditions. What better solution could be found than to occupy these people in their own craft, giving them a stimulant to overcome boredom. Those who did nothing at all (and there were many) did not know what to do with their time.

After living in close proximity for a couple of years, everyone knew each other, in spite of the slowly changing population in the camp. Some went home to England, others arriving from other camps. At the outset, the majority of people in the married quarters, had their roots in England. Others, who had arrived with later batches, were more doubtful, at one time referring to their English homes and, at others, to Germany. Although nobody expressed political opinions openly, one knew exactly who was who.

At this late period in 1943, Bender was called to the Commandant's office. The ensuing conversation was in connection with his thirteen-year-old daughter, who was a pupil of the camp school, administered by German teachers. In his friendly way, the Commandant opened the conversation. "Well, Mr Bender, I've brought you here to discuss an aspect which concerns your daughter. I have it on authority that she never takes part in the German lessons in our school. I would like to find out the reason for this, and at the same time, I must stress the fact that the German language will always be an asset to those who can speak it. Why is it your daughter does not attend the German lessons?"

Feeling somewhat uneasy, Bender cleared his throat and replied. "I know that the German language is an asset, sir, and I would like my daughter to learn it thoroughly, but it all depends where and how it is taught. In the camp school," he went on, "there are still teachers with leanings towards Germany, and I don't wish my daughter to be taught by totalitarians."

"Your explanation is a sound one," the officer replied. Then, unexpectedly, said — "If you are not prepared for your daughter to learn German in the camp, I may be able to find ways and means of sending her to boarding school outside."

Bender was staggered when he heard this, unable at first to believe that it was possible for an internee's daughter to be educated at boarding school amongst free people. Recovering his equilibrium, he asked — "Where is the school you have in mind, sir?" All the time wondering what this was going to cost him financially. When he learnt that it was the Buchan High School for girls in Castletown, not far from Port Erin, he was delighted. Thanking the officer for his interest and assistance, he hurried home to discuss the matter with his wife.

All evening they sat together debating the wonderful proposition, and by next morning were all in agreement. As quickly as possible Bender made his way to the chief's office. Some hours later, in a private car, the Commandant and Bender set out for Castletown. After seeing the Headmistress, they were shown over the school. When they returned to the camp it was a foregone conclusion that Luise would start a new education. After passing her entrance examination, she left the camp a few days later for the new school. At last she was able to study to her heart's content in congenial surroundings amongst other girls of a similar nature. Although only a few miles away from her parents, whenever she paid a visit to the camp, even she had to apply to the Home Office in London for an entry-permit.

How many more months, Bender wondered, would he have to spend in the camp? He had lodged one application after another to obtain his release, but in spite of the support from reputable business people on the mainland, so far it had been in vain. In particular, the company chairman, to whom he had furnished details for a new factory in New Zealand, had made every effort to secure the internee's services. As a last resort Bender sent a further application, stating that he was prepared to accept any job the Ministry of Labour and National Service might offer him in England. One month went by, and then another, but still nothing happened. Not until he was called by an Intelligence officer for an interview did he raise new hopes.

Soon after this meeting, completely out of the blue, Herr and Frau Bender received orders to pack their bags for the journey home. It caused great excitement, tinged with faint regret at leaving behind a relatively comfortable camp life. On account of the short notice, the packing had to be done in a hurry. The little business had to be wound up, the weaving loom and yarn stocks sold to another internee.

The day of departure arrived, and one bleak November morning, with much waving and good wishes from their friends, the couple left the boarding house on the hill.

Once again, after three-and-a-half years, on the 25th November, 1943, the Benders stepped on to English soil. On the journey from Fleetwood to Hyde, they wondered what sort of a reception they would receive when they arrived. How would English people react at having enemy aliens in their midst whilst the war was still raging? It was with mixed feelings that they arrived at their home, not knowing what to expect. However, they were pleasantly surprised at the welcome given them by some of their best friends.

The Benders' house had been officially locked up in 1940

but soon after, a German bomb had fallen in the vicinity, demolishing much of the property belonging to their friends. A new house had to be found for the unfortunate victims and with the consent of the local authorities, they had taken over the aliens' house. They had been living there for three years, but just before the internees returned, they had been offered a council house.

Some were pleased to see the Germans back; others were nonplussed, not caring one way or the other. On the first morning, Herr Bender fulfilled his first duty by reporting to the Labour Exchange. For some time there was not a suitable job for him, and although he trudged from factory to factory, all the managers and directors who had known him in the early days as a company director, could not bring themselves to offer him the menial jobs available. Week after week passed by, during which many people crossed his path, a few of whom were not ashamed to shake hands with him in public. Others, however, would only speak to him when nobody else was about, or even look straight through him as if they had never known him. One went so far as to remark in his presence that the only good German was a dead one.

Marianne, who had also been in search of work, was more fortunate in obtaining a job in a grocer's shop. The manager was more than satisfied with her efforts, and after only a few weeks, remarked that in time she would make a good manageress. However, when two of the directors of the chain-store appeared on the scene one day, they sacked her on the spot, their reason being that they could not afford to have a German employed during a war. With tears in her eyes, she crossed the road to a jewellers, where the understanding Jewish proprietor offered her a good and permanent post.

In the end Bender also found a job in an acquaintance's furniture factory at a salary of £3.15.0 a week. Every morning, with his lunch tin under his arm, he would set out for the works, which were on the same site as Bender's ribbon factory. On entering the main gate he would join the stream of workers, many of whom were lads and lasses who had previously worked for him, making for the timber shed where he laboured with heavy loads of wood all day long.

And so Herr and Frau Bender were able to earn a living.

What did it matter how hard they had to work, so long as they were together in their own home amongst free people? Nevertheless, on account of the war, they kept to themselves, avoiding public places, as advised by the police. Their papers and cameras were returned to them, including the harmless R.A.C. road maps, which the judge had used when trying to brand Bender as a spy at the 1940 tribunal.

Their neighbours were as friendly as in pre-war days, Frank still living on one side and Eric on the other. Neither they, nor their families, were the least worried at having Germans living amongst them. The pattern of war had changed, as the armies of the dictators were now on the retreat everywhere. All this was reflected in the minds of the British people; there was hope now for an early finish. The bombing of the British Isles was less severe, the Germans getting it back a hundredfold. Around Christmas the Benders experienced their first real air raid, when doodlebugs, launched from the North Sea, passed over their house; only one dropped in the vicinity, hitting a lonely farm in isolated country. This was the only big bang they experienced during the whole of the war.

Conscientiously, Bender stuck to his job as a labourer, although gradually the strain of unloading the heavy timber began to tell. His doctor told him to give it up, keeping him on the sick list for sixteen weeks, until he had found a suitable job more in his own line. During that time, the patient tried everything to secure work, receiving managerial offers from as far away as South Africa and New Zealand, preferring, however, to stay in the British Isles where he and his family had lived happily in pre-war days. His own ribbon firm, which had been taken over by the Custodian of Enemy Property, did not require his services, as English directors were now in charge. The job he took was a relatively small one, offered to him by the chairman with whom he had corresponded from the camp. The object was to develop the firm's patented machines for post-war bulk production. It was an interesting and satisfying job, amongst his own kind of people in a Manchester factory, where he did not have to tramp through sawdust all day long.

1944 passed quickly with Bender in normal circulation again, looking forward each morning to his train journey to town, where he met the same jovial chaps, who exchanged pleasantries in true Lancashire fashion.

When 1945 came he advanced to research-engineer. The machines were ready and so was the new factory in the north-east, and, packing their belongings, the Benders left the Cheshire district, and settled down on Tyneside amongst the Geordies. The move practically coincided with the end of the war, and filled with fresh incentive the production manager soon got into his stride on the new trading estate, training a relatively raw labour force in the most modern production methods. Very soon he was appointed general manager, and could look forward to a comfortable future. The Home Office, after all, made him British and, altering his name to Charles Bender, he became a Britisher amongst the British.

Germany lay far behind him. His father had died in 1940, though his brother and sister were still alive. His native town of Ronsdorf, however, lay in ruins, having been bombed to smithereens on 30th May 1943.

# REFLECTION

Many years have passed since the end of the last war, and the days of rationing long since over. The British nation now enjoys a more affluent existence, whilst social standards have levelled themselves out, to a certain extent. The Benders can still be found in circulation, absorbed into the British community. During his days of retirement, Bender had ample time in which to reflect on his whole life, reaching the conclusion that in a certain way, he had an advantage over others in that he had lived, as it were, two lives in one. He knew the German nation inside out and, to some extent, the British. How often, over the years, he had been approached by English friends with the casual remark that there was not so much difference between the British and the Germans — that they were more like cousins. To a minor degree, this might have been the case hundreds of years ago with the Anglo-Saxon race. Nowadays, however, there is a vast difference, which has been amply illustrated by twentieth century history. As individuals, the Germans are good-natured people but, *en masse,* they are so easily led into disaster by men such as the Kaiser and Adolf Hitler. In this book, German extremities have been illustrated to the full. They prefer to knock their heads against stone walls rather than to negotiate. Bender never forgot a remark made to some of his British acquaintances by a top German businessman at the end of the war: "I wish, politically, that the German nation had the backbone you British have. As we have proved in two major wars, we are either on top of the world, or down in the dumps." The British method of thinking and administration, whether in politics or business, is so vastly different. On democratic principles they slash out their policies in committee, achieving what they want in the end. There is also far more complacency in the British character, which rarely forces the issue, but rather negotiates in order to avoid catastrophic events. The start of the last two wars gives a typical example of the unpreparedness of the British, and whilst the Germans were invading other countries, the British were planning for final victory. For proof of this, one has only to read through history.

Personal characteristics also become apparent when comparing German and British individuality. A German likes to gesticulate when he speaks, and his conversation is normally fast and loud, sometimes with an arrogant sting; he likes to be heard. A Britisher is far more reticent. A good illustration of this is often seen in trains, restaurants or hotels, where he prefers to take an empty table rather than join strangers. His home is his castle and where he is most jovial, enjoying the company of his close friends. He is a sportsman throughout, and would rather turn to the back page of the daily paper first, than look at the front page for important world events. As a sportsman he can quickly forget a lost game, treating war similarly, by shaking hands with his previous enemies as soon as the struggle is over.

It took more than thirty years for Bender to shed most of his German peculiarities, but to this day, when conversing with strangers, they soon detect the Continental volume of speech and the foreign accent. The latter is something one can never cast off and, though it may be said that Bender speaks English with a German accent, whilst on holiday in Germany recently, he was told that he spoke German with a Geordie accent. For a foreigner to live amongst the British creates no problem. Bender and his family have been treated well wherever they have lived. Although legally British this still does not mean that he can consider himself entirely British. He has always to be careful when expressing himself in company. For instance, he dare not say — "Our cricket team has won the Ashes," or "Our Air Force has bombed so and so," as, to an Englishman, this would sound absurd. In actual fact, a naturalized person who becomes British by his own choice and conviction, should be a better Britisher than the one who acquired the nationality through birth, without any effort on his own behalf. A born and bred Britisher is always British, all other nationals outside the Commonwealth being foreigners. To call a British-born subject a foreigner, is not very acceptable, even when travelling in foreign countries.

Within the British Isles, there also exists a certain divergence, where a Geordie becomes a foreigner to a Cockney. For the southern people, the north of England finishes somewhere around York; to them, all that which is beyond, where it is cold, rough and bleak, in a countryside dotted with dirty pit-heaps, is a veritable no-man's-land.

Some of the happiest days Bender and his wife spent in England were amongst the wonderful people of Northumberland. This county became their home, and having travelled through practically every other part of the country, it is in Northumberland that they really felt they belonged. The Geordies are a fine race and, whether businessmen, dockers, miners or farmers, they offer hospitality to strangers freely. Hardy as they are, it takes some time for a stranger to break the crust, but once he is accepted, he finds open houses everywhere. Their kindliness is somewhat reflected in their language, with that singing crescendo at the end of each sentence, but should they resort to the proper Geordie dialect, no southerner could understand them.

The countryside is one of the finest in the British Isles, though unappreciated by many people in the south. Here, one finds the cradle of Christianity; mountains and moorlands of great beauty; the ancient Roman Wall dating back to when Christ was born. The whole area is steeped in history, and in every town, village or hamlet, one may come across some kind of ancient treasure. What a pleasure one derives from motoring, or walking, high up over the moors and fells, along twinkling rivers and burns, frequented by trout and salmon. Bender enjoyed nothing better than to sit on a river bank, watching nature and wild life, at the same time concentrating upon his fishing, waiting for the thrill of a tight line with a salmon or sea trout at the end. High up into the Cheviots he would go, where crystal clear burns cascaded over the rocks, harbouring fine trout by the dozen, a paradise for any angler. Here, amongst thinly distributed population, everything is unspoilt, and the stocky, healthy farmers of northern Northumberland, are one of the finest class of people to be met.

What a wonderful life one can live if there is peace. Bender's generation can look back over practically seventy years, ten years of which were spent in two raging wars. Strife, quarrel and fighting have been mankind's reward in the past. In early history, conflicts were easily settled with the bow and arrow, but the invention of war machinery has never halted, until, not so very long ago, man killed man by suffocating and exterminating one another with the deadliest of poisonous gases, a method which even the ancient tribes of Africa have never equalled. The last war brought us nearer to the annihilation of mankind and had the Hydrogen Bomb been invented a little earlier, it could have been the end of living existence. Now that we have reached an era with weapons too destructive to think about, we come to a point which should lead to a better and safer future.

Old generations go, new ones come; the choice of 'to be or not to be' rests in the hands of our younger people. Will it be total extermination, or lasting peace in a world which one may call ' Utopia '?